Barcelona and Madrid

Barcelona and Madrid

Social Networks of the Avant-Garde

Aránzazu Ascunce Arenas

Lewisburg
BUCKNELL UNIVERSITY PRESS

Published by Bucknell University Press
Co-published with The Rowman & Littlefield Publishing Group, Inc.
4501 Forbes Boulevard, Suite 200, Lanham, Maryland 20706
www.rowman.com

10 Thornbury, Plymouth PL6 7PP, United Kingdom

British Library Cataloguing in Publication Information Available

Library of Congress Cataloging-in-Publication Data

Ascunce Arenas, Aránzazu, 1974-
   Barcelona and Madrid: social networks of the avant-garde / Aránzazu Ascunce.
      p. cm.
   Includes bibliographical references.
   ISBN 978-1-61148-424-3 (cloth : alk. paper) — ISBN 978-1-61148-425-0 (electronic)
   1. Barcelona (Spain)—Intellectual life—20th century. 2. Madrid (Spain)—
Intellectual life—20th century. 3. Avant-garde (Aesthetics)—Spain—Barcelona—
History—20th century. 4. Avant-garde (Aesthetics)—Spain—Madrid—History—20th
century.
   5. Barcelona (Spain)—Relations—Spain—Madrid. 6. Madrid (Spain)—Relations—
Spain—Barcelona. I. Title.

   DP402.B265A84 2012
   946'.41074—dc23

                                                                  2011052012

Printed in the United States of America

This book is dedicated to my parents,
Consuelo Carmen and Gil Ascunce,
who have taught me preseverance.

~

Contents

Illustrations

~

Acknowledgments

First and foremost, I would like to thank God for giving me the power and strength to see this project through. Second, I would like to thank my family and friends who have accompanied me along this journey since the beginning or who have miraculously appeared along the way. Third, I would like to thank my teachers and mentors who have guided and instructed me in the art and science of academic research and writing. Finally, I would like to thank key individuals and institutions that have supported me at various stages in very practical ways.

My nuclear family has been witness to the writing this book from beginning to end. I especially thank my parents whose faith in me has been steadfast. I would also like to thank my brothers, Gil Ignacio and Gabriel Ascunce, who have been my most honest critics. Not too long before my beloved grandmother, Hilda Isabel Ascunce—she too a professor of Spanish language and linguistics— passed away two summers ago at age ninety-one, she assured me that this book would be published. She was right. My cousin, Marie Arenas, who is more like the sister I never had, has opened the doors of her home and her heart during my many stays with her while undertaking research in Spain. I am forever thankful to you all.

There are several beloved friends, dear to my heart, whom I would like to acknowledge for their continuous encouragement over the years: Alicia López Operé, Arantxa Leziñena Loizu, and Gonzalo Escarpa. With each of them, I have greatly enjoyed our passionate discussions about my book virtually, over the phone, and face-to-face. Also, I would like to especially thank those colleagues and friends who have read my manuscript in full or in part and have given me their invaluable feedback: Gloria Beatriz Rodríguez, June Naughton, and Josep Minguell. I also extend my gratitude to my dear friends in Barcelona and Madrid who have supported me in many practical ways. In Madrid, I especially thank my friend Professor Ángel Álvarez who really has been like an angel to me in the last five years. Thank you to my friend Julio Reija, a first-class poet and talented graphic designer, for agreeing to create an original piece of artwork for the cover of this book. In Barcelona, thank you to my former professor Jaume Subirana, who was the first to introduce me to Catalan studies and to teach me Catalan when I was an undergraduate student. Two other special friends in Catalonia include Miquel Visa, who made his private library available to me, and Enric Escudero Guilló who so kindly cared for me the summer I lived in Gràcia with him and his circle of fervent Catalanist friends.

Professor Andrew A. Anderson, one of the top contemporary scholars of the Avant-Garde in Spain, directed the initial stages of research required for writing this book. I am grateful for his invaluable guidance and his reliable mentorship throughout the dissertation writing process. I would also like to thank the secondary readers of my dissertation: Professors Matthew Affron, Enrico Cesaretti, and David Haberly, all of whom were extremely generous with their time and specialized knowledge. Thank you also to Professors David Gies, Javier Herrero, and Fernando Operé for your constant, enthusiastic encouragement both during and after graduate school.

A special note of thanks to the many librarians who have assisted me in the hemerotecas (periodical libraries) at both the *Biblioteca Nacional* in Madrid and the *Biblioteca de Catalunya* in Barcelona; the Transatlantic Library at the *Residencia de Estudiantes*; the fast and friendly inter-library loan service staff at Alderman Library at the University of Virginia, especially Severyn Hanusz; and the Scholar's Lab at the University of Virginia, especially Nancy Krechner.

Last, but not least, I would like to thank the institutions that have funded various grants that have made this book possible including the University of Hawaii, the University of Virginia, the Fulbright Program, and the Mellon Foundation.

~

Chronology:
Barcelona and Madrid, 1900–1939

This chronology highlights details discussed in this book. It brings attention to a series of events that serve as landmarks for understanding the Avant-Garde in Spain from two focal points, Barcelona and Madrid, simultaneously. The following events are not limited to literary history, but also include events related to art, law, politics, the press, social history, sports, and urban works. The timeline spans from 1900 until 1939, but it is focused on the years between the arrival of the first news of Italian futurism in Spain (1909) and the debut of Dalí and Buñuel's surrealist short film, *An Andalusian Dog* (1929), which was screened first in France, then in Spain. The events listed in each year are also organized in chronological order (from January to December, but without indicating the months, in order to simplify the format and because not in every case is that information available).

The objective of this chronology is to easily keep track of the activities that are relevant to a study of the Avant-Garde in both Barcelona and Madrid, but in some instances, also beyond. Barcelona and Madrid were not the only two cities to adopt the Avant-Garde spirit in Spain, but for the purposes of this book, the chronology remains fixed on just these two. The entries are not described in detail, since their contents are discussed at greater length in the chapters. These events have been compiled over nearly one decade and from a wide array of sources, but especially academic books, art exhibit catalogues, and my own research in various archives.

A friend remarked that this chronology is problematic because of its abbreviated nature. Again, the items included in it are explained in greater detail and contextualized in the body of the book. To my knowledge, no other dual cultural chronology of the Avant-Garde in Barcelona and Madrid of this extent exists. It was a resource that I wish would have been available to me as I conducted my research. Since it was not, I have taken the liberty and risk of creating one. It is a first attempt. My hope is that it will be useful, first, to detangle some of the knots that result when composing the complicated tapestry of early twentieth-century history in Spain, and second, to understand the complex connections at play here by watching how intimately these two histories coil around one another, like strands of deoxyribonucleic acid.

1900	Picasso, first individual show, Els Quatre Gats, Barcelona
	Picasso's first trip to Paris
1901	Picasso moves to Madrid; from Madrid he travels to Barcelona and Paris
	Arte Joven, artistic magazine founded by Picasso and a Catalan friend, Madrid
	Lliga Regionalista political party established, Barcelona
	First general strike in Barcelona
1902	Picasso extends a stay in Paris, where he lives with Max Jacob
	General strike in Spain, sought eight-hour day and recognition of right to strike
	Alfonso XIII comes of age at sixteen to rule as King of Spain
	First Barcelona vs. Madrid football match in Copa del Rey
1903	Picasso returns to Barcelona
	First Salon d'Automne of Paris, organized in protest of state-sponsored art shows
1904	Gabriel Alomar gives his first lecture on *futurisme*, Barcelona
	El Poble Català (Barcelona, 1904–18), periodical
	Picasso moves to Paris indefinitely
	Jardines lejanos, poetry book by J. R. Jiménez
1905	Bolsheviks founded by Vladimir Lenin
	Die Brücke, formation of expressionist artists group in Dresden, Germany
	Salon d'Automne, Paris; fauvism first used to define works of artists shown
	Garba (Barcelona, 1905–6), periodical
	Military assault on Catalan press: *Cu-Cut* and *La Veu de Catalunya*
	Gran Vía, a major boulevard in Madrid, is expanded
	La República de las Letras (Madrid, 1905–?)

1906   *Noucentisme*, Barcelona; major aesthetic and cultural movement
        takes root
        E. D'Ors published first "glosari" in Barcelona newspaper *La Veu
        de Catalunya*
        Attempted murder of King Alfonso XIII
        Centre Nacionalista Republicà, a political group, founded in
        Barcelona
        Law of Jurisdictions enacted (until 1931)
        Solidaritat Catalana, a political movement, established in Bar-
        celona
        Estudis Universitaris Catalans established, Barcelona
        La Nacionalitat Catalana, book by E. Prat de la Riba
        First Congress of the Catalan Language hosted in Barcelona
        Josep Dalmau opened his first art gallery in Barcelona
1907   *Les Demoiselles d'Avignon*, Picasso
        Law of Jurisdictions repealed
        Futurisme (Barcelona, 1907), periodical
        Renacimiento (Madrid, 1907); G. Alomar published "Futurismo"
        articles
        Institut d'Estudis Catalans established, Barcelona
        Celso Lagar exhibited in Madrid
        Diego Rivera, Mexican artist, in Madrid until 1909
1908   Via Laietana, urban project to widen road, begins, Barcelona
        Partit Republicà Radical, a political party founded by Lerroux in
        Barcelona
        Prometeo (Madrid, 1908–12), periodical
        Futurisme (Tarrasa, 1908), periodical
        L. Bagaría moved to Madrid (until 1938)
1909   Solidaritat Catalana dissolved
        España Futura (Madrid, 1909–10), periodical
        Futurism manifesto by Marinetti published in *Le Figaro*, Paris
        Italian futurist manifesto translated and published in Madrid
        (*Prometeo*)
        General strike in Spain
        Military defeated in a Rif War battle in Morocco
        Tragic Week, Barcelona
        Prime Minister Maura resigned
1910   CNT, an anarcho-syndicalist trade union, established in Barcelona
        Marinetti's futurist manifesto for Spaniards published in Madrid
        (*Prometeo*)
        Residencia de Estudiantes founded, Madrid

Futurisme (Penedés, 1910), periodical
J. M. Sucre's first visit to Madrid
C. Lagar moved to Madrid; visited Barcelona
Les Arts i les Artistes, an artistic group, founded in Barcelona
Sociedad de Amigos del Arte, an artistic group, founded in Madrid

1911   General strike in Spain organized by CNT
Law of the Lock enacted by government and suppressed CNT
Association of Basque Artists, an artistic group, established in Bilbao
C. Lagar moved to Paris
The Handsome Woman, novel by Eugeni D'Ors

1912   Picasso, Dalmau Gallery
Cubist Art, Dalmau Gallery
Revista de Catalunya (Barcelona, 1912–34), periodical
Mancomunitat proposal approved, Barcelona
Prime Minister Canalejas assassinated, Madrid
Collection of Marinetti manifestos translated and published in Spanish, Valencia
Campos de Castilla, poetry collection by A. Machado
Over one hundred thousand Spaniards exiled to Latin America

1913   Barradas arrived to Barcelona from Uruguay via Italy
Normes Ortogràfiques, Pompeu Fabra
Escola Català d'Art Dramàtic established, Barcelona
Mancomunitat established, Prat de la Riba elected first president
Del sentimiento trágico de la vida, Unamuno

1914   World War I (until 1918). Many artists living in Paris exiled to Spain
Revista Nova (Barcelona, 1914–16), periodical
Mancomunitat constituted, Barcelona
National Library of Catalonia established, Barcelona
Escola Superior dels Bells Oficis established, Barcelona
Niebla, Unamuno
Greguerías, R. Gómez de la Serna
Meditaciones del Quijote, J. Ortega y Gasset
Platero y yo, J. R. Jiménez
La Esfera (Madrid, 1914–31), periodical
J. M. Sucre visited Madrid
Barradas moved to Barcelona

1915   *Vell i Nou* (Barcelona, 1915–21), periodical
Themis (Vilanova i la Geltrú, 1915–16), periodical
La Revista (Barcelona, 1915–36), periodical

España (Madrid, 1915–24), periodical
Los Quijotes (Madrid, 1915–18?), periodical
Iberia (Barcelona, 1915–18), periodical
Integral Painters art exhibition, Madrid
Residencia de Señoritas established, Madrid
Pombo weekly gathering founded, Madrid (until 1936)
J. M. Sucre visited Madrid
Lipchitz in Madrid
Lagar, Dalmau Gallery; planism

1916   Basque Association of Painters exhibited in Madrid, then Barcelona
Jack Johnson vs. Arthur Craven Dada boxing match, Barcelona
Per Catalunya i L'Espanya Gran, manifesto by C. Riba
Picabia in Barcelona (until 1917)
Troços (Barcelona, 1916), periodical
Cervantes (Madrid, 1916–20), periodical
Strikes organized by CNT and UGT
Miró meets Dalmau and Picabia in Barcelona

1917   Legionaires art exhibit, hosted first in Madrid, then Barcelona and Bilbao
Dada (Zurich/Paris, 1917–20), periodical
Russian Revolution
General strike in Spain, organized by UGT (Unión General de Trabajadores)
Juntas de Defensa in response to summer strikes established by Spain's military
Censorship of the press
391 (Barcelona, 1917–24), periodical
Un enemic del Poble (Barcelona, 1917–18), periodical
La Nau (Barcelona, 1917), periodical
Ballet Russes, Barcelona and Madrid
Picasso visited Barcelona and Madrid
Campos de Castilla, second edition of poetry book by A. Machado
Luis Buñuel entered Residencia de Estudiantes, Madrid (until 1925)
Torres-García and Barradas, Dalmau Gallery
C. Lagar, Galería General de Arte, Madrid; planism
Diccionari Ortogràfic, Pompeu Fabra

1918   *L'Esprit Nouveau* (Paris), periodical
D'ací, d'allà (Barcelona, 1918), periodical
Arc-Voltaic (Barcelona, 1918), periodical
Miró, first individual show, Dalmau Gallery, Barcelona

Barradas, Laietanes Gallery, Barcelona; vibrationism
L'Instant (Barcelona/Paris, 1918–19), periodical
Barradas moved to Madrid
Huidobro moved to Madrid, published *Hallali, Tour Eiffel, Poemas árticos*
Pombo, R. Gómez de la Serna published book about his weekly literary gathering
Jorge Luis Borges and sister, Norah, in Madrid and involved in Ultra (until 1921)
Humo de fábrica, Salvat-Papasseit
Gramatica Catalana, Pompeu Fabra
Lagar, Laietanes Gallery, Barcelona
Lagar, Ateneo, Madrid
Lagar moved to Bilbao
Columna de Foc (Reus, 1918–20), periodical
First Saló Tardor (Autumn Salon), Barcelona
Influenza epidemic

1919   Statute of Autonomy of Catalonia approved
Ultraísmo, avant-garde movement, Madrid
Salvat-Papasseit manifesto, "Concepte del poeta," published in Barcelona
Cosmópolis (Madrid, 1919–22), periodical
Lorca entered Residencia de Estudiantes, Madrid
Canadiense strike, Barcelona
Metro opened in Madrid
Eight-hour workday law passed
Employer lockout
Unió de Sindicats Lliures, a political organization, established in Barcelona
Poemes en ondes hertzianes, book of poems by Salvat-Papasseit
Barradas moved to Madrid; introduced to Lorca
C. Lagar moved to Paris indefinitely

1920   *El maleficio de la mariposa*, Lorca, Teatro Eslava, Madrid
Barradas, Dalmau Galleries
Alfar (La Coruña, 1920–54), periodical
Manifiesto ultraísta vertical, Guillermo de Torre
Reflector (Madrid, 1920), periodical
Poemes i cal·ligrammes, poetry collection by Junoy
"Contra els poetes amb minuscula," Salvat-Papasseit futurist manifesto
Sucre introduced to Dalmau

Over one thousand strikes in Spain
Miró's first visit to Paris; met Picasso; stayed until 1925
1921   Communist party established
Twenty-one assassinations in thirty-six hours in Barcelona
La Nova Revista (Barcelona, 1921–29), periodical
Proa (Barcelona, 1921), periodical
Ultra (Madrid, 1921–22), periodical
Prime Minister Dato assassinated, Barcelona
Miró, Dalmau Gallery, Barcelona
Miro's first solo exhibition in Paris
Creación/Création (Barcelona/Paris, 1921–24), periodical
L'irradiador del port i les gavines, poetry book by Salvat-Papasseit
Índice (Madrid, 1921–22), periodical
Tableros (Madrid, 1921–22), periodical
Espejos, poetry book by Juan Chabás
España invertebrada, long essay by Ortega y Gasset
El movimiento V.P., poetry book by Cansinos Assens
Los cuernos de Don Friolera, experimental play by Valle-Inclán
Battle of Annual, Morocco, defeat of Spanish military
1922   *Prisma* (Barcelona/Paris, 1922), periodical
"Segon manifest catalá futurista," S. Sánchez-Juan
Acció Catalana, a political movement, founded in Barcelona
Notas marruecas de un soldado, first book by Giménez Caballero
Dalí entered Residencia de Estudiantes, Madrid (until 1926)
La Publicitat (Barcelona, 1922–39), daily newspaper
Benito Mussolini marched to power in Rome
Dissolution of Juntas de Defensa in Spain
Horizonte (Sevilla, 1922–23), periodical
Concurso de Cante Jondo organized by Lorca and Falla, Granada
Les conspiracions, book of poetry by Salvat-Papasseit
La gesta dels estels, book of poetry by Salvat-Papasseit
Poemas de abril y mayo, book of poetry by Sucre
Sleepwalking Dreams, painting by Dalí
Bernat Metge Foundation established, Barcelona
1923   Salvador Seguí (CNT leader) assassinated
Ambos (Malaga, 1923), periodical
Parábola (Burgos, 1923–28), periodical
Revista de Occidente (Madrid, 1923–36), periodical
Coup d'état, Barcelona (September), beginning of Primo de Rivera dictatorship
La gaceta de las artes gráficas (Barcelona, 1923–38), periodical

Hélices, book of poetry by Guillermo de Torre
Vértices (Madrid, 1923), periodical
Dalí expelled from San Fernando School of Fine Arts in Madrid
El poema de la rosa al llavis, poem by Salvat-Papasseit
Group de Sabadell, Barcelona
Banquet for L. Bagaría, Madrid

1924   Surrealism, Paris
Manifesto in Defense of the Catalan Language signed by Castilian intellectuals
La Sociedad de Cursos y Conferencias, a cultural organization founded in Madrid
Gaseta de les Arts (Barcelona, 1924–30), periodical
Ronsel (Lugo, 1924), periodical
National Telephone Company of Spain established
Unión Patriótica established, only political party during Spanish dictatorship
Revista de Catalunya (Barcelona, 1924–31), periodical
Salvat-Papasseit died
Tobogán (Madrid, 1924), periodical
La Mà Trencada (Barcelona, 1924–25), periodical
Fluid, book of poetry by S. Sánchez-Juan
La sagrada cripta, second tome of R. Gómez de la Serna's records of Pombo
Marinero en tierra, collection of poetry by R. Alberti
Versos humanos, collection of poetry by G. Diego
Manual de espumas, collection of poetry by G. Diego
La sombrilla japonesa, collection of poetry by I. Vando Villar
Metro opened in Barcelona

1925   *Revista de Poesía* (Barcelona, 1925–27), periodical
Plural (Madrid, 1925), periodical
Lorca's first visit to Catalonia (Barcelona, Cadaqués)
Louis Aragon lectured at the Residencia de Estudiantes in Madrid
Mancomunitat abolished by Primo de Rivera government
Failed assassination attempt of King Alfonso XIII
Football Club stadium closed, Barcelona
Society of Iberian Artists, Palacio de Hielo, Madrid
Venus and Sailor. Homage to Salvat-Papasseit, painting by Dalí
Dalí, first solo exhibition, Dalmau Gallery, Barcelona
National and Foreign Modern Art, Dalmau Galleries, Barcelona
Surco y estela, collection of poetry by Gutiérrez Gili

Literaturas europeas de vanguardia, critical review of new poetry by
  G. de Torre
Deshumanización del arte, long essay about new art by J. Ortega y
  Gasset
Versos humanos, collection of poetry by G. Diego (Nobel Prize for
  Literature)
Barradas moved to Barcelona; established Ateneillo de Hospitalet
  (until 1928)
Buñuel, Hinojosa, Moreno Villa, Palencia, Pérez Ferrero moved
  to Paris
First exhibiton of surrealism painting, Paris

1926   Modern Catalan Art, Círculo de Bellas Artes, Madrid
Ciutat (Manresa, 1926–28), periodical
Barradas, Dalmau Gallery, Barcelona
L'Amic de les Arts (Sitges, 1926–29), periodical
Mediodía (Seville, 1926–29), periodical
Dalí traveled to Paris for the first time; introduced to Picasso
Gaudí died
Dalí expelled indefinitely from San Fernando
Gasch and Dalí introduced
Litoral (Malaga, 1926–29), periodical
Dalí, Dalmau Gallery

1927   *La Gaceta Literaria* (Madrid, 1927–31), periodical
La Nova Revista (Barcelona, 1927–29), periodical
Verso y prosa (Murcia, 1927–28), periodical
La rosa de los vientos (Tenerife, 1927–28)
Barradas, Dalmau Gallery, Barcelona
Lorca visits Cadaqués and Barcelona
Lorca introduced to many Catalans, such as Foix, Gasch, and
  Montanyà
Lorca Drawings Exhibit, Dalmau Gallery, Barcelona
Mariana Pineda, play by Lorca, Teatro Goya, Barcelona
Papel de Aleluyas (Huelva/Seville, 1927–28), periodical
Guillermo de Torre moved to Buenos Aires
The Catalan Book Fair, National Library of Spain, Madrid
Constel·laciones, collection of poetry by S. Sánchez-Juan
Gertrudis, collection of poetry by J. V. Foix
La branca nua, collection of poetry by V. Solè de Sojo
Perfil del aire, collection of poetry by L. Cernuda
Canciones, collection of poetry by Lorca
Homage to Góngora, Seville

1928   Carteles, Giménez Caballero's art exhibit at Dalmau Gallery,
        Barcelona
        Obras de vanguardia, Dalmau Gallery, Barcelona
        Gallo (Granada, 1928), periodical
        Manifest Groc, anti-art manifesto launched by Dalí in Barcelona
        Circunvalación (Mexico, 1928), periodical
        "Els 7 davant El Centaure," anti-artistic conferences hosted in
        Sitges
        Marinetti visited Barcelona and Madrid
        Barradas moved to Uruguay
        Homentage a Rafael Barradas, Dalmau Gallery, Barcelona (Au-
        gust–September)
        Les Arts Catalans (Barcelona, 1928–29), periodical
        Radicions i poemes, collection of poetry by C. Sindreu
        Romancero gitano, collection of poetry by Lorca
        Cántico, collection of poetry by J. Guillén
        Hércules jugando a los dados, novel by E. Giménez Caballero
        Yo, inspector de alcantarillas, novel by E. Giménez Caballero
        La flor de California, collection of poetry by J. M. Hinojosa
1929   Mirador (Barcelona, 1929–37), periodical
        Hélix (Vilafranca del Penedès, 1929–30), periodical
        Spanish School of Paris, Botanical Gardens, Madrid
        International World Fair, Barcelona
        Ibero-American Fair, Seville
        Atlántico (Madrid, 1929–30), periodical
        Wall Street Crash (October)
        Lorca visited New York City
        Poeta en Nueva York, collection of poetry by Lorca
        Sobre los ángeles, collection of poetry by R. Alberti
        Julepe de menta, novel by E. Giménez Caballero
        Novísimas greguerías, collection of poetry by R. Gómez de la Serna
        Meridiano (Huelva, 1929–30), periodical
        Dalí, Goemans Gallery, Paris
        Un chien andalou, film by Dalí and Buñuel that premiered in Paris
        Barradas dies
1930   Castilian intellectuals' visit to Barcelona
        General Primo de Rivera resigned; died six weeks later in exile
        Second Surrealist Manifesto signed by A. Breton in Paris
        La rebelión de las masas, essay by Ortega y Gasset
        Catalunya endins, book by J. Esterlich
        Cataluña ante España, book by E. Giménez Caballero

Lorca finished writing *El público*, one of his most abstract theatrical texts

L'Age d'Or, second film by Buñuel and Dalí

1931   Second Republic of Spain declared

King Alfonso XIII fled Spain

Esquerra Republicana de Catalunya, a political group, established in Barcelona

AC (Barcelona/Madrid/San Sebastian, 1931–37), periodical

Ismos, book by R. Gómez de la Serna

Trabalenguas, book by E. Giménez Caballero

1932   *KRTU*, J. V. Foix

General Dictionary of the Catalan Language, Pompeu Fabra

Miró moves to Barcelona (until 1936)

1933   Hitler rises to power

Spanish Falange founded by José Antonio Primo de Rivera, son of former dictator

Art (Lleida, 1933–34), periodical

1935   Lorca's last visit to Barcelona to open his play *Yerma*

Quaderns de Poesia (Barcelona, 1935–36), periodical

1936   Failed military overthrow led by Franco

Outbreak of Spanish Civil War

Lorca assassinated

1939   End of Spanish Civil War

Beginning of Franco dictatorship (until 1975)

Outbreak of World War II (until 1945)

Introduction

Much of the success of avant-garde artists has to do with the people with whom they were connected. The individuals who composed the circle of friends that practiced and promoted the Avant-Garde in Barcelona and Madrid did not function in a vacuum. In fact, much of their survival depended on the quality and quantity of their ties with other like-minded individuals beyond their own group. This book is a work in cultural studies, because it identifies and analyzes the ways in which members of these various networks functioned by using concepts borrowed from the discipline of network studies, without leaving literature, history, language, or politics out of the picture. The book's argument is placed within the cultural context of the Avant-Garde in Spain. It takes into account the cultural, social, and political environment of those who promoted this movement. It also takes into consideration their various instruments and modes of communication, such as literary magazines, pamphlets, personal letters, poetry, manifestos, conferences, informal meetings, and art objects. This book is a cultural contextualization of the Avant-Garde that simultaneously takes into account the multiple social networks connecting Barcelona and Madrid.

The representatives of avant-garde Barcelona and Madrid not only identified with one another, but they connected with each other so as to sustain this new way of expressing themselves and being. The members of both of these groups expanded their networks in order to make new connections with like-minded individuals, regardless of the potential limitations of nationality, geography, social class, age, culture, sexual preference, religious affiliation, or politics. The direction of the expansion of networks is bilateral: Madrid networks reached out to Barcelona and vice versa. It is also multidirectional. These networks expanded out to other centers in Spain, like Seville and La Coruña, and to other cities in Europe and the Americas. In building a system with the intention of breaking with the past, members of the Barcelona and Madrid vanguard networks sustained a revolutionary movement that helped change the cultural identity of Spain and Catalonia. Regardless of their differences, the promoters of the Avant-Garde in Barcelona and Madrid shared a progressive spirit in which the act of crossing and breaking borders was fundamental. As a result of the development of personal and professional relationships, cultural unity was promoted in the name of overall change.

This book is an exploration of the networks connecting people and groups centered in Barcelona and Madrid that were associated with the Avant-Garde, through the consideration of literary, visual, political, and journalistic texts. It reveals a complicated web of dialogue, assumptions, cultural clashes, political impasses, and misunderstandings. The protagonists of both cities adopted avant-garde ideologies to associate themselves with and differentiate themselves from others, depending on the political climate and personal circumstances. The common link that connected the Barcelona and Madrid avant-garde networks was a shared spirit of rupture, resistance, and renewal of art, culture, literature, and society. By considering the Avant-Garde with a more broad and multifaceted vision, a more complicated version of history emerges, but also one that more closely resembles the truth.

The purpose of chapter 1 is to address the Avant-Garde generally and in relation to Spain. After considering the definition of the word *avante-garde*, this part of the book describes those vanguard movements with the greatest impact in Spain. Some of the ideas of these groups and tendencies were imported from abroad, but others were made in Spain. Key characteristics and some of the principal goals of these movements are introduced. Then a description of how people participated in these movements is provided. It is argued that the vanguard artists in Spain forged a new, more modern identity, one that could be defined as interconnected, because of the necessity to transcend differences in order to persist. Three conclusions about the Avant-Garde in Spain as a result of widening the analytical lens are presented at the end of this chapter, each of which will be addressed in the subsequent chapters of the book in a more thorough manner. But first, some other critical concepts must be discussed.

Chapter 2 is an introduction to the basic measures and key concepts of network studies. The nature and properties of links are explained, such as direction, intensity, frequency, strength, and symmetry. These terms are described through the specific example of the relationship, or cluster, between three individuals. The critical vocabulary of network studies is presented by looking at the connections that link Federico García Lorca (a Spanish poet from the south of Spain who lived in Madrid and visited Barcelona on several occasions), Sebastià Gasch (a Catalan art critic who lived in Barcelona and published frequently in Madrid), and Rafael Barradas (a Uruguayan painter who lived in Barcelona and Madrid and played an active role in both avant-garde networks). Using this "cluster" as an example to introduce concepts borrowed from the discipline of network studies, several other people must inevitably be introduced in order to explain the Lorca-Gasch-Barradas connection, including Joan Miró (a Catalan painter who lived in Paris), Salvador Dalí (a Catalan painter who lived in Barcelona, Madrid, and Paris), Lluís Montanyà (a Catalan journalist who lived in Barcelona), and Josep Dalmau (a Catalan art merchant and gallery owner). The multiplexity of connections evident in this example strengthens the book's argument that the avant-garde networks of Barcelona and Madrid were more connected than we have been led to believe. The chapter ends by mentioning other critical nodes in the two vanguard systems. Some are well known, such as Pablo Picasso, but most others are not, as is the case with Joan Salvat-Papasseit and Luis Bagaría.

Before moving ahead with the main analysis of the systems connecting avant-garde Barcelona and Madrid, chapter 3 outlines the political panorama at the time. First, this section offers some introductory explanations regarding the historic rivalry between Barcelona and Madrid. It looks back to the Spanish monarchy's centralization policies throughout the fifteenth through eighteenth centuries, which resulted in gradual losses of autonomy, rights, and power in Catalonia in relation to the Spanish crown. In order to understand the turmoil of the early twentieth century, several key facts about the nineteenth century are mentioned, including the Carlist Wars, the overthrow of the Spanish monarchy, and the establishment of the First Republic, all in the shadow of the Industrial Revolution. Spain's military loss to the United States in 1898 had grave effects on Barcelona, Madrid, and their relations; each city came up with its own ways of dealing with the loss of the empire. In Catalonia, several cultural and political movements surfaced, such as *modernisme* and *noucentisme*. In Madrid, intellectuals and politicians responded with regenerationism, while writers came together to find solutions to this crisis, forming what is known as the Generation of '98. Urban strife seemed constant as tensions increased between Barcelona and Madrid. Spain was involved in an unpopular war in North Africa, and in the rest of Europe, many civilians were also losing their lives in World War I.

Chapter 4 draws attention to periodicals that were critical in connecting the avant-garde networks of Barcelona and Madrid. Known as "little magazines," these periodicals where necessary to the survival of the movement. It was within their pages that trends would be introduced and debated. These magazines also provided some of the platforms on which relationships formed and evolved between members. In addition, these little magazines maintained the network that sustained them. Three patterns emerged in the study of over one hundred little magazines from the time period in question. First, there is a clear intention to dialogue, immediately prior to the appearance of the first avant-garde movement in Spain. The direction of this tie is bilateral; in other words, from Madrid to Barcelona and vice versa (1904–9). Second, during the years in which the avant-garde movements were introduced to Spain, there is an increase in communication between Barcelona and Madrid through these periodicals (1909–23). Third, there is a distinct shift away from the two major urban centers and to the peripheries (1923–29), which also happens to coincide with the dictatorship of General Miguel Primo de Rivera. The periodicals in Barcelona and Madrid turn inwards, and we find publications of avant-garde periodicals in cities throughout Spain, such as Huelva, Malaga, Manresa, Murcia, and Seville.

The primary concern of chapter 5 is the art world of the Avant-Garde in Spain. This section of the book begins with a brief introduction to cubism and surrealism in Spain through the examples of two artists, Pablo Picasso and Salvador Dalí, paying special attention to their connections. The scene is set for describing the readiness of Barcelona and Madrid for accepting avant-garde artistic ideas and practices. This chapter is divided into five sections, each of which provides an example of the relationships between Barcelona and Madrid in the context of avant-garde art. The first section is dedicated to one of the major bridge builders between these two cities, Rafael Barradas, who actively contributed to the art scene in both of these cities. The second section of this chapter discusses differences in showing practices, buying behaviors, and artistic attitudes before addressing three crucial art shows in describing the dissonances and resonances of the avant-garde circles in Barcelona and Madrid. These three shows were the Iberians (Madrid, 1925), Modern Catalan Art (Madrid, 1926), and Spaniards Residing in Paris (Madrid, 1929). Like Barradas, the role of Salvador Dalí as a major bridge figure is also discussed.

Chapter 6 concludes with a case in point. One man, Ernesto Giménez Caballero, made unparalleled efforts to connect Barcelona and Madrid during the 1920s. He did so mostly through his periodical, *La Gaceta Literaria* (Madrid, 1927–32), but also through events he organized, such as the

Catalan Book Fair (Madrid, 1927). This final chapter is divided into three main sections. The first describes his attitudes prior to the launching of his periodical, one of the principal organs for the diffusion of information about the Avant-Garde in Spain. The second section deals with his periodical and two events related to it: first, a celebration of the periodical's first anniversary in Barcelona, and second, organizing and executing the Catalan Book Fair in Madrid. The systematic inclusion of Catalan culture in *La Gaceta Literaria* is explained as one of his goals for the periodical, but also as a matter of necessity due to financial compromises with influential members of a political party from Catalonia. There is a clear shift in the attitude toward Catalans and Catalonia on behalf of Giménez Caballero and his periodical after the fall of the dictator, General Miguel Primo de Rivera. If, in the early days of *La Gaceta Literaria*, he proclaimed that ineffective communication was Spain's greatest ill, in the end, he claimed that it was actually separatism.

The hope is that readers will feel that they are getting both sides of the story; that they are learning about the avant-garde circles of Madrid and Barcelona simultaneously. The intention is to shed light on the more global and interconnected nature of the Avant-Garde network in Spain. This system consists of at least two centers, Barcelona and Madrid, instead of just one. Furthermore, there is an emphasis on all that connected the two largest cities of the Iberian Peninsula during turbulent and bellicose times. Finally, readers may realize that much more work of this comparative kind remains to be done in Spain, between different regions, or autonomous communities, that are so widely different, and also in relation to Portugal. Rather than take an isolationist stance, the intent is to be more encompassing of the linguistic variety, long history, and ancient traditions that make this part of the world so culturally rich and extraordinary.

CHAPTER ONE

~

Introduction to the Avant-Garde

Avant-garde is a French word that was first used to describe a military concept. According to its original meaning, it refers to the first (*avant*) line of defense (*garde*) in battle. Those who made-up the avant-garde were the soldiers who stood in the front line of fire. They were the ones who attacked first, the ones most prone to injury and death. During the first half of the twentieth century, French thinkers adopted this military term to describe those who fearlessly attacked old ways of doing things, especially in the arts and politics. These nonconformists rejected old models for organizing society. They were more interested in new political paradigms like anarchism, socialism, fascism, and communism. In the arts, those who purposefully broke the rules of rhyme in poetry or rebelled against the laws of perspective in painting were not automatically considered to be avant-garde. In the context of the early twentieth century, the time period that concerns this book, one who was avant-garde generally belonged to a group that was created for the express purpose of combating the old and celebrating the new. One who was considered to be avant-garde was usually related to a group or school, like cubism, futurism, or surrealism. Analogously, one cannot truly be a gang member without belonging to a gang. Sure, there may have been avant-garde artists and writers who were loners (even though it is difficult to think of one in the case of Spain), but the vast majority of them belonged to an interconnected group, or network. The purpose of this book is to show how the cultural phenomenon of the Avant-Garde in Spain functioned as a system of multiple networks, one of which was centered in Barcelona and the other in Madrid.[1]

1

If we only consider one city or the other, as is normally done when addressing the Avant-Garde in Spain, we cannot see that the various vanguard groups of both of these cities belonged to a much larger, more complex whole. This book is my attempt to articulate the bigger picture.

The time period during which the various avant-garde movements (there were countless of them throughout Europe, and many in Spain) first originated and practiced (the beginning of the twentieth century) is known as the Avant-Garde.[2] The many different styles of these new artistic and literary movements share a similar spirit and a desire for freedom that was difficult to acquire with conventional formulas. This moment in Spain was not just about what was going on in Barcelona, and it was not just about what was happening in Madrid. It was about what was going on between them, especially in the context of everything that was going on around them. To understand Spain's Avant-Garde more fully, we must consider the activity of Barcelona *and* Madrid as well as the political, cultural, and social circumstances of the moment. The avant-garde styles that most influenced Barcelona and Madrid, in chronological order, include cubism, futurism, expressionism, dadaism, planism, constructivism, vibrationism, creationism, ultraism, and surrealism. There were other "isms" practiced in other countries, but these were the ones that had the greatest impact in Barcelona and Madrid.

The first four of these isms—cubism, futurism, expressionism, and dadaism—were imported. Cubism had a considerable impact in Spain. If there were a dictionary of Spanish visual culture, it would be one of the main entries, due in large part to the great success of Pablo Picasso (Spanish, 1881–1973) whose cubist works can be found in museums all over the world. The movement's seminal work is a painting by Picasso (*Les Demoiselles d'Avignon*, 1907), who was living in Paris at the time that he created it.[3] Most of the early explorations of this mode of artistic expression were happening well before the First World War in France, not Spain. The pioneers of cubism include French painters (e.g., Georges Braque, Robert Delaunay, Albert Gleizes, Jean Metzinger, Fernand Léger) and poets (e.g., Guillaume Apollinaire, Blaise Cendrars, Jean Cocteau, Max Jacob, Pierre Reverdy), all of whom were centered in Paris.

The other three of these first four isms—futurism, expressionism, and dadaism—also were ideas from abroad: Italy, Germany, and Switzerland, respectively. The poet Filippo Tommaso Marinetti (Italian, 1876–1944) authored in 1909 the first manifesto that defined futurism. As the movement's name implies, futurists loathed everything from the past and praised everything that was new: speed, movement, energy, technology, youth, and the industrial city. In poetry, the main futurist idea of the word freed from the page was practically applied through experiments in typography. In the visual arts, artists strived to express movement and the dynamism of objects. Expressionism was a German aesthetic movement defined in 1910 that rebelled against naturalism and realism. In the visual arts, it was an outright rejection of impressionism and was greatly influenced by fauvism in its use of colors. Dadaism was a direct product of the First World War. Of all the isms, it is the most nihilistic in its attempt to destroy traditional methods of representation. The movement began in Switzerland (Zurich) during the Great War, and then quickly spread to Germany (Berlin, Cologne), France (Paris), Spain (Barcelona, Madrid), and the United States (New York).

The next five isms mentioned above—planism, constructivism, vibrationism, creationism, and ultraism—were made in Spain. Planism, constructivism, and vibrationism are three styles invented by three individual painters who challenged traditional modes of representation, each in their own way. Celso Lagar (Spanish, 1891–1966), Joaquín Torres-García (Uruguayan, 1874–1949), and Rafael Barradas (Uruguayan, 1890–1929) crafted these three methods of expression, planism, constructivism, and vibrationism, respectively, as personal responses to their lessons in cubism and futurism. These three artistic styles did not have nearly the same following or impact as cubism, futurism, or dadaism. Yet they are important to mention because they are styles particular to Spain's Avant-Garde and they are representative of the avant-garde aesthetic in Spain as a whole.

Creationism was a poetry style defined by the poet Vicente Huidobro (Chilean, 1893–1948), who moved to Madrid in 1918 after living in Paris, where he had direct contact with the creators of cubism. His goal was to discover the essence of poetry by eliminating anecdotes and other sentimentalisms. When he arrived in Madrid at the end of the First World War, the climate was just right for others to appreciate his new ideas about the construction of meaning in poetry. Poets in Madrid were on their way to inventing their own style, inspired by cubism, futurism, and dadaism. The poetic movement of ultraism surfaced in Madrid in 1919 as a style that was influenced by all the isms that came before it. While it was practiced primarily in poetry, visual artists also experimented with its concepts. As in creationism, the metaphor was increasingly cherished, as was reinforcing visual elements of poetry, while the anecdote became increasingly less important.

Finally, André Breton (French, 1896–1966) defined another ism in Paris in 1924: surrealism. This style has become almost synonymous with the meaning of the word *avant-garde*. The goal of this aesthetic was to explore the subconscious in order to gain a better understanding of the function of thought. According to his first manifesto, Breton defines the revolution as follows: "Surrealism is based on the belief in the superior reality of certain forms of previously neglected associations, in the omnipotence of dream, in the disinterested play of thought."[4] Surrealism entered the scene in Spain when the painter Salvador Dalí and his filmmaker friend Luis Buñuel shocked the world with their experimental short film, *An Andalusian Dog* (1929). Up until this point, there were mentions of surrealism in the press that covered such news in Spain, but it was not fully understood and certainly not practiced by many. Surrealism is the most well-known avant-garde style, which explains why oftentimes this term is used erroneously to describe all the experimental styles that led up to and came after its discovery.

A shared belief in a series of ideals is one of the key characteristics of the Avant-Garde and its corresponding spirit. One of these was living a nonconformist lifestyle that was opposed to high culture as well as commercial, bourgeois, and mainstream values. Many supporters of the Avant-Garde fought for sociopolitical and cultural reform by instigating an artistic revolution. They sought the innovation of both the form and content of artistic production through both creative experimentation and rational theorization, as evident in their many manifestos. The goal of all of these isms was to experience freedom from the restrictions of old models of representation. As a whole, the Avant-Garde fought against sentimentalisms, linear narrative, and the anecdote. Consequently, their work was often provocative, shocking, and misunderstood.

Promoters of the Avant-Garde were united by an exaltation of abstraction, the subconscious, rationality, freedom, purity, imagination, youth, play, sport, and passion. Through experimentation they searched for the essence of things, including both subjects and objects, and they philosophized about their musings in architecture, music, poetry, sculpture, theater, and prose (especially manifestos, novels, and journalistic essays). Over the course of his life, Salvador Dalí, for example, wrote about his work, his society, and himself almost as much as he painted. In literature and the visual arts, members of the Avant-Garde experimented with the use of multiple and simultaneous points of view, free rhyme, innovative typography, metaphors, symbols, and mixed media. The destruction of old models of representation was achieved by inventing new ones that were more appropriate in commenting on and expressing the realities of a life that was in severe political, economic, and social crisis, as was certainly the case in Spain.

While young people today use a variety of gadgets and systems to communicate, those who were members of the Avant-Garde in Barcelona and Madrid also felt an urge to form groups and networks, but without our same technology. They connected, identified, and interacted with one another through their participation in the creation of this new art that included literature, dance, music, architecture, sculpture, and painting. They demonstrated their involvement and leadership in various networks by participating in political and cultural events and the press, especially as seen in their contributions to the specialized press that sustained the Avant-Garde. Through their many roles in various activities, oftentimes in multiple cities, they became members of a much larger social network and an international movement that forged a new, more modern identity, which defined twentieth-century culture in opposition to the nineteenth-century one.

The reason why social networking sites are so effective today is because membership in these virtual communities reveals hidden connections. Once this happens, the opportunity for networking with people who have common interests will increase one's chances for finding a job, friends, a partner, or community. Naturally, the more connections one can make, the larger one's network and the greater one's chances of finding what he or she is looking for, whether it be companionship or employment, for example. The practice of expanding the number of one's contacts (professional or personal) is achieved by making more connections through contact with other individuals also registered in the same networking sites. As we will see in the chapters to come, the members of the various avant-garde circles of Barcelona and Madrid expanded their networks by making connections with like-minded people, irrespective of their nationality, social class, gender, or political beliefs. If today's social networking culture helps people connect and create community, the forms of communication practiced at the beginning of the twentieth century by members of the Avant-Garde in Barcelona and Madrid helped sustain a revolutionary movement that changed the face of Spain and Catalonia's twentieth-century cultural identity and history. Furthermore, the many artistic isms that arose throughout Europe during the first three decades of the twentieth century may have gone unnoticed, had there not been a system of social communication networks connecting them while circulating knowledge and information about them.

The cubist painter Juan Gris (Spanish, 1887–1927) is one avant-garde painter who offers an example of what this changing face of a more interconnected and modern Spain could have looked like. Gris, who was born in Madrid, moved to Paris at the age of nineteen. In what was then considered the artistic and cultural capital of the world, he befriended a fellow Spaniard, Pablo Picasso. In 1912 Gris painted a cubist portrait of Picasso as a sign of his friendship and respect for one of the leaders of this revolutionary style. The experimental work of Gris was exhibited at an art show in Madrid in 1929 that, for the first time in Spain, featured the work of several avant-garde

Spanish painters who were living in Paris. One of these works is a drawing titled *Espanyol*, which means Spaniard.[5] Interestingly, Gris (or his agent) spelled this word in Catalan, not in Spanish, which would have been *Español*. The fragmented profile of this young and strong male figure strongly resembles the shape of the Iberian Peninsula, where both Spain and Catalonia are located. The eyes, ears, and lips are clustered in the center of the work, drawing attention to the acts of seeing, hearing, and speaking, as if to suggest that these actions should be characterizing features of the new Spaniard. Already, these were fundamental skills mastered by most avant-garde artists to communicate, stay connected, and stay relevant. The modern Spaniard was one who was interconnected not only in his or her city but beyond it.

By definition, that which is avant-garde pushes, crosses, and, in some cases, destroys boundaries in order to defeat the enemy, conquer new frontiers, gain power, and seek a new, fresh paradigm of culture. The Avant-Garde spirit in Spain consisted of a desire to break not only aesthetic boundaries but also geographic, linguistic, physical, political, social, and cultural ones. The way in which the story of the Avant-Garde in Spain has been told so far insists on focusing on one city or the other. Histories rarely take into account the elaborate system of networks connecting the avant-garde movements of both cities. By failing to do so, they effectively deny the movement's essence. By denying or neglecting to pay attention to the relationships between the avant-garde networks of Barcelona and Madrid, the movement in Spain as a whole would be stripped of its progressive spirit, in which boundary crossing is of principal importance. By telling each side of the story separately, the Avant-Garde movement in Spain comes across as overly simplistic and uninteresting. What makes these years so fascinating is the speed of the advances in the creation of new art and literature, especially in comparison to the century that preceded it, and the original ways in which artists and poets were incorporating these changes into their work.

One reason why the Avant-Garde of the 1920s in Spain should not be overlooked is because it challenges the story of separation of Barcelona and Madrid that has been perpetuated for so many centuries. By keeping these two cities divided when addressing Spain's Avant-Garde as a whole, or Catalonia's Avant-Garde, the divisions between them will not only persist but also multiply. Some have considered that one of the greatest weaknesses of Spain's Constitution is that it fails to assign to any governing body responsibility for promoting interregional cooperation.[6] This book serves as my testament to encourage scholarship in support of interregional understanding in Spain. It also aspires to shift attitudes about the historically antagonistic relationship between Barcelona and Madrid, in general.

Figure 1.1. Drawing by Juan Gris, titled *Spaniard.*

With the recent sporting victory of Spain in the 2010 World Cup, we have witnessed that it is possible to overcome the kind of national differences that keep Spain divided, as long as the different parties agree on the same goal. And by this, I am referring to the fact that more than half of the players on the Spanish national team played for F.C. Barcelona during the regular season. For two players, Carles Puyol and Xavi Hernandez, this victory also belonged to Catalonia, as they ran around the field with the Catalan flag after the game. The objective of the groups and individuals who made up the avant-garde networks of Barcelona and Madrid was not always clear, nor did everyone always agree on its terms, but the desire to tear down old walls and build something entirely new was certainly present. In some instances the vanguard promoters proved to be successful; in others, they failed to produce the desired results, usually due to a cause outside of their control, such as political turmoil, poor infrastructure, or lack of funding for basic resources. The efforts of avant-garde artists and writers in early twentieth-century Barcelona and Madrid resulted in a rapid progression of culture that still seems shocking today.

A study of the system of networks connecting avant-garde Barcelona and Madrid reflects the sociopolitical and cultural realities of early twentieth-century Catalonia and Spain. The loss of Cuba, Puerto Rico, the Philippines, and Guam to the United States Navy in 1898 meant the end of the Spanish Empire with its fifteenth-century origins. In Madrid, a centralized vision of the state was important for the demoralized collective ego. It seemed to ease the blow of losing their global grip. The central government in Madrid saw the culture of Castile, that representing the center of Spain, as the core of Spanish identity. On the other hand, Catalans saw themselves as having a unique identity different from that of the rest of Spain. Catalans were frustrated with Madrid, because its centralist politics denied them certain autonomous rights, as well as greater independence and power.

The divide between Catalans and Castilians, or non-Catalan Spaniards, just as with Barcelona and Madrid, has existed for centuries. As a result of this division, and the history behind it (to be discussed with more attention in the next chapter), it was difficult for many in Madrid to understand and accept a distinct Catalan culture in their reformulations of Spanish identity after the disastrous colonial loss to the United States. During the first half of the twentieth century, most artists and writers in Barcelona looked in the direction of Europe and toward the continued construction of their own national and cultural Catalan identity. A close look at the nature of relationships between the cultural networks of Barcelona and Madrid during the inception of the Avant-Garde reveals two visions of Spain that did not always coincide, and two cultures that conflicted, drifted apart, and even avoided dialogue at times.

Despite the conventions, an analysis of the interactions and production between networks in these two communities reveals that the avant-garde networks of Barcelona and Madrid were dynamic and deeply interconnected, even if just spiritually. It makes perfect sense that the Avant-Garde would challenge the centuries-old boundaries around identity and Spanish culture. And because of what the Avant-Garde stood for, this research posits that, contrary to traditional interpretations and documenting of vanguard production and interactions, members of this generation of artists and writers forged a new cultural identity that characterizes twentieth-century Spanish and Catalan culture. Those who promote conventional ideas about artists and writers adhere to the above division, arguing that much like Spanish society, many artists and writers in Madrid were influenced by a centralized vision of Spain. And in Barcelona, it is believed that by contrast, many artists and writers found it difficult to accept a national identity that omitted the Catalan component.

Indeed, one hundred years ago, governments and institutions, and even artists themselves, took few initiatives to promote encounters between artists and writers of the two cities in question. Even with the establishment of a national network of telephone lines, communication between the two cities was not easy. Train rides were long, mail was slow, and plane trips were a luxury. However, despite the logistical obstacles that made effective communication difficult, much evidence about the interactions that did occur between these two communities reveals that the human dimension and the intensity and authenticity of relationships between avant-garde artists and writers from both cities created an authentic web of personal and professional relationships that promoted unity. These networks opened new horizons for these visionaries in their views of national culture and identity and their contributions to them. The networks gave them hope for progress and helped them face one another in reconstructing a new identity. The story of separation between Barcelona and Madrid continues. In the summer of 2010, just a few days after Spain's victory at the World Cup, the Constitutional Tribunal of Madrid blocked Catalonia's Statute of Autonomy. Today's politics continue to reflect more divisions than links between these two capital cities and their respective communities. Yet human relationships between people of both cities move beyond the existing political tension, which often serves only as a way to aggravate differences of opinion, promote violence, and feed ignorance. This transcendence of difference was often the case among Avant-Garde promoters in Spain.

This book explores the web of relationships between networked groups and individuals centered in Barcelona and Madrid who were connected to the Avant-Garde as a whole in Spain and beyond. It is pieced together from a variety of sources, consisting of literary, visual, and political texts (e.g., periodicals, art exhibit catalogues, photographs, letters, lectures, paintings, drawings, manifestos, and speeches). The original question that initiated this project—did the avant-garde artists and poets in Barcelona and Madrid know about one another?—led to the discovery of many connections linking the two cities' distinct vanguard movements. Investigating the way in which this matrix of relationships worked revealed a complicated web of dialogue, presumptions, misinformation, and culture clashes. Others have already attempted to map out the networks of individuals and institutions related to the Avant-Garde in one city or the other. The objective here is to consider the avant-garde networks of Barcelona and Madrid more holistically, focusing on the complexities of connections and disconnections, and what these reveal about Spanish and Catalan cultural identity, progress, and modernity.

When and where did the Avant-Garde movement begin in Catalonia and Spain? The telling of this account might begin at various points in time, or with various artists or art works in particular. There is no point in agonizing about beginnings. Instead, we can take heed of the words of the Iberian medievalist, Rosa María Menocal: "Why do we not begin, more simply and cleanly, in some indisputable *media res* and from there go bravely forward into the future, rather than backwards to where the question of the source of that particular river may lie?"[7] Avant-garde ideas from abroad, such as Italian futurism, infiltrated Spain's borders as early as 1909, when Filippo Tommaso Marinetti's manifesto was translated into Spanish and published in Ramón Gómez de la Serna's literary review, *Prometeo*, in Madrid. Yet three years earlier, two visual artists, Pablo Picasso and Pablo Gargallo, were already experimenting with proto-cubist ideas in Catalonia. My concern is not to determine where or when exactly this movement began, but rather to understand the nature of the relationships between the people and institutions that promoted avant-garde practices in both cities. Who were the bridge figures? How did they communicate? How often did they communicate? What were the results of these communications? Why were some communications more effective than others? What was the relationship between the avant-garde experiments and the realities of daily life? A study such as this, with a wide-angle lens, reveals that the difficulty of developing and maintaining positive relationships between the avant-garde networks of these two cities is directly related to the severe political tensions and cultural misunderstandings that kept them divided for centuries. As we shall see, artists and writers from both Barcelona and Madrid used avant-garde ideologies to either bring them closer together or keep them divided, depending on the political climate and personal circumstances.

At the heart of the Avant-Garde in Spain and amongst its supporters, centered in either one of these two cities, is a common denominator that transcended their national allegiances or nation of origin. Crossing a range of boundaries (age, class, geography, language, politics, and sexuality), they all believed in the radical renovation of art, culture, literature, and society at large. And the tools of the Avant-Garde helped them work toward this goal. The individuals and works that make up this book share a common faith in the ideas of rupture, resistance, and renewal. These Avant-Garde members tackled tradition through their magazines, books, art shows, banquets, performances, conferences, and frequent gatherings. Many of the believers in this Avant-Garde spirit communicated with one another as best they could before and during the Miguel Primo de Rivera military dictatorship (1923–30) and up until a second military overthrow by General Francisco Franco (1936). And precisely because the Avant-Garde was a minority cultural movement in both cities, the strength of their faith in their purpose was essential to its survival. Like other faith systems, the Avant-Garde in Spain depended on its prophets, especially during hard times, to communicate their message efficiently and wisely. It also depended on its disciples. These individuals—their works, their interactions, public statements, affiliations, and the coming together of all of these aspects—are the focus here.

The present research reveals an elaborate web of communications between Barcelona and Madrid evident in three major areas. The first of these consists of literary and artistic periodicals, also known as "little magazines." These documents have been given this name due to their generally limited circulation and short life span. At times, the periodicals only consisted of one or two issues, like the little magazine created by Federico García Lorca in Granada (with the help of his Catalan friend, Salvador Dalí), called *Gallo* (Rooster), which was published only on two occasions. The bulk of this research stems from the study of one hundred of these little magazines from Barcelona and Madrid, in which a plethora of links that tied both of these cities together both in theory and practice emerged. For instance, some of these experimental publications published in both Catalan and Spanish as a way to bridge the linguistic divide between these two centers, while also drawing attention to boundary-crossing journalists and artists, like Sebastià Gasch and Rafael Barradas. Catalans who crossed over into the Spanish press of Madrid included Salvador Dalí, Sebastià Gasch, Tomàs Garcés, and Josep Maria Sucre. Non-Catalan Spaniards who crossed over to the press of

Barcelona were Ramón Gómez de la Serna, Ernesto Giménez Caballero, Gerardo Diego, and Benjamin Jarnés.

The second source of information regarding the connection between poets and artists in both cities consists of the documents and publications related to art shows of the Avant-Garde in Spain. Many of the poets of this time were visual artists and vice versa. The marriage between poetry and art during this time was a happy one. Proof of this coexistence is seen in many of the little magazines that included illustrations alongside literary texts. The early career of Salvador Dalí exemplifies this crossover between the visual and the written word. One of the ways in which he, a Catalan, got his foot in the door in Madrid was by publishing illustrations in many of the city's specialized periodicals. In addition to studying the relationship between artists and poets within the pages of the little magazines, exploration of major collective and individual art exhibits that directly address the subject of national identity sheds light on the relationship between the avant-garde circles in Barcelona and Madrid. In some cases, a catalogue for the show was available, as well as photographs; in other cases, the primary sources of information are reviews, letters exchanged between friends, and other more marginal documents.

In this overall widening of the scope of our analysis of the Avant-Garde in Spain, the number of contacts between Barcelona and Madrid increases. Only with this panoramic lens can we even begin to consider the connectedness between their respective networks. In a similar way, while concerned with two of the threads of the web that connected avant-garde Barcelona and Madrid, those being art and poetry, this book is also interested in the cultural moment in general. In order to keep up with the quickly changing styles (cubism, futurism, dadaism, etc.), it was imperative that artists and poets communicate not only with one another, but also with all those who made up the various avant-garde circles in Barcelona and Madrid. While friendships were important, networking was vital for the survival of the movement and for the people involved. Artists and poets are the first who come to mind when thinking about the Avant-Garde. But there were others who contributed to the movement with funding, infrastructure, opportunity, and moral support, such as journalists, politicians, and business people.

As a result of widening the scope beyond artists and poets, other documents beyond the little magazines and art exhibits were helpful in understanding the communication between the avant-garde circles of both of these cities. For instance, many promoters of the Avant-Garde in Spain met regularly at cafes or in private homes. These social gatherings, commonly known as *tertulias*, were an integral part of the intellectual fabric of urban culture in both cities. Ramón Gómez de la Serna was the organizer of one of the most famous of these, called Pombo. Any visitor to Madrid who was associated with the Avant-Garde during this period very likely made an appearance at the Café Pombo at least once. The reason why we know so much about what went on every Saturday night in the same meeting place for many years is that Gómez de la Serna kept judicious records.[8] Today, these published and edited notes are available in two data-packed tomes. Here we can discover who was at Pombo and what they discussed. Gómez de la Serna considered these weekly meetings to be more than just social gatherings, which is probably why he went to great lengths to document details about every weekend for years. He had the foresight to recognize that what was happening every Saturday night, under his direction, was historic and crucial to the forging of modern Spain's new identity.

As a result of using this wide-angle research method described above, three facts about the relationship between the avant-garde networks in Barcelona and Madrid became clear. First, Barcelona's avant-garde network materialized before Madrid's. In literature, for instance, the influence of Italian futurism among a small group of Catalan poets is pronounced. The Italian founder of this avant-garde style, F. T. Marinetti, maintained correspondence with several Catalans, including J. V. Foix, Joan Salvat-Papasseit, Josep Maria Junoy, and Sebastià Sánchez-Juan. The impact of Italian futurism was so great in Barcelona that a Catalan variant evolved (c. 1912–20). This Catalan variant was also influenced by literary cubism and late symbolism. Some of the poets who participated actively in this movement include Joaquim Folguera, Josep Maria Junoy, Joan Salvat-Papasseit, Carles Sindreu, and Vincenç Solé de Sojo. Like Marinetti, Salvat-Papasseit authored several futurist manifestos, signing his name as one word: "poetacatalanvanguardista," meaning: Catalan-avant-garde-poet. As described later on, the Avant-Garde in the visual arts also manifested itself early on in Barcelona, much sooner than in Madrid, primarily because of the art shows organized by one gallery owner, Josep Dalmau. It is widely acknowledged that at the beginning of the twentieth century, Barcelona was the center of new art practices in Spain, a major stop en route to Paris, as was the case for so many Spanish (non-Catalan) and Catalan avant-garde artists, namely Joan Miró, Pablo Picasso, Juan Gris, and Pablo Gargallo.

The second fact that became apparent as a result of my methodology was that Spain's major avant-garde movement, *Ultraísmo* (1919–23), was exceptionally diverse in terms of the nationality of its promoters. *Ultraísmo* was founded in Madrid, but its impact went well beyond the capital's borders. Also called Ultra, this avant-garde style closely associated with Madrid warmly welcomed newness. The founding manifesto makes this clear: "invocan la colaboración de toda la juventud literaria española" (we invoke the collaboration of all of Spain's young literati).[9] Periodicals that promoted Ultra, like *Ultra*, *Grecia*, and *Cervantes*, published in languages other than Castilian. Ultra also found expression in a wide variety of artistic genres, such as woodcuttings, sculpture, and collage. In terms of the nationality of its members, the movement included people from many parts of Spain, Europe, and Latin America. Some of the Catalans who participated in the Ultra movement include Joan Salvat-Papasseit, Sebastià Gasch, and Salvador Dalí. Some of the foreigners who lived in Madrid and promoted Ultra were Rafael Barradas (Uruguayan), Jorge Luis Borges (Argentinean), and Vicente Huidobro (Chilean).

The third point that clearly arose as a result of adopting a wider-angle lens in the analysis of the Avant-Garde in Spain was unexpected. Once the original excitement of Ultra fizzled in Madrid, avant-garde periodicals shifted away from the cities, in this case Barcelona and Madrid, and into the peripheries. By 1924, Ultra was no longer the fashion in Madrid, and from 1923 to 1930 a military dictatorship there ruled Spain. Avant-garde magazines appeared in Spanish-speaking areas of the country, like Andalusia and the Canary Islands, that were geographically far from Barcelona and Madrid. During the dictatorship, Ultra radiated as far as Mexico and Argentina, thereby increasing ties with Spanish speakers across the Atlantic and broadening its network. A similar shift occurred in Catalonia with the publication of major avant-garde periodicals in Catalan-speaking cities beyond the urban limits of Barcelona, like Sitges, Manresa, Vilafranca, and Lleida. With this shift to the peripheries, direct links between Barcelona and Madrid decreased, but the network in Spain as a whole increased.

Members of the avant-garde networks in Barcelona and Madrid did not function completely independently of one another. In fact, just the opposite is true. In some cases, Avant-Garde promoters from Barcelona and Madrid collaborated directly with one another to create a variety of innovative projects. The most emblematic case of a Catalan avant-garde promoter collaborating with a non-Catalan Spaniard counterpart is that of Salvador Dalí and Federico García Lorca, but there were many others.[10] That which united these diverse individuals was a common Avant-Garde spirit, with its elements of opposition to the established order, commitment to change, break with tradition, and rupture with the past; formal experimentation; connection to the world outside of Spain; rejection of *modernismo*, *noucentisme*, and naturalism; and provocation and revolution. In the end, these individuals were capable of overcoming differences (political, national, linguistic, geographic, etc.) to unite and create something completely new together: a mutual understanding between two historically antagonistic cities and cultures under the common flag and language of the literary and artistic Avant-Garde. Collectively, the stories of the many artists and their works detailed throughout this book provide the basis for my conclusion that the connections between these networks not only existed, but that they had a significant impact on the evolution of Spain and Catalonia's cultural identity throughout the twentieth century.

Notes

1. Please note that when referring to the movement as a whole, I capitalize the whole word (e.g., the Avant-Garde, the Avant-Garde movement). When referring to particular segments, features, or elements of the movement, I leave the word in lowercase letters (e.g., avant-garde style, avant-garde artists).

2. For a compilation of manifestos and other founding documents of European avant-garde movements translated into Spanish, see Ángel González García et al., *Escritos de arte de vanguardia 1900–1945* (Madrid: Istmo, 2003).

3. One of the things that must have shocked viewers (then and today) when standing in front of Picasso's *Les Demoiselles d'Avignon* is its huge scale (8' x 7'8") (243.9 x 233.7 cm) as described in New York's Museum of Modern Art Web site. The title of the painting directs us to the red-light district in Barcelona where Avignon Street (Carrer d'Avinyó) is located, which suggests that the five women are prostitutes. The size of each of these figures is larger than life. *Les Demoiselles d'Avignon* is part of the permanent collection of the Museum of Modern Art in New York City. *Les Demoiselles d'Avignon*, Museum of Modern Art, http://www.moma.org/collection/object.php?object_id=79766 (accessed July 15, 2011).

4. "Surrealist Manifesto," http://wikilivres.info/wiki/Surrealist_Manifesto.

5. Joan Gris, *Espanyol* (Madrid: *Españoles Residentes en París*, 1929).

6. Luis López Guerra, "National and Regional Pluralism in Contemporary Spain," in *Iberian Identity: Essays on the Nature of Identity in Spain and Portugal*, ed. Richard Herr et al. (Berkeley: Institute of International Studies, University of California, Berkeley, 1989), 27.

7. Rosa María Menocal, "Beginnings," in *The Cambridge History of Spanish Literature*, ed. David Gies (Cambridge, UK: Cambridge University Press, 2004), 58.

8. Ramón Gómez de la Serna, *Pombo* (Madrid: Trieste, 1986), and *La sagrada cripta de Pombo* (Madrid: Trieste, 1986).

9. Jaime Brihuega. *Manifiestos, proclamas, panfletos y textos doctrinales: Las vanguardias artísticas en España, 1910–1930* (Madrid: Istmo, 1981), 37–38.

10. On the relationship between Federico García Lorca and Salvador Dalí, see two comprehensive accounts: Ian Gibson, *Lorca–Dalí: el amor que no pudo ser* (Barcelona: DeBolsillo, 2004), and Agustín Sánchez Vidal, *Buñuel, Lorca, Dalí: el enigma sin fin* (Barcelona: Planeta, 2004).

CHAPTER TWO

~

The Avant-Garde as Network

Let us look at the interconnected literary and artistic vanguard groups of early twentieth-century Barcelona and Madrid concurrently. In doing so, we will instantly see a complicated web of connections linking these two cosmopolitan centers. We also will see how experimental literature and the arts were instrumental in reformulating both Barcelona and Madrid's cultural identities in a dynamic, complex, and highly interconnected process. While there may not have been a high level of information exchange between these two centers on a daily basis in the way we might see today, there were real, legitimate, and significant connections between individuals and groups linking these two cities. One case that illustrates this point can be found in the life and work of Ernesto Giménez Caballero, one of the leaders of the avant-garde network in Madrid.

Just weeks after the remarkable success of the Catalan Book Fair in Madrid, Ernesto Giménez Caballero, one of the main organizers of this extraordinary event, which will be discussed in more detail in the final chapter, made an important trip. He flew to Barcelona on Iberian Airlines to exhibit his "literary posters" in the most cutting-edge art gallery in Spain. Each one of the literary posters depicted a contemporary writer, critic, editor, or artist using mixed media, especially colorful paper and newspaper cutouts. After allegedly being hassled by military police at the Barcelona airport, he convinced the authorities that he was simply returning a cultural visit. The Catalans had just exhibited their books in Madrid, and now he was exhibiting his artwork in Barcelona. He was allowed to display his literary posters at the Dalmau Galleries from January 8 to 20, 1928, but only under the supervision of police officers. On the opening day of the exhibit, Gustavo Gili, a successful Catalan book editor, purchased all of Giménez Caballero's posters for an undisclosed amount. But before Giménez Caballero handed them over to Gustavo Gili, he exhibited the posters in Madrid at an art gallery located in an exhibiting space of the Ediciones Inchausti publishing company.

The contemporary poet Pedro Salinas attended this second showing of Giménez Caballero's innovative approach to literary criticism through visual art. In an article published by Giménez Caballero in Madrid, he describes a dialogue he had with Salinas.[1] According to this account, Salinas remarked that the collection would be more complete if it included a poster that reflected on Spain's new literary movement as a whole, not just some of its protagonists. Giménez Caballero responded to Salinas's challenge at the closing ceremony of the Madrid exhibit. In his response, the creator of these literary posters argued that the center of Spain's experimental literary activity and cultural production was not Barcelona, as highly suggested by the Catalans during their recent Book Fair in Madrid, but Madrid.

To argue his point, he drew the "Theorem of New Spanish Literature" on a blackboard. This image would later be published in his periodical *La Gaceta Literaria*, accompanied by a fragment of his talk.[2] He depicted the Iberian Peninsula as a pentagon that contained various networks in the form of five small triangles from which the "new Spanish literature" was emerging. According to his visual, verbal, and written explanation, none of the three main triangles inside the pentagon are connected. In other words, there are no points of connection between the various groups creating new literature on the peninsula. In fact, he uses this image, the public occasion as well as the follow-up published article, to prove that Madrid is the center of Spain's new literary phenomenon. While Giménez Caballero was relatively safe making this argument from his hometown of Madrid, he chose not to make the same argument at the Dalmau Galleries in Barcelona several months earlier. Or at least there are no indications that he did so, at least not publicly.

Giménez Caballero begins to prove his "theorem" by asserting that the shape of Spain is that of a pentagon. Inside this figure, he drew five triangles. The first triangle is located to the north and covers the region of Catalonia. Outside of the pentagon, there is an arrow to the right above the geometric shape representing Catalonia, to suggest that this region functioned like a funnel for all of the ideas pouring in from the rest of Europe. In order to measure the size and shape of each of the triangles, he uses the literary and cultural periodicals, which he considers to be "el núcleo absoluto donde se insertan numeradores y denominadores" (the absolute nucleus where nu-

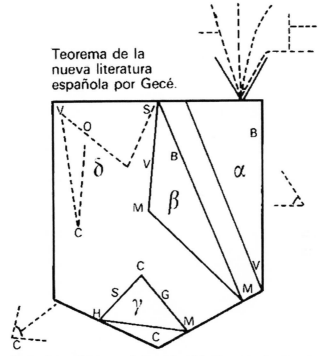

Figure 2.1. *Theorem of New Spanish Literature* by Ernesto Giménez Caballero.

merators and denominators can be found). He uses the periodicals to mark the figure's coordinates.[3] The coordinates, then, are indicated on the map using the initial of the city from where the periodical originates. Therefore, the "G" is an abbreviation for Granada, the city where *Gallo* is published.[4]

Once he determines the coordinates for each of the triangles, he labels each of them: Alpha (α) = Catalonia and Valencia; Beta (β) = Castile and Murcia; Gamma (γ) = Andalusia; (δ) Delta = Galicia and Portugal.[5] Before defining their value, he compares them in the following manner: First, "α < β > γ > δ" (alpha is less than beta, which is greater than gamma, which is greater than delta; or Catalonia/Valencia is less than Castile/Murcia, which is greater than Andalusia, which is greater than Galicia/Portugal). Second, "β > α > γ > δ" (Castile is greater than Catalonia, which is greater than Andalusia, which is greater than Galicia and Portugal). Third, "γ < α < β < δ" (Andalusia is less than Catalonia, which is less than Castile, which is smaller than Galicia).

In conclusion, he determines that the new literary movement in Madrid is greater than that in Barcelona, which is greater than that in Andalusia, which is greater than that of Galicia and Portugal. Yet he does not offer any proof or explanation as to how he came up with any of these calculations. His evaluation is completely subjective, even though he would like to seem objective by using the guise of geometry.

The triangle that corresponds to the new literary movement in Catalonia and Valencia is nearly "all political," he states in the already referenced article, and not so literary. Not only did he disapprove of the fact that both the *Nova Revista* and *L'Amic de les Arts* published entirely in the "vernacular," that is, in the Catalan language, but he loathed it. As we will see in the final chapter of this book, Giménez Caballero distrusted periodicals that centered themselves exclusively on Catalan issues. He strongly believed that the new literary movement had to be inclusive of the peninsula's plurality of cultures and languages and that the different regions of Spain had to collaborate. There was no room for separatisms in his vision of Spain's new literary movement. In his theorem he explains that the triangular area that corresponds to Madrid can be characterized as having everything that the one that corresponds to Barcelona does not, especially its "desdén por la política" (dislike of politics). Giménez Caballero goes on to say that if Madrid's cultural periodicals included any politics, it was so lyrical that one could argue that it was more literary language than anything else. The only politics of Madrid periodicals such as *Revista de Occidente* and *La Gaceta Literaria* was to "correct" Barcelona's disdain toward Madrid. Giménez Caballero believed this could be achieved not through traditional politics, but through avenues opened up by collaborating in the new literary and artistic movement, organizing events like the Catalan Book Fair in Madrid, and getting them covered in the press of both cities.

Rather than enter into dialogue with the Catalans, Giménez Caballero would often impose his idea of what he thought was correct on them. It is almost as if he truly believed that just because he included Catalan news in the periodical he directed (*La Gaceta Literaria*), the Barcelona press would reciprocate—as if the historic tensions between the two cities could be solved overnight and without any true dialogue. His mission, through his bimonthly periodical, was to fight for an "indigenous Spain"; that is, a nation composed of many subgroups, including Castilians, Catalans, Portuguese, Sephardic Jews, and Latin Americans.[6] For this reason he called for the "trinity of peninsular languages," the three languages being Spanish, Catalan, and Portuguese, in order to achieve the "Iberian ideal of cooperation founded on geography and culture."[7] No other periodical involved in the new literary movement in Spain worked so diligently toward creating a more unified Spain through the arts. The value he placed on this "higher" mission may be one of the reasons why the beta triangle, the one corresponding to Madrid, is greater than the alpha or the one corresponding to Barcelona. We can only deduce that this is the reason why he considers Madrid to be greater Barcelona, based on the variables he introduces into his equations.

When the editor of *La Gaceta Literaria* differentiates between Barcelona and Madrid by accusing the people of Barcelona of being more influenced by the ideas that funnel in from France and Italy, in contrast to Madrid's "autochthonous influences," he places more value on all that is Spanish than that which is "foreign."[8] In Madrid, new ideas come from writers and intellectuals like José Ortega y Gasset, Miguel Unamuno, Azorín, Pío Baroja, Juan Ramón Jiménez, Eugeni D'Ors, Ramón Gómez de la Serna, Antonio Machado, and Ramón Pérez de Ayala. Without further explanation, Giménez Caballero concludes that ultimately, the new literary movement in Spain is one that is defined by its limits. He was setting himself up to be the hero of uniting a divided Spain through his multilingual periodical. Correspondingly, he considered his periodical and his city to be the center of Spain's literary and artistic vanguard movement.

Ernesto Giménez Caballero was not the only one who took a centralizing stance in shaping the development of the Avant-Garde phenomenon in Spain. A few years earlier, the Madrid-born poet and literary critic Guillermo de Torre published the first book-length study written in Spanish describing all of the major European literary and artistic avant-garde movements: *Literaturas europeas de vanguardia* (Literatures of the European Avant-Garde) (1925).[9] In this lengthy text, he describes every artistic and literary avant-garde style in Europe, including Madrid's *Ultraísmo* movement, but fails to mention Barcelona at all. According to the histories that Ernesto Giménez Caballero and Guillermo de Torre construct, Barcelona played little to no role in the development of Spain's Avant-Garde as a whole. However, if we place the literary and artistic networks of Barcelona and Madrid on the same playing field, rather than dismissing one or the other, a system of connections linking these two centers is revealed. Seen in this way, the new literary and artistic movement suddenly plays a much larger role in the development of Barcelona and Madrid's identity politics at the beginning of the twentieth century. More importantly, we can see how the relationships between the people and groups involved in reshaping the identities of these two urban centers at the level of this literary and artistic revolutionary movement, known as the Avant-Garde, were dynamic, complex, and highly interconnected. Giménez Caballero, for one, could not claim that Madrid was the heart of the Avant-Garde movement in Spain without mentioning its relationship to Barcelona. Specifically, he argued that the new literary movement in Spain was greater in Madrid than in Barcelona.

In a more contemporary account of artistic activity in Spain, Jaime Brihuega's indispensible *Las vanguardias artísticas en España: 1909–1936* (The Artistic Avant-Gardes of Spain) (1981) offers an impressive report of invaluable documentation.[10] But, the way in which he presents this data implies a disconnection between these two cities, as if it were a given. The art historian compiles a year-by-year account (in some instances a month-by-month, sometimes day-by-day, listing) of the many exhibitions, books, periodicals, meetings, happenings, lectures, individuals, and political acts associated with the origins and development of the Avant-Garde in Spain. This rendering implies that both communities operated within independent and mutually exclusive orbits of cultural production, similar to the way in which Ernesto Giménez Caballero depicted it in his theorem of new literature in Spain. While there may not have been excessive communication between writers and artists from these two cities on a daily basis, it does not mean that there were no links.

The difficulty of recounting the dynamic nature of Spain's cultural scene during the beginning of the twentieth century is apparent from the start of Brihuega's account. He begins his narrative with 1909, the year that the first futurist manifesto written by the Italian poet Filippo Tommaso Marinetti was translated into Spanish, in a literary periodical edited by Ramón Gómez de la Serna called *Prometeo* (Madrid, 1904–12). The original Italian manifesto was published in the Parisian newspaper *Le Figaro* on February 20, 1909:

> 1909.—Partimos de la publicación del Manifiesto Futurista en 'Prometeo.' Ese mismo año, en marzo, Gabriel Alomar había dado la noticia de la aparición de este manifiesto en París, diecisiete días después de su publicación en 'Le Figaro.'

> (1909.—We begin with the Futurist Manifesto in 'Prometeo.' This same year, in March, Gabriel Alomar announced the appearance of this manifesto in Paris, seventeen days after it appeared in 'Le Figaro.')[11]

This art historian would like to begin his annotated chronology of the history of the Avant-Garde in Spain with the publication and Spanish translation of the Italian futurist manifesto in Madrid. Yet, in good faith, he cannot do so without making a reference to Barcelona. The Catalan writer Gabriel Alomar, living in Barcelona at the time, had already philosophized about another type of futurism, a Catalan futurism, several years before Marinetti. As Brihuega points out, Alomar reported the news of the Italian futurist manifesto in Barcelona about one month before Ramón Gómez de la Serna did so in Madrid (April 1909).[12] In fact, Alomar broke the news of the Italian manifesto in Barcelona (March 9, 1909) before it was even reported in Marinetti's homeland, Italy (March 11, 1909, in the periodical *Poesía V*).

After the chronological complications involved in explaining the Marinetti (Paris)–Alomar (Barcelona)–Gómez de la Serna (Madrid) triangle that is necessary to mention when describing the inception of futurism in Spain, Brihuega settles for simplicity. In order to avoid such future entanglements, he opts for a city-based chronology and chooses as his starting point the year 1911. He avoids further confusion by focusing on the avant-garde developments in Spain on a city-by-city basis. In doing so, he establishes Madrid as the central axis of his chronology. Brihuega traces the cultural history of the vanguard movements in Spain by centering his timeline in Madrid, while Barcelona and other cities are treated laterally. He maintains this structure throughout the book, until he reaches the year of the onset of the Spanish Civil War (1936), when his account ends.

Separating these major events in Spain by city oversimplifies the time period, causing the impression that avant-garde activity in each city operated on its own, as if there were no contact or communication connecting them. The other cities in Spain that Brihuega mentions—Barcelona, Bilbao, La Coruña, and Seville—all seem to function independently, like nerve centers feeding off the central medulla of Madrid. This organizational structure gives his readers a sense that all avant-garde artistic activity in Spain originated in Madrid or depended on it, which is certainly not the case. This disconnected account, like so many others, further exaggerates the distance between these cities, leading the reader to believe that there was no dialogue of any kind. Indeed, a significant geographical and cultural distance divided Barcelona and Madrid, but they were not completely unaware of one another, as evident in the daily press and specialized periodicals and other evidence gathered for this study. The artistic and literary visionaries of Barcelona and Madrid, just like many others who participated in the new literary and artistic movement of both cities—politicians, doctors, philosophers, business people, journalists—did not function in complete isolation from one another. In fact, the case is quite the opposite—they oftentimes acted and behaved in relation to one another.

Introduction to Network Studies

The Avant-Garde in Spain is a cultural phenomenon comprised of networks, not isolated groups as presented in Ernesto Giménez Caballero's theorem explaining the new direction of literature and the arts, as discussed above.

Up until now, many have approached the artistic and literary movements that evolved throughout Europe during the first three decades of the twentieth century—cubism, futurism, expressionism, dadaism, and surrealism—as discrete and separate entities, instead of interconnected systems. To isolate them from each other denies their essence. Those who practiced the Avant-Garde in Spain were a diverse group of individuals. Many lived in Barcelona and Madrid, but they resided in others cities as well. One aspect of this diversity was that some of these artists and writers were born in Spain, but others were not. Some of them came from wealthy families, but others had more humble beginnings. Most of them traveled, and many of them contributed to literary and artistic periodicals from a variety of cities in Spain and beyond. Considering the dominant, more conservative cultural scene at the time, believers in and practitioners of the Avant-Garde in Spain were a minority. In order to stay alive, so to speak, they networked with other believers, regardless of nationality, city of origin, age, social status, religious beliefs, or sexual preferences. In studying this cultural phenomenon as a network of networks, a hierarchy of power is revealed. In order to make out these distinctions, different questions must be asked, new evidence collected, and alternative ways to describe and analyze social structures must be adopted.

When we think about social networking today, we think of Internet sites like Facebook and Twitter. Within these digital universes, we can easily discover and quickly connect with friends. We can post pictures and describe exactly what we are doing right now. We can document our lives and share them with anyone who cares to know. Anthropologists and sociologists have been studying and theorizing about patterns of human relationships and how they function since the 1960s. More recent network analysis focuses on how groups and individuals communicate information and knowledge. Analysts study the links among social systems then provide visual renderings of these relationships. The purpose of these maps is to probe the underlying deep structures connecting and dividing social systems.

Those who study social networks generate hypotheses, collect data, analyze results, and propose theories about how humans communicate. It has been critical to explore the area of network studies in order to articulate and understand how the social networks between the people and groups of avant-garde Barcelona and Madrid behaved. Just like the subjects of structural network analysis, actors of the Avant-Garde in Spain were also enmeshed in complex social networks cutting across national, geographical, and linguistic boundaries. The methodology used in this analysis focuses on links between nodes in both cities in order to better define the nature and function of the cultural movement in Spain as a whole. As pointed out by network analysts,

the basic strength of the total network approach is that it permits simultaneous views of the social system as a whole by analyzing the parts that make
up the system.

In general, a network requires two key elements: relational ties and nodes.
Both of these foundational elements surfaced in my search for relationships
that connected people, groups, events, organizations, literary reviews, and
art journals from Barcelona and Madrid. For instance, there were people and
periodicals that functioned as centers of information and its dissemination.
Then there were links that connected these various centers. Consequently,
the conceptualization of the cultural moment in question here is as a system
of networks. Analyzing the individual parts of the Avant-Garde movement
allows for simultaneous views of the system as a whole. It also permits the
connections and disconnections between the individual parts to emerge from
the data. It was not one or five individuals responsible for the communication that occurred between these two cities, as has been suggested in the
past, but many more; however, there were some that were more influential or
powerful than others. If one individual played a key role in communicating
news with people from the other city, let us say in the direction of Madrid
to Barcelona, it was likely that this person in Madrid knew at least four
other people in Madrid who together may have known at least ten people in
Barcelona. In this way, as relationships between individuals that comprised
these systems of contacts were identified, the web of connections became
increasingly complicated. At the same time, it revealed deeper structures of
behavior between the people of Barcelona and Madrid that ran parallel to
Spain's political struggles at the beginning of the twentieth century.

Network analysis, in the strictest sense of the discipline, is much more
analytical than what I intend to do here. Traditional network analysts compile data on the number of times one individual, for instance, wrote letters
to another. Then they enter this data into a computer program to create a
graph or map. The purpose of creating these maps is so that researchers can
represent and explore the nature and properties of certain relations. While
I do not plan on entering my data into a network analysis software program
at this time, I have borrowed some of the key concepts of the discipline to
approach the kinds of relationships that surfaced in my research. A node,
for example, can be a person, group, or organization, and it is one of the
fundamental concepts of networks. In this study, nodes are leaders of the
Avant-Garde in Madrid and Barcelona, or influential periodicals, important
art exhibits, or major cultural events.

According to network analysis, once the nodes have been determined,
links that connect them are identified and described. Nodes can be linked

directly or indirectly. A direct link occurs when two nodes connect without the assistance of a third node. Indirect links occur with the assistance of another node. Networks can be sparsely or highly connected. If the system is very insular, it is sparsely connected. But if the network is open to communication, it is described as being a highly connected system. Networks also can be centralized or decentralized. The centrality of the network depends on whether the people that compose the network are vital in relation to the others in the group. The extent to which an actor is central to a network depends on factors such as the number of direct links with other actors or the actor's proximity to, or ability to easily reach, all the other actors in network. Within network analysis we must ask ourselves questions such as: Is it just one individual running the network, or is it multiple people? How is this individual connected to the other actors in his or her network? And how do these relationships affect the overall behavior of the network?

The way the avant-garde movements in Spain worked was that one individual would be the editor of a literary review that disseminated these new ideas and practices, but usually that was not all he did.[13] Oftentimes this individual was also a poet, journalist, artist, writer, politician, teacher, or student. Also, it was rare for this person to work in isolation. The periodical this person directed did not exist in a vacuum, nor did he or his staff. The literary periodical competed and co-existed with several other journals within the same city and neighboring towns. Most scholars have treated the avant-garde system in Spain as if it were decentralized. Yet, one of the main objectives of periodicals devoted to the new literary and artistic movement in Barcelona and Madrid was to connect with other avant-garde enthusiasts outside of their own city. If we were to create a new version of Ernesto Giménez Caballero's map of new literature in Spain, it would consist of several centers, all connected to one another, similar to what a telephone map from the late 1920s (fig. 2.2) looked like.

Desire for interconnectedness is clearly evident in the fact that most of the cultural periodicals from this period included a section dedicated explicitly to reviews of journals, books, art shows, and performances in the city they represented and, in some cases, in others as well. Being informed of what was happening in other avant-garde circles was of primal importance to the survival and strength of the movement as a whole. If it were not so important to connect with other believers or competitors, most of the editors would not have bothered wasting time, space, or money on such a section in their journals. In some instances, these sections would initially be situated at the end of the journal, but were later transposed to the front of the periodical. The placement of these reviews in the journal demonstrates readers' interest

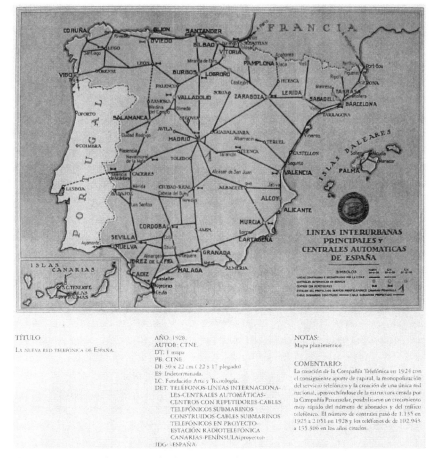

Figure 2.2.   Map of Spain's Telephone Network.

TÍTULO

LA NUEVA RED TELEFÓNICA DE ESPAÑA.

AÑO: 1928.
AUTOR: CTNE.
DT: 1 mapa
PB: CTNE
DI: 50 x 22 cm (22 x 17 plegado)
ES: Indeterminada.
LC: Fundación Arte y Tecnología.
DET: TELÉFONOS-LÍNEAS INTERNACIONA-
LES-CENTRALES AUTOMÁTICAS-
CENTROS CON REPETIDORES-CABLES
TELEFÓNICOS SUBMARINOS
CONSTRUIDOS-CABLES SUBMARINOS
TELEFÓNICOS EN PROYECTO-
ESTACIÓN RADIOTELEFÓNICA
CANARIAS-PENÍNSULA(proyecto)-
IDG: -ESPAÑA-

NOTAS:
Mapa planimétrico

COMENTARIO:
La creación de la Compañía Telefónica en 1924 con
el consiguiente aporte de capital, la monopolización
del servicio telefónico y la creación de una única red
nacional, aprovechándose de la estructura creada por
la Compañía Peninsular, posibilitaron un crecimiento
muy rápido del número de abonados y del tráfico
telefónico. El número de centrales pasó de 1.135 en
1925 a 2.051 en 1928 y los teléfonos de de 102.943
a 155.306 en los años citados.

in knowing about the world outside of their little magazine. This desire to
be informed of the quick developments and introduction of new avant-garde
styles demonstrates that overall, the movement, as a system or network, desired to be more connected than disconnected.

The links that connect the nodes are central to studying networks because
they define the nature of the communication between them. Relational
ties have numerous properties, such as strength, symmetry, and multiplic-
ity. Within formal network analysis, lines on a graph or chart traditionally
represent the relations between nodes. These lines are known as links, ties,
or arcs. Relations can be directional or nondirectional; binary or valued; uni-
plex or multiplex; tangible or symbolic. All of these major network concepts

developed by Daniel Brass in 1995 are useful for understanding the complex relationships between the artistic and literary networks of Barcelona and Madrid during their avant-garde moment at the beginning of the twentieth century.[14]

Following the lead of network analyst Barry Wellman, first I would like to describe how social networks are measured at the most basic level.[15] The first of seven main concepts is direction. For instance, an indirect link that connects two nodes consists of two people, or actors, linked to one another through a third. The connectivity of a network is the extent to which actors in networks are linked to one another, either by direct or indirect ties. As applied to a specific case in Spain's Avant-Garde, Federico García Lorca was a poet from the south of Spain who moved to Madrid as a young man to study. A second actor, the Uruguayan painter Rafael Barradas, met Lorca in Madrid in 1919 at the place where Lorca was living, the Residencia de Estudiantes (Students' Residence). Barradas introduced Lorca to a third actor, the Catalan art critic Sebastià Gasch. Barradas first lived in Barcelona, moved to Madrid, and then returned to Barcelona. When Barradas moved to Barcelona for the second time, he sent a telegram to his friend Gasch inviting him to meet Lorca, who was visiting Barcelona. Gasch and Lorca were the same age and like minded. Barradas was almost ten years older than both and saw the opportunity for a friendship between these two people whom he admired and who were both involved in the new literary and artistic movement, but residing in different cities. Using network analysis terminology, then, Lorca and Gasch were linked indirectly by Barradas. This relational tie can also be described in the opposite direction: Gasch was indirectly linked to Lorca through Barradas. All three actors, Barradas, Lorca, and Gasch, can be considered as nodes of the same overall network (the Avant-Garde in Spain), which was made up of at least two other avant-garde networks: (1) the one in Barcelona that included Barradas and Gasch, and (2) the Madrid system that also included Barradas and Lorca. In time, Lorca became a member of the Barcelona network and Gasch of Madrid's, precisely because of this original connection and the friendship that developed as a result.

Since Sebastià Gasch is the lesser known of the Barradas–Lorca–Gasch cluster discussed here, a few biographical notes are in order. Sebastià Gasch (Barcelona, 1897–1980) was one of the most astute modern art critics of his era. Early on in his career, he wanted to be a painter. He associated himself with one of several modern art schools in Barcelona, called El Cercle de Sant Lluc (Saint Lluc's Artistic Circle), which officially hired him as their librarian in 1923. It was through his connections here that he met the Catalan avant-garde painter Joan Miró (Barcelona, 1893–1983), about whom he wrote his first published article as an art critic in the Barcelona press (*Gaseta de les Arts*, December 1925). Over the course of the following year, Gasch went on to write with great objectivity about the works of similarly innovative artists and poets, such as Salvador Dalí, Rafael Barradas, and Federico García Lorca. Even though Gasch was a firm believer in cubism, new architecture, and new film, he also is known to have once said: "¡Vanguardismo! La palabra odiosa no ha producido únicamente paradojas" (Vanguardism! That hateful word has produced nothing but paradoxes).[16]

Gasch is unique in that he published most of his journalistic essays in one of two journals: *L'Amic de les Arts*, centered in a beach town located just outside of Barcelona called Sitges, and *La Gaceta Literaria*, which was located in the center of Madrid. In this second publication he edited his own section titled "Gaceta de arte" (Art Gazette) (1929). We can also find his byline in other cultural periodicals from Barcelona (*D'Ací d'allà, Les Arts Catalanes, Butlletí, Fulls Grocs, Gaseta de les arts, Hélix, Mirador, La Nova Revista, L'Opinio, Quaderns de Poesia*); as well as newspapers (*La Veu de Catalunya, La Publicictat*). He also published in periodicals based in other places in Spain (*Gallo, Mediodía, Papel de Aleluyas, Verso y prosa*) and outside of Spain (*1928* [Havana]; *A.C., Atlántico, Amauta, Circunvalación* [Mexico]; *OC, Democracia* [Rosario, Argentina]). In 1928, he signed the infamous anti-artistic manifesto, *Manifest Groc* (Yellow Manifesto) along with Salvador Dalí and Lluís Montanyà.[17]

In an interview with a journalist from the Catalan newspaper *La Nau* (March 17, 1928), Dalí gives Gasch credit for having the original idea for the *Manifest Groc* after long hours of conversations with him in Barcelona.[18] Nevertheless, it would be Dalí who would write the first version of said document in February 1928.[19] Despite his devotion to anti-art, Gasch vehemently renounced surrealism. By 1932 his beliefs diverged so much from those of his friend Dalí that the two parted ways indefinitely. From this brief description, we can already see that Salvador Dalí was another node involved in the Barradas–Lorca–Gasch cluster connecting the avant-garde networks of Barcelona and Madrid, but his involvement will be discussed in more detail later.

After direction, frequency is the second element to consider in studying networks. Frequency measures how many times or how often a link occurs. After Barradas introduced Gasch and Lorca, the two avant-garde enthusiasts exchanged letters frequently over the next few years. The frequency of a link determines its strength. Again, as explained by Barry Wellman, the strength of a relationship consists of the amount of time, emotional intensity, intimacy, or reciprocal services between two actors. In Lorca's letters to Gasch, we can see the strength and frequency of their link by the intimacy he expressed in these letters. Notice the increasing level of emotional intensity of Lorca when directing himself to Gasch over time: "Querido Sebastián Gasch; Querido Gasch; Querido amigo Gasch; Mi querido Gasch; Querido Sebastián; ¡Mi querido Sebastiá!; ¡Querido Gasch!; ¡Querido!; Queridísimo Gasch; Mi queridísimo Sebastián" (Dear Sebastian Gasch; Dear Gasch; Dear friend Gasch; My dear Gasch; Dear Sebastian; My dear Sebastian! Dear Gasch! Dear! My very dear Gasch; My very dear Sebastian!).[20] At the beginning of the relationship, Lorca addressed himself to Gasch formally, using both his first and last name. As the relationship developed, he used either his first or last name. The "dear" became "dearest," and exclamation marks are introduced. The frequency, intimacy, and intensity of these exchanges indicate a strong link between these two actors of this one particular cluster.

Another measure of frequency is stability, or the existence of the link over time. In the case of Lorca and Gasch, after they met in 1927 they were friends until Lorca's assassination in 1936. If their correspondence is a measurement of the stability and frequency of this link, the period of greatest intensity in their relationship occurred between 1927 and 1928, during Lorca's inception to the Catalan avant-garde network and during Gasch's initial involvement with that of Madrid. Based on the collection of letters between Lorca and Gasch, it appears that Lorca spent more time writing to Gasch than the other way around. One reason for this imbalance could be that when Lorca and Gasch first met in Barcelona, Lorca was just starting a literary periodical in his hometown in the south of Spain. The mission of this literary review was to be "anti-local" and "anti-provincial." It was to be a magazine from Granada but intended for an audience well beyond Granada. In other words, Lorca expected that his local network in the south of Spain would reach Madrid and Barcelona.

Lorca needed help getting this ambitious project off the ground. He also needed people who would be willing to work for free and who were connected to the right circles in Barcelona and Madrid. At the same time, Lorca also wanted his review to be of the highest caliber. Lorca knew that Gasch was a well-respected art critic, and as we can read in his letters, he highly valued Gasch's work. Lorca also preferred to fill his magazine with articles written by friends, not strangers. In the end, Lorca and his brother Francisco only published two issues of his little magazine, called *Gallo* (February 1928, April 1928). Interestingly, the last issue includes a Spanish translation of the "anti-artistic" Catalan manifesto signed by Salvador Dalí, Sebastià Gasch, and Lluís Montanyà. Lorca has been credited with the translation, but it is possible that he had a little help from his Catalan friends, either Salvador Dalí or Sebastià Gasch.

Lorca seemed to have intended *Gallo* to function as a way to inform others about the relationships he had recently established with Barcelona and Catalonia. The Catalan painter Salvador Dalí drew the icon of the rooster, the Catalan art critic Lluís Montanyá wrote an article about new Catalan literature, and the Catalan art critic Sebastià Gasch wrote about Picasso.[21] If Madrid and Barcelona seemed distant, the geographical divide between Granada and Barcelona was even greater. With this experimental magazine, Lorca minimized the gap between the north and the south while simultaneously strengthening his network with the Catalans. Evidently, Lorca intended to bridge the gap between the cultures of Andalusia and Catalonia. As he mentioned to Gasch in one of his letters, Lorca believed that these two regions were the sources of Spain's vanguard movement. Lorca planned to devote an entire issue of *Gallo* to Dalí, and if there was enough money, another issue to avant-garde painting from Catalonia and Andalusia. Lorca knew that what he was doing with his journal was revolutionary, and that most would not understand. Lorca expected his reading public to be enraged by his proposition of approximating the two cultures, "aunque haya gente que rabie, patalee y nos quiera comer" (even though people will be livid, kicking and screaming and wanting to eat us alive).[22] The avant-garde circles of Andalusia and Catalonia were united by these individual friendships, but also because of the strides these friends took to create the two periodicals preoccupied with the avant-garde spirit, *Gallo* and *L'Amic de les Arts*.

The network between Lorca and Gasch is one of multiplexity, because as time passed they became linked by more than one relationship (i.e., Lorca is friends with Dalí, who is also friends with Gasch). In other words, even though Barradas introduced Lorca and Gasch, once they became friends they realized that they were also connected through other friends and colleagues; their networks started to merge based on previous links and common interests, thus creating a larger system beyond their local base. At the beginning of the Lorca and Gasch friendship, they sought each other out for advice and worked together. Lorca introduced Gasch to his friends in Granada by telling them about him and publishing his work in his literary journal from Granada. He also spoke about Gasch in Madrid. At the same time, Gasch wrote about Lorca's drawings that he liked so much within the pages of the Barcelona cultural magazines. So while Lorca was promoting Gasch in Madrid and Granada, Gasch was promoting Lorca in Barcelona and beyond. As a result, the relationship between these two nodes—Lorca and Gasch—created a whole series of other nodes, links, and clusters.

The final measure used to study social networks is symmetry or reciprocity, which values the extent to which the relationship is bidirectional or mutual.

In the case of Lorca and Gasch, their relationship at the beginning was symmetrical and mutual. Lorca would ask Gasch for advice and vice versa; or Lorca would encourage Gasch and vice versa. As their friendship grew, Lorca encouraged Gasch to keep writing in Spanish despite his insecurities with the language, while Gasch supported Lorca in developing his drawing skills, even though he felt more confident as a musician and writer. One of the ways Gasch encouraged Lorca was by reviewing his drawings in the most active avant-garde journals in Barcelona (*L'Amic de les Arts*) and Madrid (*La Gaceta Literaria*). At the same time, Lorca encouraged Gasch to continue writing for the journals in Madrid. Lorca felt that Gasch's knowledge and understanding of the Avant-Garde was much more necessary in Madrid than in Barcelona. In January 1928, Lorca explains:

> Yo siempre digo que tú eres el único crítico y la única persona sagaz que he conocido y que no hay en Madrid un joven de tu categoría y de tu conciencia artística, ni tampoco, es natural, de tu sensibilidad. Por eso no debes tener ningún reparo con tus artículos (siempre preciosos y utilísimos) en la *Gaceta Literaria*. Tú haces mucha falta y debías publicar todavía mucho más. En cuanto a tu castellano, te aseguro que es noble y correcto y llena el fin para que lo utilizas. Pero mucho más importante que el idioma que usas son tus ideas . . . Y en Madrid, querido Sebastián, haces mucha más falta que en Barcelona, porque Madrid pictóricamente es la sede de todo lo podrido y abominable, aunque ahora literariamente sea muy bueno y muy tenido ya en cuenta en Europa, como sabes bien.

> (I always say that you are the only critic and the only astute person that I know and that there is no young person in Madrid of your quality and of your artistic conscience, nor, it's clear, of your sensibility. This is why you should have no qualms with your articles [always lovely and very useful] in the *Gaceta Literaria*. You are very needed and you should publish even more. In regards to your Spanish, I assure you that it is noble and correct and the means justifies the end. But much more important than the language are your ideas . . . And in Madrid, dear Sebastian, you are much more needed than in Barcelona, because Madrid pictorially is the seat of everything that is rotten and abominable, although now literarily very good and considered throughout Europe, as you very well know.)[23]

Lorca and Gasch were the kind of friends who encouraged one another regarding their respective goals and pushed one another to overcome their fears. The fact that Gasch would take Lorca's advice and vice versa shows that they respected one another as professionals, but also as believers in the Avant-Garde. In another letter from Lorca to Gasch, he admits, "If it wasn't for you, the Catalans, I would have never kept drawing."[24] Lorca and Gasch were also the kind of friends who thanked one another. The strength and quality of the relationships between Lorca and his Catalan friends in Catalonia, such as the one with Gasch, encouraged him to overcome fears and cross major boundaries in his professional and personal life. Lorca respected and admired his Catalan friends and their feelings were mutual. He learned from them and in turn he spoke to his friends in Madrid and Granada about them, thus expanding his network and theirs.

Beyond the basic social network measures mentioned above, actors can play a series of roles including star, liaison, bridge, gatekeeper, and isolate. To summarize, a star is an actor who is highly central to the network (e.g., Lorca is central to the Madrid network, Gasch to the Barcelona network, Picasso and Miró to the Paris network). A liaison is an actor who links two or more groups that would otherwise not be linked, but is not a member of either group. A bridge is a member of two or more groups (e.g., Barradas is a member of both the Madrid and Barcelona networks), while a gatekeeper is an actor who mediates or controls the flow between one part of the network and another (e.g., Giménez Caballero). Finally, an isolate is an actor without links, or relatively few links to others. There are very few cases of isolate roles in Spain's overall Avant-Garde.

Other kinds of communication linkages between nodes within a social network include migratory and embedded knowledge.[25] The first consists of information in easily moveable forms that encapsulate the knowledge that went into its creation (books, designs, machines, blueprints, and individual minds). Following the example stated above, the drawing that Lorca dedicated to Gasch, *Leyenda de Jerez* (Legend of Jerez), in 1927 is an example of a text that functions as migratory knowledge, because it was shown in an exhibit in Barcelona and it was published in a journal. Another example could be a prose poem that Lorca wrote and dedicated to Gasch, "Santa Lucía y San Lázaro," which was the only literary text Lorca wrote from January to August of 1927. On the other hand, embedded knowledge is more difficult to transfer; as defined by the network analyst scholar Joseph Badarraco, it "resides primarily in specialized relationships among individuals and groups and in the particular norms, attitudes, information flows, and ways of making decisions that shape their dealings with each other."[26] An example of embedded knowledge could be conversations that occurred between various actors of the Avant-Garde that would be shared with others but of which there is no evidence.

It is clear from Lorca's letters to Gasch that their relationship functioned as a way of uniting the distant worlds of Barcelona and Madrid, as well as those of Catalonia and Andalusia. Lorca wrote to Gasch: "Como ves, cada día Andalucía y Cataluña se unen más gracias a nosotros. Esto es muy importante y no se dan cuenta, pero más tarde se darán." (As you can see, each day Andalusia and Catalonia are less distant thanks to us. This is very important and most do not realize it, but in time, they will.)[27] As Lorca points out, the cultural unity achieved by this friendship was neither recognized nor understood by their peers in Granada, Barcelona, or Madrid. Yet, for him, it was a critical element of their friendship. Through their common faith in the Avant-Garde, they were uniting their different cultures. In an article he published in *L'Amic de les Arts*, a Catalan journal out of Sitges, just outside of Barcelona, Gasch laments the small-mindedness of the "Little Catalaners," or Catalans, who are clueless about what is happening on the other side of the Ebro River; in other words, the land that is south of Catalonia.[28] Their friendship, united by a common vision defined by new ideas developing in the literature and the arts, tackled problems, found solutions, and created a unity that most could not achieve, especially not politicians.

Lorca was so spiritually united with his Catalan compatriots of the Avant-Garde that he once declared himself a fervent Catalanist. His links with Catalonia were strengthened by two trips there. The first was in 1925, and the second was a much longer stay (approximately four months) in 1927, both during the dictatorship of General Miguel Primo de Rivera. Barradas prompted Lorca's first trip to Barcelona when he invited Lorca to give a talk at the *ateneo*, or athenaeum. The fact that Salvador Dalí, his friend from the Residencia de Estudiantes in Madrid, invited Lorca to spend a few days with him in Cadaqués while he was in Catalonia was surely a motivating factor to make this long journey during his spring recess from school, instead of returning to Andalusia where his family lived, as was customary.

During Lorca's 1925 trip to Barcelona and to the Dalí family summer home in Cadaqués, which took place during Holy Week, Lorca read his play *Mariana Pineda* three times to audiences that Dalí and his father organized for him. Although these readings were informal, they eventually led to a performance of the play in Barcelona's Teatro Goya two years later with Dalí in charge of set design and the talented and popular Catalan actress Margarita Xirgu in the leading role. Barcelona staged the play that Lorca dreamed of performing in Madrid. Theater companies in Madrid feared that military censors could read this text as an affront to Primo de Rivera's regime. With this experience of staging the controversial play, Lorca discovered that the Catalans in Barcelona were more open than the powers that be in Madrid. This support was crucial for him and his confidence as a young aspiring artist. Lorca's second trip to Catalonia was much longer, since he was there primarily to prepare for the opening of *Mariana Pineda*.

When *Mariana Pineda* opened in Barcelona on June 24 of 1927, another Catalan, Josep Dalmau, invited Lorca to exhibit twenty-four of his drawings at his gallery. By the time of this second visit to Barcelona, Lorca's supporters there included Dalmau, Dalí, Rafael Benet, J. V. Foix, Josep Carbonell, M. A. Cassasayes, Lluís Góngora, Regino Sainz de la Maza, Lluís Montanyà, Joan Gutiérrez Pili, and, of course, Sebastià Gasch. According to Lorca, his main attraction to Barcelona was his friends, as he notes in a letter to Gasch, "Barcelona me atrae por vosotros" (I am attracted to Barcelona because of you all).[29] We can be sure that Lorca loved his friends in Catalonia. Lorca spent the month of July in Cadaqués with the Dalí family, the same month that an experimental piece of prose written by Dalí, "San Sebastián," dedicated to Lorca, was published in *L'Amic de les Arts*. After this particular publication, Dalí became a regular contributor to this Catalan journal. Perhaps the fact that Dalí was connected to other avant-garde networks outside of Catalonia made him an attractive choice as a journalist for the editor of this magazine that supported the Avant-Garde. Using network studies terminology, then, Lorca's ties to the Catalan Avant-Garde network were mutual, multiplex, and strong.

While Lorca remained friends with Gasch, this was not the case with Dalí. When Lorca published his poetry collection, titled *Romancero gitano* (Gypsy Ballads), in 1928, it received rave reviews in the press nationwide. Dalí, on the other hand, did not agree. He was greatly disappointed with the book. Dalí's letter to Lorca, filled with stinging criticism, suggests that perhaps something else was bothering Dalí, perhaps something that could have happened between these two good friends during Lorca's second, much longer, stay in Catalonia in 1927. Something must have sparked Dalí to cause such a mood change toward his dear friend who had been the subject and inspiration of so many of his foundational early works and who had become so close to the Dalí family. In this letter we can see how Dalí felt that Lorca committed treason with this collection of anecdotal gypsy ballads, thereby denying everything the two friends had been fighting for as avant-garde artists. With this letter, Dalí wounded Lorca for life, and it marked the beginning of the end of their close friendship.

Dejected and demoralized, Lorca retreated to his family's rural home in Andalusia and put his pen down for almost an entire year. His parents were so worried about their son's emotional state that they sent him across the Atlantic in hopes of brightening his spirits. Echoes of a conflicted poetic voice struggling to escape from an inferno are heard in the collection of poems that he wrote there, *Poeta en Nueva York* (Poet in New York). At the same time, Dalí and Luis Buñuel (another close friend from Lorca's days at the Residencia de Estudiantes in Madrid) released their debut Surrealist film, *An Andalusian Dog*, without the help of their good friend Lorca. In their minds, Lorca had given the public what they wanted with his book *Romancero gitano*, rather than stay true to the Avant-Garde spirit. But Lorca had that extraordinary human quality: the ability to overcome and make the best of things. When he returned to Spain, he exceeded everyone's expectations, produced his best work, and continued to befriend Catalans; one of the strongest examples being that of the talented actress Margarita Xirgu, who continued to collaborate with him on stages worldwide.[30] Even so, Lorca kept his distance from Barcelona. He would not return there until September of 1935 for the opening of his play *Yerma*.

Other Considerations and Critical Nodes

How did the nodes of various avant-garde networks in Barcelona and Madrid identify and communicate with one another? What language did they speak? What tools did they use? Joaquim Molas, a contemporary Catalan scholar, author of one of the few more panoramic studies of the avant-garde literary movement in Catalonia, sheds some light on these questions. Molas describes the removal of boundaries between art and literature as one of the inherent characteristics of the Avant-Garde:

> Las vanguardias borraron las fronteras entre las diversas formas de expresión . . . entre la pintura y la literatura . . . por su parte, los poetas, con la idea de hacer nuevas exploraciones de tipo estético, para romper con la rutina tradicional del discurso o para hacer frente a la crisis de la palabra, reforzaron la escritura con toda clase de componente gráficos, la sustituyeron por su representación plástica y, a la larga, por el propio objeto que designa.

> (The avant-garde erased boundaries between different forms of expression . . . between painting and literature . . . poets did so, on their end, with the idea of making new discoveries of the aesthetic kind, to break with the traditional routine of discourse or to confront the crisis of the word, they reinforced writing with a whole class of graphic components, they substituted traditional written discourse with a plastic representation, and in the end, with the object itself that it described.)[31]

Avant-garde poets confronted the "crisis of language" that was so characteristic of modernism by incorporating imagery into their writing. In order to do so, the boundaries dividing art and literature were erased. Their boundary-breaking experiments in search of a new mode of representation resulted in losing the word itself. The signifiers became the signified. The poem became the image. If the breaking of formal and traditional boundaries was an inherent characteristic of the Avant-Garde, would it be a stretch to think that the actors who practiced these ideas also challenged other kinds of limits (cultural, political, linguistic, and geographic)?

If these poets were to break with the past and with traditional poetic discourse, how would they communicate? What was their common language? Throughout this period of experimentation, the poets and artists of Barcelona and Madrid often communicated with one another through a code language of images inspired by the lexicon proposed in cubism. To be fluent in the language of images allowed them to communicate effectively with all of their spiritual peers regardless of nationality or mother tongue. The grouping of these images on the printed page or on the painted canvas functioned like symbols on a map. Poets experimented with drawing, as is the case with Federico García Lorca, and artists experimented with writing, as did Salvador Dalí. To speak the language of the Avant-Garde required learning a new form of expression: one centered on the image, free of descriptions, anecdotes, sentimentalisms, and narrative. The goal was to break with the direct mimicking of reality. The Avant-Garde was fueled by a desire for rupture, especially with the bourgeois and academic models; it was motivated by research and experimentation; finally, it was concerned with sharing, or publicizing, its members' experiments and findings of innovative aesthetic styles beyond their own networks.

Just like the poets and artists who wanted to remove the boundaries between the old and the new in literature and the arts, there was also an intention on the part of many of the actors of each city's movement to permeate the physical boundaries that divided them politically, linguistically, and culturally. Therefore, when we define the main characteristics of Spain and Catalonia's Avant-Garde, one key concept emerges: interconnectivity or connectedness. The Avant-Garde, arguably the most influential cultural movement of the twentieth century in Spain, with its all-star cast of artists and writers such as Pablo Picasso, Juan Gris, Joan Miró, Salvador Dalí, Luis Buñuel, and Federico García Lorca, was the result of an intended and, in some cases, achieved communication, collaboration, contact, and networking with others who shared these actors' beliefs in the same kinds of new ideas. One of the aspects of being avant-garde in Spain was crossing over and entering new territories in art, literature, politics, and culture with an enthusiastic spirit. Oftentimes it also involved crossing geographical boundaries, thus forming a complex series of networks connecting the various groups. Communication across borders may not have been the motivation of their art, but it was certainly a consequence. It also was a mode of survival, since the Avant-Garde was a minority movement.

A good number of the protagonists of the Avant-Garde in Spain traveled to Barcelona or Madrid to meet, work with, befriend, and, in some cases, collaborate with their spiritual peers. Some of these individuals were native to either Barcelona or Madrid, but others were (originally) from places as diverse as Irún in the Basque Country, Palafrugell in the interior of Catalonia, or Montevideo, Uruguay. Nevertheless, these cultural nomads resided in Barcelona or Madrid at one point or another. They were all visitors to or residents of either Madrid or Barcelona, and they all made it a point to meet their peers while visiting the other city. Generally, the purpose of the contact between these artists and writers was for them to learn about the other and return to their respective local networks and disseminate news. We can call this behavior "networking." Their trips, contacts, friendships, exhibits, and projects all play a fundamental role in understanding the essence of the origins and development of Spain's dynamic Avant-Garde moment. To overlook these contacts would result in a distorted view and incomplete understanding of the cultural movement as a whole.

Federico García Lorca and Salvador Dalí stand as the two best-known bridge figures, or nodes, involved in the cultural networking between Barcelona and Madrid, but they were not the only ones.[32] Even though they are often treated as exceptional cases, Lorca's activity in Catalonia and Dalí's pursuits in Madrid are emblematic of a mode of conduct that was inherent to the Avant-Garde in Spain and Catalonia. In order for their communication to be effective, they had to speak the same language of the Avant-Garde, as well as share a similar spirit and network. In the case of Lorca and Dalí, we know they first met in Madrid as students at the Residencia de Estudiantes, where they both lived. Neither one was a native of Madrid. Lorca was from the south of Spain (Andalusia) and Dalí from the north (Catalonia), but they shared all of the three aforementioned qualities: aesthetic language, spirit, and networks. It is not surprising that they became so close.

If we look at the specific case of this friendship, we will find that they collaborated, traveled, performed, and published together. Because of their relationship, the distance between Barcelona and Madrid was greatly reduced. But the Lorca-Dalí link is just one within the much larger cosmos of Spain's Avant-Garde. Like Lorca and Dalí, lesser-studied writers like Luis Bagaría, Rafael Barradas, Ernesto Giménez Caballero, Joan Salvat-Papasseit, and Sebastià Gasch formed friendships that bridged gaps dividing Barcelona and Madrid. As a result of these relationships and the networks they generated, the ideas that sprang forth from these individuals traveled across cultural, geopolitical, and linguistic borders. Together, they formed a larger network of a human system with the unified goal of combating tradition while creating new modes of representation. Their desire and ability to permeate boundaries through traveling, writing, painting, publishing, and networking were crucial to the development of improved communication between the artistic and literary networks of Barcelona and Madrid. Unfortunately, the way the Avant-Garde in Spain has been documented and described over the last century has made it challenging to determine the relationships that made up this overall network connecting Barcelona and Madrid.

Another famous bridge figure who connected Barcelona and Madrid but who predates Lorca and Dalí is one of the original initiators of the European artistic avant-garde movement, Pablo Picasso (Malaga, 1881–1973). Picasso lived a comfortable middle-class life in Andalusia until his father took a post in the city of La Coruña in the northern region of Galicia, Spain, as an art professor in 1891. Four years later, Picasso's only sibling, Conchita, died of diphtheria, and the family moved to Barcelona. His father enrolled his only son at the Llotja School of Fine Arts in Madrid, where he visited El Prado Museum frequently. Two years later, Picasso presented his painting *Science and Charity* at the Fine Arts General Exhibition in Madrid, and he was accepted to the San Fernando Academy of Fine Arts. After falling ill with the scarlet fever, he returned to Barcelona. On the invitation of his friend Manuel Pallarès, he moved to Horta d'Ebre in Catalonia for eight months. When he returned to Barcelona in 1899, he joined the artists and poets who frequented the tavern Els Quatre Gats (The Four Cats), a meeting place of modernists. This group of artists shared close ties to the Parisian symbolists. By associating himself with this group of painters and intellectuals, he was inherently rejecting the academic style of painting of his father. In 1900 he had his first solo show at Els Quatre Gats, consisting of 150 *modernista*-style portraits with an art nouveau influence. These small pictures depicted his Catalan friends and other leading figures like Ramon Casas, Santiago Rusiñol, Miquel Utrillo, and Pere Romeu, who happened to be the four founders of the club.[33] That same year Picasso made his first trip to Paris, where he attended the Universal Exhibition. He spent Christmas in Barcelona and the New Year in Malaga before moving to Madrid, where he intended to stay for one year.

During this second stay in Madrid in 1901, Picasso founded a small journal named *Arte Joven* (Art of the Youth) with his Catalan friend Francesc d'Assís Soler, which ran five issues. He returned to Barcelona, followed by a second trip to Paris, where he showed sixty-three works alongside the Basque painter Francisco Iturriño in the gallery of Ambroise Vollard. He returned to Barcelona, and in 1902 took a third trip to Paris, where he lived and worked with the symbolist writer Max Jacob. In 1903 he went back to Barcelona and in 1904 moved to Paris indefinitely. Picasso's work from 1901 to 1903, known as the Blue Period, reflects the major changes he was going through as a young man looking for his way as he worked feverishly and traveled back and forth between various cities, especially Barcelona, Paris, and Madrid.

A recent art show at the Metropolitan Museum of Art in New York City displayed the Picasso works in the museum's permanent collection (thirty-four paintings, fifty-eight drawings, a dozen sculptures and ceramics, along with two hundred of the museum's four hundred prints). This show emphasized the importance of Picasso's early friendships with Catalans, especially with Pedro Mañach, Jaime Sebartes, Ricard Canals, and Carles Casagemas. One of the important results of these friendships was an easier transition to Paris. In Barcelona, Picasso found a network of like-minded individuals centered at Els Quatre Gats tavern, something that was harder for him to find in Madrid but that he was willing to create with the attempt of founding a small journal with his Catalan friend Francesc d'Assís Soler. Barcelona was where the Picassos had their home, the place he would always call home after many of his trips, his headquarters, a cultural center that was open to change. Then, at the age of twenty-three, in the spring of 1904, he took a leap of faith. He left behind the comfort and security of Barcelona and moved to Paris permanently. This was the artistic capital of the world and a major avant-garde center. Soon thereafter, Picasso became a critical node in Paris for the young artists and writers of Spain who aspired to follow his lead.

The complexity of describing a node and the nature of communications between one node and another can be seen in the case of one of the leaders of the Madrid avant-garde network: Ramón Gómez de la Serna (Madrid, 1888–1963). No history of the avant-garde movement in Madrid is complete without including him or his work. The filmmaker Luis Buñuel considered him (not Dalí, Picasso, Miró, or Lorca) to be "the man who most influenced our entire generation."[34] Even today, he stands as one of the only Madrid natives ever to be mentioned in Catalan literary histories.[35] He is also one of the few Madrid-born poets who published in the Barcelona avant-garde press, even though it was not very often. Gómez de la Serna is considered by many to have founded the Avant-Garde movement in Spain (not Catalonia) when he published a translated version of F. T. Marinetti's first futurist manifesto in his monthly periodical, *Prometeo* (Madrid, 1908–12).[36] As a result of his correspondence with Marinetti, over the course of a year, the Italian futurist wrote a manifesto specifically addressed to Spaniards that appeared in Gómez de la Serna's journal, *Prometeo* (no. 20, 1910), but nowhere else in Spain, not even Barcelona. Gómez de la Serna enthusiastically supported this radical way of writing poetry, inspiring him to publish more of his experimental poems, which he called *greguerías*. For Gómez de la Serna, Italian futurism represented a new kind of literature that had nothing in common with the introspective and overly emotional writings of the Generation of '98 authors or the extravagant poetry of *modernista* writers. Italian futurism was liberating. It dismantled boundaries of representation and freed the word from all its previous constraints in an original way. Yet Marinetti's ideas did not stick in Madrid, while in Barcelona, Italian futurism found much greater resonance.

Even though Ramón (as everyone called Ramón Gómez de la Serna) visited Barcelona only once, and only briefly, he fostered significant ties with Catalans from his headquarters in Madrid.[37] He formed and maintained many relationships with individuals from all corners of Spain and throughout Latin America and Europe. Besides being a tireless letter writer, he was also the editor of a magazine, a frequent contributor to the press both in and outside of Madrid, the leader of a popular literary club, a public speaker, and inventor of the catchy *greguería*—brief, image-based metaphoric lines of prose usually involving humor. His capacity to weave so many intricate webs between people from all walks of life was the result of his untiring, creative, and charismatic personality, in addition to his unbreakable faith in the Avant-Garde. Gómez de la Serna mediated the flow of information within the Madrid avant-garde network through his various activities, especially the weekly social gathering he hosted, without ever spending much time away from Madrid and without becoming a core member of any other avant-garde network. Other avant-garde actors from Spain and Catalonia came to him, not the other way around. People referred to him as "the Pope," and to his literary gathering place, discussed more in depth later, as "the Sacred Crypt" or "the Tabernacle."

Even though Gómez de la Serna did not visit Barcelona until 1930, he was still connected to the avant-garde network there. In order to determine the nature of his relationship to the Barcelona avant-garde network, it would be useful to examine two of his strongest links: first, his contributions to the Catalan-language press, and second, his role as the leader of the well-known Pombo *tertulia*, or literary gathering. Members of the first avant-garde circles of Barcelona probably initially heard about Gómez de la Serna as the first in Spain to publish Marinetti's futurist manifesto, in his Madrid-based periodical *Prometeo*. Gómez de la Serna initiated a correspondence with Marinetti that resulted in the latter writing a special manifesto addressed exclusively to Spaniards that was published in the same magazine the following year.[38] Gómez de la Serna was one of the first writers from Madrid to take a serious interest in Marinetti. Avant-garde enthusiasts in Barcelona keeping up with Madrid's press (e.g., *Prometeo*) would have taken note.[39]

Rather exceptionally, Gómez de la Serna was one of the few representatives of Madrid's small avant-garde network who published in Barcelona's press, and he did so in two of the key Catalan avant-garde journals, namely *Un enemic del Poble* (Barcelona, 1917–19) and *Hèlix* (Vilafranca del Penedés, 1929–30), both of which were primarily Catalan-language periodicals. He was one of the only Madrilenians to publish in Joan Salvat-Papasseit's two-page "subversive sheet," *Un enemic del Poble*, even if it was only on two occasions.[40] Much later, *Hèlix* published Gómez de la Serna's work alongside that of other Spanish writers, such as the novelist Benjamín Jarnés, Ernesto Giménez Caballero, and the journalist Ledesma Ramos. His contributions to both *Un enemic del Poble* and *Hèlix* were printed in Spanish. Outside of these two exceptional cases, Gómez de la Serna's work can also be found in almost every other city and town in Spain that had an avant-garde periodical. The exact link between Gómez de la Serna and the Barcelona avant-garde remains a mystery. One possible connection could have been Marinetti, who visited and maintained contact with avant-garde enthusiasts in both Barcelona and Madrid. Another possible connection could have been through the Catalan journalist Josep Maria de Sucre.

Josep Maria de Sucre (Barcelona, 1886–1969) was a member of the Catalan avant-garde network who visited Madrid during the period in question (approximately 1909–29). Younger than the Catalan futurist Gabriel Alomar, and a good friend of the established *modernista* poet Joan Maragall, Sucre was a government worker, poet, painter, art critic, journalist, and curator. For twenty years, from 1903 to 1923, Sucre's day job consisted of documenting criminals for the city government of Barcelona. His early books, all written in Catalan, include *Un poble d'Acció* (1906), *Apol-noi* (1910), *Joan Maragall* (1921), *L'ocell daurat* (1922), and *Poema barber de Serrallonga* (1922). His Spanish collection of poetry, *Poemas de abril y mayo* (1922), caught the attention of Joan Salvat-Papasseit while convalescing in a tuberculosis sanatorium near Madrid. After meeting the Barcelona art gallery owner and collector Josep Dalmau in 1920, Sucre's painting flourished. He exhibited in Dalmau's Galleries on three occasions.[41] He also helped Dalmau organize several exhibitions, such as Ernesto Giménez Caballero's literary posters (January 1928) and the *Homage to Rafael Barradas* (August–September 1928). Another one of his contributions was organizing the banquet to celebrate the opening of Lorca's exhibition of twenty-four drawings at the Dalmau Galleries (1927). As an art critic, Sucre wrote numerous catalog introductions and reviews of art shows, in addition to making introductory speeches during art openings.

Sucre's first trip to Madrid was in 1910, and although the motive for his visit and the length of his stay are unknown, it is a fact that he met Gómez de la Serna while he was there. As president of the Ateneu Enciclopèdic Popular of Barcelona (1912–15), Sucre organized a cultural excursion from Barcelona to Madrid, including visits to Toledo and the Escorial. The theme of the 1914 trip was the Renaissance artist El Greco, and it is possible that he met up with Gómez de la Serna again while he passed through Madrid. According to Sucre's memoirs, he attended the opening of Pombo as a literary club that took place in 1915.[42] Almost a decade after his first visit to Madrid, Sucre published a poem dedicated to Gómez de la Serna in the last issue of Salvat-Papasseit's *Un enemic del Poble* (no. 18, May 1919). Written in Catalan, the poem takes the reader on a virtual tour of Madrid's cultural landmarks, including Gómez de la Serna's Pombo Café. Sucre is one of the few Catalans associated with the Barcelona avant-garde network who visited Madrid on several occasions, met Gómez de la Serna, befriended him, and possibly facilitated publishing his work in Barcelona. Sucre maintained a sustained working and publishing relationship with the writers in Madrid up until approximately 1929, when he published his last of many articles in *La Gaceta Literaria* (Madrid, 1927–32).[43] His articles appear in this periodical, one of Madrid's strongest supporters of the Avant-Garde movement, from beginning to end. Sucre functions as a node connecting the avant-garde networks of Barcelona and Madrid because of his friendship with Gómez de la Serna, but also because of his later collaborations in the cultural press of Spain and abroad, writing in both Spanish and Catalan.[44]

Sucre began his career under the influence of *modernisme*, frequenting Els Quatre Gats, Barcelona's famous *modernista* meeting place for revolutionary, anti-bourgeois painters like Pablo Picasso and Joaquim Sunyer. Most critics agree that Sucre abandoned his *modernista* tendencies around 1910 or 1911. His aesthetic and ideological turn from the neo-romantic to the avant-garde may very well have been directly related to his 1910 trip to Madrid, where he met Gómez de la Serna, who had recently translated and published the first Italian futurist manifesto. The year that Sucre and Salvat-Papasseit met is unknown, but it could not have been too much after his third trip to Madrid in 1915. The first letter to Sucre included in Salvat-Papasseit's correspondence is dated December 1917. Interestingly, in this postcard, Salvat-Papasseit explains why he and Sucre could not visit Barradas, who had promised to paint a portrait of Sucre. If Barradas was planning on painting a picture of Sucre, he must have been a close friend or, more probably, Sucre was one of the Catalan avant-garde network nodes who also happened to be connected to Madrid.

Further research shows that Sucre and Salvat-Papasseit collaborated on several projects as they both experimented with notions of the Avant-Garde.

For instance, Sucre wrote the prologue for Salvat-Papasseit's posthumous essay collection, *Mots propis* (In My Own Words) (1917–19). Sucre left Els Quatre Gats to join a new circle of friends that included Salvat-Papasseit, Barradas, and Torres-García. After 1925, he regularly attended Barradas's literary gathering in the outskirts of Barcelona every Sunday. He was one of the group's core members. He wrote about Barradas's influence and importance within the modern art movement on multiple occasions, from various platforms, and in both Spanish and Catalan. By the end of the 1920s, he was one of Madrid-based *La Gaceta Literaria*'s main correspondents in Barcelona, just as he was for *Alfar* out of La Coruña in Galicia. His main responsibility at *La Gaceta Literaria* was to review new Catalan books.

If we describe the links between Gómez de la Serna and the Barcelona network using network terminology, we can also describe the nature of the relationship between these various nodes. In the case of *Un enemic del Poble*, the link seems unidirectional. Gómez de la Serna may have been connected to Barcelona through Sucre's early visit to Madrid (1910) and their subsequent friendship. Gómez de la Serna published in the Catalan periodical with which Sucre was associated (February and May 1918), but did Gómez de la Serna reciprocate by publishing the magazine's editor, Salvat-Papasseit, in Madrid? Was it Gómez de la Serna who informed the other avant-garde actors in Madrid of this Catalan avant-garde poet who was founding avant-garde periodicals and publishing books of poetry inspired by Italian futurism? Is there symmetry in this link? In the face of so many questions left unanswered, the frequency of the tie between Gómez de la Serna and Salvat-Papasseit is not very strong, since the work of Gómez de la Serna only appeared in two of the eighteen issues of *Un enemic del Poble* and no where else, until ten years later in a journal published outside of Barcelona. However, we must also keep in mind that the period between 1918 and 1929 was also the period of the Primo de Rivera dictatorship in Spain (1923–30), when relationships between the avant-garde networks of Barcelona and Madrid became estranged.

Gómez de la Serna was one of the few Madrid experimental poets to publish in the Barcelona avant-garde press, but seen from the other direction, the first person to publish him in the Barcelona avant-garde press was also one of the founders of the Catalan literary avant-garde movement: Joan Salvat-Papasseit (Barcelona, 1894–1924). It was his intention to use *Un enemic del Poble* (1917) as a platform to publish the experimental work of others outside of Barcelona, regardless of their nationality, so long as they spoke the same language of the Avant-Garde. Salvat-Papasseit, however, was not concerned with creating any sort of new nation, vanguardist or otherwise, based on some sort of common spirit. Just one year prior to the publication of the first issue of *Un enemic del Poble*, another group of poets in Barcelona was already incorporating and practicing the lessons they learned from the Italian revolutionary poet, Marinetti, in 1909. With the added influence of dadaism, an artistic and literary movement created in Zurich in 1916 that responded directly to the atrocities of World War I, and exposure to the experiments of French exiled avant-garde artists who practiced these radical poetic philosophies and forms of expression, like Francis Picabia, the Catalans were the first in Spain to found literary journals strictly devoted to promoting these new styles (e.g., *Troços*, 1916, directed by Josep Maria Junoy).

Poets like Junoy and Salvat-Papasseit were instantly attracted to Marinetti's "words in freedom" and futurism's goal of increasing the expressivity of language through the minimization of adjectives, adverbs, finite verbs, and punctuation. Also interesting for these Catalan poets were the onomatopoeia and typographical experimentation proposed by futurism. After founding three avant-garde magazines (some of the first in Catalonia and Spain) and publishing several books of experimental poetry, such as *Poemes en ondes hertzianes* (1919), Salvat-Papasseit published the "First Manifesto of Catalan Futurism" (1920), which he signed: "poetavanguardistacatalà," or Catalan-avant-garde-poet. Four years later, his plans to revolutionize Catalan poetry were cut short.[45] Tuberculosis took the poet's life at the age of thirty.

Joan Salvat-Papasseit is an exceptional case for the concerns of this study, because he was a figure who strongly linked the Barcelona and Madrid avant-garde networks through a series of publications. His futurist-inspired poetry appeared in three of the foundational avant-garde literary journals from Madrid: *Grecia* (1920), *Ultra* (1922), and *Tableros* (1922). The poems in *Grecia* stand out because they are in Spanish. When a group of poets writing in the Madrid-based *Ultraísmo* style were seeking inspiration, they turned to Barcelona and found Salvat-Papasseit. This young, revolutionary poet spoke the language that both avant-garde centers could understand. One of the greatest lessons Salvat-Papasseit learned from Italian futurism was finding meaning in the sounds and shapes of words. He understood that with typography, he could create the grammar for a more universal language. Poetry had a visual component just as much as the visual had a poetic element. He was in the process of constructing this language and developing his voice when his illness worsened, at which point he took a quick detour toward a more traditional and sentimental style of poetry.

Within this context, the fact that Salvador Dalí's debut as an artist in Madrid included a painting in honor of Salvat-Papasseit, the Catalan man whom the *Ultraísta* poets in Madrid welcomed several years earlier, is much more meaningful. In a way, Dalí was following Salvat-Papasseit's lead. He connected to the Madrid avant-garde network by making a direct reference and paying tribute to the revolutionary Catalan who preceded him. With this painting, *Venus and Sailor*, Dalí sent a direct message to a carefully targeted audience in Madrid. Did they remember Salvat-Papasseit in Madrid? Like Salvat-Papasseit, he too was a Catalan avant-garde poet, but in the visual arts. Salvat-Papasseit was also the author of manifestos. All three of his periodicals served as launching pads for several of them. Dalí would follow a similar programmatic line. Only eight months prior to showing *Venus and Sailor* at the Modern Catalan Art Exhibition in Madrid (1926), a subject to be discussed at greater length in the fifth chapter of this book, Dalí was more than likely the author of the counter-manifesto published in conjunction with the first collective show to introduce avant-garde art to Madrid, known as the Ibéricos, or Iberians, of 1925.

Dalí's target audience in Madrid included people like Gómez de la Serna, who had already collaborated with Salvat-Papasseit. Gómez de la Serna was well known among avant-garde enthusiasts because of the literary club, or *tertulia*, that he founded in an underground bar in Madrid. The café was located on one of the most heavily populated pedestrian streets in Madrid, Calle Carretas, where today one can walk up or down the long hill reading quotations by Spain's great writers that have been engraved into the ground. Gómez de la Serna founded this club in 1914 and he hosted it every Saturday evening, beginning with dinner at ten o'clock, followed by hours of drinking, smoking, and discussion. As mentioned earlier, Sucre, the Catalan avant-garde enthusiast, attended the opening of Pombo in Madrid. More than a social and literary gathering, there was a spiritual element associated with it. The space earned the name of the "Sacred Crypt," and it was presided over by the "Pontiff," as Gómez de la Serna's followers called him. The faithful attendees often invited other friends to introduce them to the revolutionary styles of art and literature that Gómez de la Serna promoted. Salvat-Papasseit's name does not appear in the Pombo registers, but it is possible that he knew about Pombo from friends who had visited (like the likeminded poets Junoy and Sucre). He also may have heard about Pombo during his brief stays outside of Madrid while he was interned at a sanatorium there.

Besides eating, drinking, smoking, and debating, the "pombianos" (as they called themselves) never knew what to expect on Saturday nights. Many of them have recorded in their memoirs that the best days were those when Gómez de la Serna published a new book, because he would distribute and dedicate free copies to all those in attendance until there were none left. An evening at Pombo also involved drawings, readings, planning of

«El absurdo», por todos menos yo.

Figure 2.3.   Exquisite Cadaver, titled *Patria* [Homeland].

banquets, heated discussions, and even duels. One of the activities that took place in Pombo was drawing. In his description of Pombo, Serna explains that images were always present in this literary gathering. One participant would draw something simple on a page, to which the others would add something else. Serna did not participate in any of these drawings, he explains, because somebody had to stop them from continuing all night long. These communal drawings had a therapeutic effect on those involved; they were "hygienic."[46] In his journal of Pombo happenings, Gómez de la Serna offers two examples of these "absurd" drawings, one of which I have reproduced here. Titled *Nationhood*, this figure bears a striking similarity to Gómez de la Serna.

This drawing created by a group of *pombianos* in 1918 clearly reflects two key features of Avant-Garde spirit: the primacy of the image and humor. The drawing has two titles. The original, *Patria* (homeland), printed with the same pen as the drawing, and the second, *El absurdo* (the absurd), in typescript edited later by Gómez de la Serna.[47] The superimposition of the second title suggests that this depiction of "homeland" is "absurd." Its absurdity, echoing beliefs grounded in dadaism, lies in the irrational combination of signs projecting out of the male figure's head: a Pentecostal flame, a writing plume, a boot, and a matchstick. Also, some of the objects are not placed where they should be, like the boot on the head or the hat under the foot. The figure is dressed in only underpants and a bowtie, and wears a crucifix. He appears to be dressed for battle, with a dagger affixed to one arm and another strap wrapped around his chest. A series of tattoos mark the large body of the figure: a person looking through a window on his stomach, and an eye on his knee; and a sign to the right of his underpants that reads: "se alquila" (for rent). Various objects project from his body like a church-like steeple balanced on his shoulder and a train traveling up his arm. It is with this same arm that the figure holds what appears to be a book titled *Flores del campo* (Flowers of the Field). The other arm is deformed, perhaps amputated. From the appendage, a faucet is dripping, allowing a seedling to grow. On the far left corner of the drawing there is a smaller figure that has been stabbed by a sword or a cross. The line coming out of his mouth could be his last breath or words. Interestingly, elements of this drawing anticipate surrealism, which was not defined until 1924, such as the tradition of drawing exquisite cadavers, and collective drawings in which one person would draw, fold the paper to conceal the drawing, and pass it on to the next person, revealing a nonsensical combination of images. If this image is an allegorical representation, then the nation it depicts, or Spain, is irrational, violent, primitive, ridiculous, and in disarray.

The Pombo tradition lasted well into the thirties, until Gómez de la Serna went into exile in Buenos Aires, Argentina, after the outbreak of the Spanish Civil War in 1936. Hundreds of artists, musicians, politicians, scientists, and writers from every part of Spain attended his Saturday night soirées, including the king, Alfonso XIII. In Gómez de la Serna's two-tome record of the *tertulia* and associated activities, he noted the appearance of several Catalans. In the first book, from 1918, Adrià Gual, Josep Maria Junoy, and Eugeni d'Ors visited the Sacred Crypt.[48] Several more Catalans appear listed in the second book from 1924, including Apa, Bagaría, Julio Casal, Tomàs Garcés, Jacinto Grau, Rafael Marquina, Josep Pla, Josep Maria de Sagarra, and Josep Maria de Sucre.[49] Appearing in the Pombo ledgers more times than any other Barcelona native by far, Bagaría was one of the club's permanent fixtures and founders. During World War I, Bagaría was crucial in communicating an anti-German sentiment through his caricatures, published nearly daily in the Madrid press. His work impacted many readers of the daily newspaper *El Sol* and the weekly journal *España*.[50]

Gómez de la Serna's high esteem for Bagaría motivated him to organize a banquet in his honor in 1923. The number of guests was so large that the event was held at a hotel, instead of in the subterranean Pombo. In a note he sent to be read in his absence, which was read aloud at the banquet by Gómez de la Serna, Miguel de Unamuno praised the illustrator; a fragment of this note reads as follows: "Bagaría me ha hecho ver en nuestra verbeneante humanidad española una trágica fetidad . . . Nos ha enseñado a mirarnos y a vernos. A vernos como fetos, y más que fetos pre-natales, fetos post-natales" (Bagaría has shown me the tragic embryonic nature of Spain's humanity . . . He has shown us how to see ourselves and one another; to see ourselves like fetuses, and more so than pre-natal fetuses, like post-natal fetuses).[51] For Unamuno, the corpus of Bagaría's caricatures, with their characteristic curved lines and bubble-like shapes, defined the very nature of the Spanish character: individualistic and isolated, yet with an exceptionally strong connection with its roots or origins. Unamuno suggests that Spaniards are like fetuses that possess all the qualities necessary in order to develop into vertebrate human beings, but they remain undeveloped. Spaniards desire a greater unity, but something tragic always ruins their plans. The balloon-like figures of most of Bagaría's characters adopt the same shape as the fertilized embryo.

Gómez de la Serna recorded the highlights of the banquet, one of them being his own speech introducing Bagaría. One of the points he made that day is that he had met the Catalan illustrator fourteen years earlier, when Bagaría worked for *La Tribuna*, a newspaper in Madrid. It appears that Gómez de la Serna wanted to make sure that everybody knew that he met the brilliant caricaturist first. Gómez de la Serna also documented the words of gratitude spoken by Bagaría during the dinner in the presence of nearly one hundred men wearing tuxedos in one of the most bourgeois hotels of Madrid. Bagaría concluded by thanking, most of all, the city of Madrid:

> Me he olvidado de rendir otro tributo de gratitud: me refiero a Madrid, a este incomparable Madrid, amable acogedor de todo esfuerzo. Su Espíritu afectuoso me hizo adivinar desde el primer momento que yo viviría y moriría en Madrid. Llegué aquí hace once años para pasar quince días, y ya veis que no llevo trazas de hacer las maletas.

> (I have forgotten to pay another tribute of gratitude: I am referring to Madrid, this incomparable Madrid, this friendly harvester of every effort. Its warm Spirit made me wonder from the first moment whether I would live and die in Madrid. I arrived eleven years ago to spend fifteen days here, and as you can see I have no intentions of packing my bags.)[52]

Life was not always so cheery for Bagaría as it was on the day of this banquet in his honor. At the beginning of his career, he worked around censors and he was not always successful. Once, the dictator Miguel Primo de Rivera sent a note to the editors of *El Sol* newspaper warning them that if they kept publishing caricatures of him, he would close down the paper. The same threat applied for any other paper that published Bagaría's drawings of the dictator. Some nights, Bagaría would share his censored drawings in the safe, embryonic, space of Pombo. Gómez de la Serna relished the secrecy of it all in his notes: "En esas noches de censura, de supresión de las garantías constitucionales, el resguardo de Pombo es admirable." (During those evenings of censorship and suppression of constitutional guarantees, the protection of Pombo was admirable.)[53]

As a painter, Bagaría exhibited in Paris in 1905, after a show in Barcelona at the Sala Parés gallery two years prior. As a caricaturist, his first one-man exhibit was also at the Sala Parés (1905), followed by a third show in the Catalan town of Tarrasa (1907), then two more exhibits in Barcelona: one at the Salon Reig (1908) and the other at Faianç Català (1910).[54] In Madrid, he exhibited at the Exposición de Pintores Íntegros (1915), where he showed portraits of writers. He also exhibited at the Ibéricos (1925) in Madrid, where he had a whole room dedicated to his works. Bagaría also showed in an individual exhibit in Bilbao organized by the Association of Basque Artists in 1916, and collectively in London (Twenty-One Gallery, 1917). His entry in the *Dictionary of the Avant-Garde in Spain* also indicates that beyond exhibiting his work, he also illustrated the cover of one of Catalan writer

Tomás Borrás's books, called *Fantochines* (Puppets), and three of Gómez de la Serna's: *Disparates* (Foolish Acts) (1921), *El incongruente* (The Incongruous One) (1922), and *Ramonismo* (Ramonism) (1923), in addition to painting the interior of a bar in Madrid: Cervecería *El Cocodrilo* (1923).

In 1930, at the tail end of the Miguel Primo de Rivera dictatorship, Bagaría joined a group of over one hundred Castilian intellectuals on a trip from Madrid to Barcelona in support of Catalan culture and freedom. Unlike Eugeni d'Ors, who was never really accepted by Barcelona after he moved to Madrid, Bagaría still maintained good ties with his natal city. Recently, one scholar has noted Bagaría's instrumental role as a bridge figure from Barcelona to Madrid: "Hijo del rico y agitado mundo cultural barcelonés de fin de siglo, el periodista catalán no sólo introdujo en Madrid la caricatura sintética, sino también un espíritu inquieto y renovador que vivificó el panorama artístico de la capital" (Son of the rich and agitated world of fin de siècle Barcelona, the Catalan journalist not only introduced Madrid to the synthetic caricature, but also a restless and renovating spirit that energized the artistic panorama of the capital).[55] Bagaría was a Catalan resident of Barcelona who moved to Madrid and joined the avant-garde network there. He functioned well within this system and was accepted by his spiritual peers like Gómez de la Serna. Consequently, Bagaría felt comfortable, welcomed, and respected in Madrid.

There are not many cases of representatives of the Catalan avant-garde who moved to Madrid and stayed there for an extended period of time. Salvador Dalí spent a handful of years in Madrid, but he eventually moved back to Barcelona. Similarly, cases of avant-garde writers and artists who moved from Madrid to Barcelona were just as rare. During this time period, it was not customary to leave Barcelona for Madrid and vice versa. Bagaría's case is exceptional. The knowledge and spirit that he brought with him from Barcelona nurtured Madrid's evolving cultural scene in a significant way. His frequent presence in Pombo and his popular drawings in Madrid's press served to link these two cities and their respective avant-garde cultures.

The fact that he was an artist, rather than a writer, could have been the explanation as to why the transition between cultures was so much easier for him, as was also the case of Salvador Dalí. Bagaría's drawings transcended the conflict between the Catalan and Castilian languages and cultures. He communicated without relying on a written language, and in the process, he created a symbolic language that the people of both cities could understand. Finally, because he was a caricaturist in the press, rather than an oil painter, sculptor, or architect, his role as a major node of the avant-garde system has remained in the background and his position as a major bridge figure has been overlooked. Looking at connections between the avant-garde worlds of Barcelona and Madrid introduces new characters into the narrative of the system as a whole. Furthermore, individuals like Bagaría, Barradas, and Gasch played leading roles as major nodes of their respective avant-garde networks precisely because of their exceptional talents as effective networkers and their excellent capacity to transcend borders and, ultimately, make the most of their situation in a home away from home.

Notes

1. For the exchange between Pedro Salinas and E. Giménez Caballero, see E. Giménez Caballero, "Theorem of New Spanish Literature," *La Gaceta Literaria*, April 15, 1928, 203.

2. E. Giménez Caballero's "literary posters" were exhibited in Madrid on March 22, 1928. The date of his conference talk was on the closing date of the exhibition, April 7, 1928. For a fragment of his talk and a reproduction of his "Theorem of New Spanish Literature," see E. Giménez Caballero, "Theorem of New Spanish Literature," *La Gaceta Literaria*, April 15, 1928, 203.

3. Giménez Caballero, "Theorem of New Spanish Literature," 203.

4. The following is a list of cities and their respective publications as indicated on Giménez Caballero's map of new literature on the Iberian Peninsula: (S)antander (*Carmen*); (B)urgos (*Parábala*); (V)alladolid (*Meseta*); (M)adrid (*La Gaceta Literaria, Revista de Occidente*); (M)urcia (*Verso y Prosa*); (S)evilla (*Mediodía*); (G)ranada (*Gallo*); (H)uelva (*Papel de Aleluyas*); (M)álaga (*Litoral*); (C)anarias (*Rosa de los vientos*); (B)arcelona (*L'Amic de les Arts, Nova Revista*). Giménez Caballero, "Theorem of New Spanish Literature," 203.

5. The triangle in the northwestern region of Spain corresponding to Galicia and Portugal is less defined because, after the closing of the periodical *Alfar*, based out of the coastal city of La Coruña, no other periodical there functioned as a representative of the "new" style of literature. Giménez Caballero, "Theorem of New Spanish Literature," 203.

6. Ibid.

7. Ibid.

8. Ibid.

9. Guillermo de Torre, *Literaturas europeas de vanguardia* (Madrid: Caro Raggio, 1925).

10. Jaime Brihuega, *Las vanguardias artísticas en España (1909–1936)* (Madrid: Istmo, 1981).

11. Ibid., 161.

12. Gabriel Alomar gave a lecture in Barcelona on June 18, 1904, titled "Futurisme" several years before Marinetti drafted his first futurist manifesto. Alomar published his lecture in the form of a small book (also titled *Futurisme*) in 1905. The

news from Barcelona of Alomar's book was picked up by the Parisian newspaper *Le Mercure*. It is possible that Marinetti could have read about Alomar's ideas by reading *Le Mercure* several years prior to drafting his own version of futurism. Some have even wondered whether Marinetti could have borrowed Alomar's title to name his own movement. While these two ideas share a similar title, they are different. This case clearly illustrates the argument of Renato Poggioli that the idea of the "future moment" was one that preoccupied many thinkers at approximately the same time during the early development of modernism in Europe. Alomar and Marinetti are only two examples of writers who made initial attempts at theorizing about the future of their nations. Please see Marjorie Perloff, *Futurist Moment* (Chicago: University of Chicago Press, 1986) for other examples of futurism throughout Europe during this same time period. Also see Renato Poggioli, *The Theory of the Avant-Garde* (Cambridge, MA: Belknap Press of Harvard University, 1968).

13. There are no cases of women directing literary and artistic journals in the nearly one hundred periodicals that were consulted for this book (see appendix I).

14. D. J. Brass, "A Social Network Perspective on Human Resource Management," in *Research in Personnel and Human Resource Management*, ed. K. M. Rowland and G. R. Ferris, 39–79 (Greenwich, CT: JAI Press, 1995).

15. Barry Wellman, "Structural Analysis: From Method and Metaphor to Theory and Substance," in *Social Structures: A Network Approach*, ed. S. D. Berkowitz and Barry Wellman, 19–61 (Cambridge: Cambridge University Press, 1998).

16. Juan Manuel Bonet, *Diccionario de las vanguardias en España 1907–1936* (Madrid: Alianza, 1995), 157.

17. On the Yellow Manifesto, see J. Minguet i Batllori, *El manifiesto amarillo: Dalí, Gasch, Montanyà y el antiarte*, trans. Joan Riambau (Barcelona: Galaxia Gutenberg, Círculo de Lectores, 2004).

18. Salvador Dalí, *La Nau*, March 17, 1928.

19. For a detailed description of Gasch's role in the events surrounding the creation of the Yellow Manifesto, see Minguet i Batllori, *El manifiesto amarillo*, 11–34.

20. Federico García Lorca, *Cartas a sus amigos: Sebastián Gasch, Guillermo de Torre, Ana María Dalí, Angel Ferrant y Juan Guerrero*. Prologue by Sebastià Gasch. (Barcelona: Cobalto, 1950), 21–48.

21. Ibid., 41.

22. Ibid., 47.

23. Ibid., 39.

24. Antonina Rodrigo, *García Lorca, el amigo de Cataluña* (Barcelona: Edhasa, 1984), 8.

25. Joseph Badaracco, *The Knowledge Link: How Firms Compete Through Strategic Alliances* (Boston: Harvard Business School Press, 1991).

26. Ibid., 79.

27. Lorca, *Cartas a sus amigos*, 41.

28. Ian Gibson, *Lorca–Dalí. El amor que no pudo ser* (Barcelona: DeBols!llo, 2004), 203–4.

29. Lorca, *Cartas a sus amigos*, 39.

30. For more on Xirgu, see Ricard Salvat, "Margarida Xirgu, su trabajo en Barcelona y Madrid" in *Dos escenarios: Intercambio teatral entre España y Argentina*, ed. Osvaldo Pellettieri (Buenos Aires: Galerna, 2006), 117–31, and his prologue to the book by Antonina Rodrigo, *Margarita Xirgu* (Madrid: Aguilar, 1988).

31. Joaquim Molas, "Las vanguardias literarias: imitación y originalidad," in *Las vanguardias en Cataluña 1906–1939: Protagonistas, tendencias, acontecimientos* (Barcelona: Olimpíada Cultural, 1992) 57.

32. Antonina Rodrigo's research, especially, has delved deep into the details of Lorca's relationship with Catalonia and its people, as played out in three book-length studies: *Lorca, Dalí: una amistad traicionada* (Barcelona: Planeta, 1981); *García Lorca, el amigo de Cataluña* (Barcelona: Edhasa, 1984); and *García Lorca en el país de Dalí* (Barcelona: Editorial Base, 2004).

33. Please see the catalogue for the 2007 art exhibit in Cleveland, New York, and Barcelona, titled *Barcelona and Modernity: Gaudí to Dalí*.

34. Quoted in Juan Manuel Bonet, "Ramón Gómez de la Serna: intento de cronología," in *Los ismos de Ramón Gómez de la Serna y un apéndice circense* (Madrid: Museo Nacional Centro de Arte Reina Sofía, 2002), 450.

35. Most significant are the multiple mentions of Ramón Gómez de la Serna in Joaquim Molas's *Literatura catalana d'avantguarda*, especially since his name appears as early as the second page of Molas's 450-page history. See Joaquim Molas, *La literatura catalana d'avantguarda (1916–1938)* (Barcelona: Bosch, 1983), 16, 27, 63, 64, 92, 94, 98, 103, 105.

36. Despite his initial interest in Spain, Marinetti did not set foot there until 1928, after at least two cancellations: one in Madrid and the other in Barcelona. When he finally did visit, he stopped in both cities. In Madrid he lectured at the Residencia de Estudiantes, the Lyceum Club Femenino, and the Círculo de Bellas Artes. Also, the director of *La Gaceta Literaria*, Ernesto Giménez Caballero, organized a banquet in his honor. In Barcelona, Dalmau greeted him with a modern art show featuring works by Albert Gleizes, Frank Burty, Francis Picabia, Enric Ricart, Rafael Barradas, Salvador Dalí, Joan Miró, Federico García Lorca, and others.

37. Given his extensive travels in Spain, Portugal, Italy, and Argentina, Ramón considered himself a "hunter of cities," but he visited Barcelona only once. This visit took place in 1930, when he accompanied a large group of "Castilian intellectuals," led by Ernesto Giménez Caballero, in support of Catalan culture during Miguel Primo de Rivera's dictatorial regime.

38. Marinetti's "Proclama futurista a los españoles" (translated by Ramón Gómez de la Serna into Castilian) is reproduced in Paul Ilie, *Documents of the Spanish Vanguard* (Chapel Hill: University of North Carolina Press), 73.

39. For more on Ramón's relationship with Marinetti, please see Andrew A. Anderson, "Futurism and Spanish Literature in the Context of the Historical Avant-Garde," in *International Futurism in Arts and Literature*, ed. G. Berghaus (Berlin: Sonderdruck, 2000), 145; and Manfred Lentzen, "Marinetti y el futurismo en España,"

in *Actas del IX Congreso de la Asociación Internacional de Hispanistas* (Frankfurt: Vervuert, 1989), 309–18.

40. The prose piece "Nuevos caprichos," by Ramón Gómez de la Serna, appeared on the front page of *Un enemic del Poble* in the February 1918 issue and was continued in the following issue, which was not until May 1918.

41. Sucre exhibited in the "Primer Saló de dibuixos i pintures d'homes de lletres no pintors" (1921), "Exposició d'Art Abstract" (September 1929), and the "Exposició d'Art Modern Nacional i Extranger" (November 1929), all of which took place at the Dalmau Galleries in Barcelona.

42. Ramón Gómez de la Serna recorded Sucre's visit to his weekly literary gathering in *La sagrada cripta de Pombo*, but without specifying a date.

43. Sucre's byline can be found in the following issues of *La Gaceta Literaria*: 4, 5, 6, 13, 15, 18, 19, 28, 39, and 42. His contributions to this Madrid-based journal can be organized into two main categories: book reviews and poetry. He wrote in Spanish and Catalan. One of his main responsibilities was to head a section reviewing Catalan books. He also wrote one art exhibit review of a show at a gallery in Barcelona. His only piece of literary criticism published in Catalan was an article in defense of Eugeni d'Ors, who had left Barcelona several years earlier.

44. Sucre founded the periodical *Occitània* (Barcelona, 1905), and contributed to *Panteisme* (Barcelona, 1911); *Teatre Català* (Barcelona, 1912–17); *Excursions* (Barcelona, ?–?); *La Revista* (Barcelona, 1917–19); *La Columna de Foc* (Reus, 1918); *Alfar* (La Coruña, 1920–54); *La Ciutat* (Manresa, 1926–28); *L'Amic de les Arts* (Sitges/Barcelona, 1926–29); *Sagitario* (Mexico, 1926–27); *La Nova Revista* (Barcelona, 1927–29); *La Gaceta Literaria* (Madrid, 1927–32); *Circunvalación* (Mexico, 1928); *Mirador* (Barcelona, 1929–37); and *L'Opinió* (?–?). This information was gathered from Juan Manuel Bonet's *Dictionary of Spain's Avant-Garde* (1995).

45. Joan Salvat-Papasseit was treated twice in a sanatorium in the outskirts of Madrid (La Fuenfría, Cercedilla). His book of poetry, *Les conspiracions* (1922), is inspired by his stay there; also see his collection of letters, *Epistolari de Joan Salvat-Papasseit*, for more details about how this illness affected his life and work. Amadeu J. Soberanas i Lleó, *Epistolari de Joan Salvat-Papasseit* (Barcelona: Edicions 62, 1984).

46. Ramón Gómez de la Serna, *Pombo* (Madrid: Visor, 1960), 177.

47. Ibid., 178.

48. Ibid., 145, 171, 120, 282.

49. See Ramón Gómez de la Serna, *La sagrada cripta* (Madrid: Trieste, 1986), 536, 137, 259, 296, 305, 306, 312, 336, 363, 370, 396, 401, 409, 416, 423, 435, 450, 474, 488, 500, 512, 519, 521, 540, 541, 593, 595, 607, 640, 702, 536, 633, 536, 702, 462, 450, 411, 536, 365, 488, 411.

50. Some of the words used by Ramón Gómez de la Serna to describe Bagaría include: "Intransigente e insurgente, remueve el espíritu de Pombo, ondea la bandera roja en el aire con sus largos brazos . . . noble . . . primitivo . . . sencillo . . . sincero, y en su alma todos los problemas están vivos con intensidad . . . incrédulo, un poco suicida, desesperado, siempre un principio de rectitud y rebeldía en su alma . . .

instintos fuertes" (Intransigent and rebellious, he stirs the spirit of Pombo, he waves the red flag with his long arms . . . noble . . . primitive . . . simple . . . sincere and in his soul problems are lived with intensity . . . incredulous, a bit suicidal, exasperated, always with moral rectitude and rebelliousness in his soul . . . strongly instinctual] in Gómez de la Serna, *Pombo*, 104–5.

51. Unamuno's letter, dated Salamanca, April 30, 1923, is reproduced in its entirety in Gómez de la Serna, *La sagrada cripta*, 474. For a detailed description of the banquet in honor of Bagaría held at the Palace Hotel in Madrid, see ibid., 474–87.

52. Ibid., 481.

53. Gómez de la Serna, *Pombo*, 189–90.

54. Bonet, *Diccionario*, 78.

55. Emilio Marcos Villalón, *Luis Bagaría entre el arte y la política* (Madrid: Biblioteca Nueva, 2004), 33.

CHAPTER THREE

~

The Crisis of Modernity

Approximately one hundred years ago, at the dawn of the twentieth century, a series of explicit revolutionary ideas in both literature and the arts, collectively known as the Avant-Garde, infiltrated Spain's borders.[1] In literary studies, it is generally known as a movement that severely broke with traditional forms of expression. In the arts, it became a language that shattered conventional modes of representation. Expressionism, fauvism, cubism, futurism, dadaism, purism, and surrealism are all avant-garde styles originating in countries like Germany, France, Italy, and Switzerland, that eventually made their way into Catalonia and the rest of Spain. Other aesthetic and literary movements, like romanticism during the previous century, shared a similar spirit of nonconformance, but the Avant-Garde differed significantly in theory and practice. In order to appreciate the complexities of avant-garde networks in Barcelona and Madrid and the relationships between them, it is necessary to understand the traditions they combated within their specific historical and cultural context. In general, the Avant-Garde offered new ways for writers and artists to express the reality of living in a time of severe political, economic, and social turmoil. The problems in Barcelona and Madrid were similar, but the people who lived and worked in these two capital cities did not deal with crisis in the same manner. These differences are seen in the art and literature they produced and in the ways they related to each other. Sometimes they sought out one another for support, other times they ignored each other intentionally, but they never took their eyes off the other for very long. Now that the main concepts of the Avant-Garde and network studies have been discussed, herein begins an account of two magnificent cities and their relationship to the Avant-Garde revolution as a whole during a particularly difficult moment in time.

The Modernization of Spain and the Rebirth of Catalan Culture

The Age of Enlightenment in Spain ended with the war against France known as the War of Independence (1808–14), also called the Peninsular War. For the first time in the history of Spain, the majority of Spaniards united in solidarity, as a result of the intrusion of a foreign emperor, Napoleon Bonaparte. As the painter Francisco de Goya so convincingly documents in his disturbing *Disaster of War* etchings series, Spaniards from all walks of life, of all ages, classes, and genders, raised arms in opposition to the French and in defense of their homeland. While the Spanish king Charles IV abdicated the throne and fled to France, liberal politicians headed south to the Mediterranean city of Cadiz, located at the most southwest corner of Spain. Here, they drafted Spain's first Constitution (1812). For nearly a decade, the people of Spain fought against Napoleon and his troops. Greatly outnumbered by the French, Spaniards invented a tactic that involved attacking and retreating, known today as guerilla warfare. This method of fighting eventually led to their victory. After thousands of casualties and the famine that resulted in urban centers like Madrid, Spaniards defeated the French Emperor, as well as Napoleon's brother, Joseph (José), who had been appointed as Spain's king (1808–13). Spaniards were now free to let the bright ideals of the Enlightenment shine in, similar to those that inspired the authors of the Constitution in Cadiz, but fate would have other plans.

One of the major consequences of the war against France at the beginning of the nineteenth century was that, in comparison to the rest of Europe, both the Industrial Revolution and romanticism arrived late in Spain. The establishment of the authoritarian rule of King Ferdinand VII (1813–33) after Napoleon's defeat explains this delay. When this monarch reclaimed the Spanish throne after his imprisonment in France during Napoleon's invasion (1808–14), he broke one of his previous promises to protect the Constitution of Cadiz at all costs. Instead, one of the first actions he took upon arriving at the seat of power was to abolish the liberal constitution, and he established an absolutist, rather than enlightened, regime. Still, many Spaniards welcomed King Ferdinand VII, called the "Desired One," as the next rightful heir to the throne, despite the fact that there was no room in his politics for liberalism.[2] It was not until after his death in 1833 that romanticism finally found free expression in Catalonia and Spain, and the Industrial Revolution gained momentum.

The despot king's death exacerbated political divisions in Spain. Toward the end of his life, King Ferdinand VII changed a law allowing women to rule the throne. His brother Carlos argued that this modification of the law was illegal. Now, instead of Carlos becoming the next ruler of Spain, it was to be Ferdinand's three-year-old daughter, Isabel, under the regency of the king's wife, Queen Maria Cristina. As a result of this political controversy, Spain divided into those who defended Carlos (the Carlists) and those who defended the queen and her daughter. As if the major wars of the previous two centuries had not been enough (i.e., the War of Spanish Succession and the Peninsular War), in addition to the numerous wars of independence in Latin America beginning during Ferdinand's reign, three civil wars erupted on the Iberian Peninsula throughout the nineteenth century. These domestic disputes, known as the Carlist Wars, ended in the overthrow of Queen Isabel II (1833–68), who was exiled to France.[3] Her son, Alfonso XII, succeeded her (1875–85) after the failure of the First Spanish Republic (1873–74).

The end of the war of independence against the French coincides with the birth of the Industrial Revolution in Spain and the urbanization of its major centers, especially Barcelona. One of the byproducts of the economic, political, and social changes associated with the Industrial Revolution in Barcelona was the development of romanticism (or, in Catalan, *romanticisme*). In opposition to the rationalism of the Enlightenment, and in conjunction with the advances of the Industrial Revolution, this literary movement had already taken root in Germany and Great Britain in the previous century. As a cultural movement specific to the nineteenth century, *romanticisme* renewed the historic autonomous culture of Catalonia. This goal was achieved in part through the use of the Catalan language as an affirmation of national identity. One example of how romanticism and a reaffirmation of Catalan identity were intertwined can be seen in the work of editors in Barcelona who feverishly translated the works of European romantic authors, such as François-René de Chateaubriand, Lord Byron, Walter Scott, and Alessandro Manzoni, into Catalan and made these texts available throughout the Catalan-speaking world.

During the period that precedes *romanticisme*, known as the *Decadència*, the Catalan culture and language were in decline. Over the course of the eighteenth century, the Castilian language, commonly known as Spanish, was systematically imposed on Catalonia by Spain's central government. However, this political imposition of Castilian over Catalan dates as far back as the fifteenth century, thus marking the beginning of the *Decadència*. The Principality of Catalonia quickly began to lose its autonomous political powers as the other kingdoms of Spain centralized, especially after the marriage of the Catholic monarchs Queen Isabel of Castile and King Ferdinand of Aragon (1469). Their marriage consolidated numerous kingdoms throughout Europe to form a Spanish Empire. The Catholic monarchs allowed historic kingdoms, like Aragon, to retain some of their ancient rights dating back centuries, but not without resistance. In one act of defiance, Catalan peasants revolted when Madrid demanded more money and troops from Catalonia in support of its war in Flanders. Known as the Reapers' War, this revolt marks a major rupture between Catalonia and the Hispanic monarchy. Catalans were under the protection of King Louis XII of France, also proclaimed Count of Barcelona, until they surrendered approximately two decades later (1640–59). Catalonia's national anthem comes from a popular song, "Els Segadors" (The Reapers), that commemorates these events.[4]

Catalonia maintained some of its historical autonomy until the War of Spanish Succession (1701–14), when the first Bourbon dynasty ruler of Spain, King Philip V, took away most of its ancient rights through the Nueva Planta decrees in 1716. In an effort to centralize the state, and in order to punish Catalonia and Aragon for siding with the opponent during the war, King Philip V stripped them of their laws, institutions, rights, and privileges. In order to enforce the new law, the entire area of Catalonia and Aragon was placed under military-based rule. The Spanish military built a fort in Barcelona called the Ciutadella, which is now a city park, in order to keep watch over continued acts of separatism. Even though the Catalan language had been used in its autonomous parliament (*Corts*) for centuries, Spanish was declared the official language for all government acts in Spain. Catalans were so impacted by these repercussions that their national holiday, September 11th, commemorates the day of the Siege on Barcelona in 1714.

It was not until Barcelona's economic boom during the Industrial Revolution that Catalonia regained some of its independence from the centralizing powers of the Spanish state. Throughout the nineteenth century, Catalans restructured their political efforts and mobilized a cultural renaissance with ideas introduced by romanticism. The purpose of this revival movement was to formulate a new Catalan identity in the wake of the pronouncement of the eighteenth-century Nueva Planta decree. This cultural renaissance placed great importance of the revival of the Catalan language. For instance, old traditions were revived, such as the medieval Catalan poetry contest called the Jocs Florals (re-established in 1859). There was also a publishing boom of books, newspapers, and other periodicals in Catalan. Three critical periodicals that helped shape this movement based out of Barcelona were *Revista de Catalunya* (est. 1862), *Lo Gay Saber* (1868–69; 1878–82) and *Renaixença* (est. 1871). The first modern daily newspaper published entirely in Catalan, *Diari Català*, was also founded (est. 1879).

This refurbished Catalan identity consisted of a romanticized vision of Catalonia that looked back at ancient traditions and used poetry, music, and theater to connect with the masses. Poetry was instrumental in transmitting oral and written messages of this cultural revival movement in search of a national identity.[5] The culmination of this literary moment occurred between 1875 and 1890 with the poetry of Jacint Verdaguer, Àngel Guimerà, and Joan Maragall. In conjunction with this cultural renaissance, politicians discussed the revival of Catalan institutions, which would elevate Catalonia to the status of its past glories. By the turn of the twentieth century, Barcelona was the most industrialized, populous, and culturally advanced city in Spain. As host of the World Exhibition in 1888, Barcelona served as an international platform from which Catalans placed a spotlight on their newly defined national identity. One of the architectural remains of this exhibition is Barcelona's Triumphal Arch. Unlike other monumental arches that commemorate military triumphs, like those in Paris or Madrid, this structure stood for the city's technological victories of their burgeoning Industrial Revolution.

Strengthened by their successes in industrialization and reenergized by their romantic revivalist movement, Catalans developed their own ideas about how to deal with the crumbling Spanish Empire, weakened by bankruptcy, civil strife, and social disarray. While the end of the nineteenth century for most of the rest of Spain was dismal, Barcelona prospered as an important industrial center. Together with the emergence of the Industrial Age, Catalan intellectuals established a cultural renaissance movement known as the *Renaixença*. After centuries of decline, Catalan culture was thriving. A poem written by the Catalan poet Bonaventura Carles Aribau titled "La patria" (The Homeland) (1833) is historically referenced as the starting point of this post-romantic revival. Notably, this year also marks the death of the despot King Ferdinand VII and the controversial succession to the Spanish throne of his daughter, Isabel II. After Catalan *romanticisme* developed during the first half of the nineteenth century with writers like Ramón López Soler and Manuel Milà, a second cultural movement, the *Renaixença*, spun from it during the second half of the same century. Chronologically, the cultural production of the Catalan *Renaixença* overlaps with that of romanticism in the rest of Spain. As we shall see, these variations of style between Catalonia and the rest of Spain, especially in relation to the center, Madrid, is a trend that persisted into the following century.

The Perpetuation of Violence at the Birth of a New Century

After the sequence of major wars that characterized the eighteen and nineteenth centuries (i.e., the War of Spanish Succession, the War of Independence, the Carlist Wars, Latin American wars of independence), the people of Spain desired urgent political and social reforms. Queen Isabel II was overthrown in the Revolution of 1868, known as La Gloriosa (The Glorious One), and in her absence a series of political experiments was initiated. In one case, Spain borrowed a prince from Italy to rule the throne (1870–73). Unable to manage so much hostility against him, Amadeo, from the Italian House of Savoy, abdicated. On the evening of his abdication, the First Spanish Republic was declared (1873). But this form of government collapsed almost instantly. This temporary political move away from the monarchy quickly ended as a result of the successful military overthrow led by General Arsenio Martínez Campos. Subsequently, the Bourbon dynasty was immediately reinstated (1875). The fifty years that followed is known, politically, as the Restoration. After so much turmoil and violence, its hope was to create a stable political system. This way of doing politics would remain in practice until the declaration of the Second Spanish Republic (1931).

Instead of restoring sovereignty to Queen Isabel II of the Bourbon dynasty, who had been exiled in France after her overthrow in La Gloriosa, her son, Alfonso XII, was selected to be Spain's ruler. A system of checks and balances was established, in the form of a house of elected officials and a single leader. Thus, a parliamentary monarchy was established that somewhat resembles the structure in place today. During the Restoration, unlike today, less than 5 percent of the population was legally allowed to vote.[6] Besides the fact that the majority of citizens were not eligible to vote, elections were notoriously decided ahead of time. According to the constantly evolving Spanish Constitution of 1876, power was to rotate every two years between the two dominant political groups, namely the conservative and liberals, leading to the popular term "Las dos Españas" (The two Spains).

One of the first major political challenges of the Restoration period was another war, but this time against the United States. The resulting loss of Spain's last colonies in the New World—Cuba, Puerto Rico, the Philippines, and Guam—in the Spanish-American War (1898) was a huge embarrassment with grave consequences. Losing these last, and treasured, colonies to the United States, confirmed that Spain was no longer the glorious, global empire of the Golden Age. Besides feeling demoralized, this military loss also led to a major economic slump. Yet, one of the main complaints of turn-of-the-twentieth-century intellectuals was that the majority of Spaniards were overly apathetic to this loss. Additionally, this disastrous colonial defeat reinforced regionalist sentiments throughout Spain and created insecurity about national unity among Spaniards. Another consequence of the defeat was that the government of Spain imposed a tax to pay for war debts. Due to the acute economic difficulties that followed the Disaster of 1898, hundreds of thousands of Spaniards abandoned their homes in search of a better life. Exile to Latin America reached its peak in 1912 with the migration of over one hundred thousand Spaniards.[7] While many looked to the other side of the Atlantic, others migrated to the more industrialized cities of Spain, primarily Barcelona, Bilbao, and Madrid.

The differences that were already being drawn between Catalans and the rest of Spain in both the political arena and in the press became more pronounced as a result of the Disaster of 1898. While most Spaniards seemed to be apathetic to the loss of the last colonies, Catalans, for the most part, were much more proactive in their response. Their main complaint was that Spain's handling of the war with the United States was irresponsible and that better terms should have been negotiated. Cuba was a major economic loss for Catalonia, and many politicians and business owners were severely affected.[8] The colonial disaster also caused a complete loss of faith in the two-party Restoration system that allowed for the alternation of power between conservatives and liberals every two years. As one historian has stated, after the Disaster of 1898, Catalan nationalists increasingly conceived of Catalonia as a "nation" and Spain as the "State."[9] Thus, 1898 clearly stands as a key year that further deepened the divide between the Catalans and Spaniards.[10]

Catalans were still riding the wave of their cultural revival movement of fin-de-siècle Barcelona. As previously mentioned, the city hosted the International World Fair in 1888; Antoni Gaudí (1882–1926) was constructing several masterpieces throughout the region; and Pablo Picasso (1881–1973) was in town. Many new periodicals exalting Catalan language and culture appeared in kiosks, such as *El Poble Català* (1904–18) and *Garba* (1905–6). The disappointment of the Disaster of 1898 caused a major shift in attitudes and tastes. Some felt that the "art for art's sake" outlook of *modernisme* did not address the preoccupations of daily life in a practical way. Catalans sought a more reasonable solution for their concerns. On one side of the spectrum, a writer from Mallorca, Gabriel Alomar, was the first person to use the word "futurism" in Spain as an aesthetic-based philosophy for the future of Catalonia at a lecture in Barcelona (1904). Alomar's ideas resulted in a series of debates published in journals that were specifically created to address the future of Catalonia in relationship to the rest of Europe.[11] Rather than look toward the past, Alomar believed that Catalan society had to look forward in order to modernize along with the rest of Europe.

At the other end of the ideological spectrum, a much larger group of Catalans believed that the future of their nation lay in models to be found at an even greater distance than those proposed by the *Renaixença*. These thinkers and writers wanted action, and they looked to the classics of antiquity for practical solutions. This collective shift of consciousness led to yet another cultural development in Catalonia, known as *noucentisme*. With this new mindset, Catalans demanded an independent and representative government, known as the Mancomunitat, in order to create an autonomous state. In 1906, the president of the Mancomunitat, Enric Prat de la Riba, published a book that defined this version of Catalan national identity, *La Nacionalitat Catalana* (Catalan Nationality). This same year, in the Catalan newspaper *La Veu de Catalunya*, Eugeni d'Ors published his first *glosari* (glosses), which were short essays that probed at the essence of Catalan culture. These popular glosses brought him fame beyond Catalonia's borders and eventually led him to Madrid.[12]

The power behind the *noucentisme* movement led to important sociopolitical initiatives, such as the creation of libraries, museums, and schools.[13] Those who promoted *noucentisme* used classicism, rather than medievalism, as their focal point: the Greek city, the polis, cities as spaces for exchange, citizens as free men, and civility. Classical images were adopted in music, art, and literature to express this new attitude toward the future of the nation. Classic myths were incorporated in politics to reinvent Catalan culture and government. The work of the *noucentistas*, those who promoted *noucentisme*, stood in stark contrast to the extravagance of Catalan *modernisme*. One just has to compare the order of Barcelona's central square, the Plaza of Catalonia, with the wildness of Gaudí's Guell Park, at the top of a hill overlooking Barcelona, both built and developed during the same decade at the beginning of the twentieth century, to experience the dramatic difference between these two competing styles. One of the reasons why the Avant-Garde movement took off so much faster in Barcelona than in Madrid was precisely because of the predominance of the *noucentisme* movement. The avant-garde writers and artists of Barcelona strongly opposed this classicist movement that dominated the general culture and politics of Catalonia. In other words, unlike the early avant-garde writers and artists of Madrid, their Catalan counterparts had a very specific battle to combat: the tradition, order, and structure promoted by *noucentisme*.

Outside of Catalonia, a general sense of national failure as a result of the embarrassing loss to the United States in 1898 led to a movement in Spain known as *regeneracionsimo* (regenerationism). Like Catalan *noucentisme*, it was a political and ideological movement with the goal of achieving modernization and stable government. Similar to the Catalans, reformers centered in Madrid sought ways to regenerate Spain's glorious past. Different areas of Spain simultaneously sought to define the essence of their more local, and in the case of Catalonia, national, identity. As a result of these concurrent introspective searches, fragmentation increased in Spain, and regenerationism never gained the momentum of a widespread national movement. It did, however, infiltrate into different areas of society, including the monarchy, politics, and the press. The force of this movement can be seen in cultural periodicals such as *España* from Madrid and *Iberia* from Barcelona, both founded in 1915 during the First World War. The national identity promoted by the regenerationists centered on a mystical idea of Castile, similar to the way *Renaixença* had looked at the glorious medieval past of Catalonia during the nineteenth century. The proposal of this mythical and romantic ideal of Castile is evident in the title and content of literary magazines such as *Los Quijotes* (Madrid, 1915–18) and *Cervantes* (Madrid, 1916–20).

The literary counterpart of regenerationism can be seen in the works of writers known as the Generation of '98. Spain's embarrassing defeat in 1898 led a group of men to embark on a quest to define Spain's problems, destiny, and role in the world. The subsequent search for individual and collective identity manifested itself in works by intellectuals associated with the regenerationist ideology, such as Azorín, Miguel de Unamuno, José Ortega y Gasset, Pío Baroja, Angel Ganivet, and others. Notably, Catalans did not outwardly participate in this literary movement, much in the same way that non-Catalans were not directly involved with the Catalan *modernisme* or *noucentisme* movements. One exception is the case of the Basque writer based in Salamanca and Madrid, Miguel de Unamuno, who shared a deep friendship and extensive correspondence with the Catalan modernist writer Joan Maragall. Unamuno and Maragall wrote letters to one another hoping to establish a periodical together that would keep readers informed about cultural and political developments in the various regions of Spain. The Unamuno-Maragall project never came to fruition, but a seed was planted and eventually a periodical inspired by this idea was created.

In addition to the domestic conflicts brought on by the Disaster of 1898, the first decade of the twentieth century in Barcelona and Madrid was plagued by violence. As one historian has stated, more often than not, "the violence seemed nonsensical, aiming to create panic rather than shape a political agenda."[14] The first strikes in Barcelona took place as early as 1901. The following year, the entire country went on strike. That same year

Alfonso XIII was named king, and four years later anarchists plotted his murder on his wedding day in Madrid. A massive military assault on the Catalan press (*Cu-Cut!*, *La Veu de Catalunya*) resulted in the enactment of the Law of Jurisdiction (1906), allowing the military full access in censoring the press. The following year an urban police force was created in Barcelona to protect its citizens.

Alfonso XIII became the king of Spain the day he was born. His mother, Queen Maria Cristina, functioned as regent until he was sixteen years of age (1902). The young Bourbon king's troubles would begin during the first decade of his reign because of Spain's involvement in an unpopular colonial war in Morocco.[15] In 1909, over two thousand Spanish soldiers were killed, leading the government to call for reservists. When hundreds of young Catalan men were recruited to fight in battle, a week of warfare broke out in the streets of Barcelona, known as Setmana Tràgica (Tragic Week) (July 25–31, 1909). The state mobilized reservists, but because there was an option to pay one's way off the list, those who could not afford the payout organized an uprising. Riots of people furious that the government was allowing the wealthy to avoid the draft broke in Barcelona and the surrounding area (i.e., Sabadell, Poble Nou, Granollers, Manresa, Mataró, and Terrassa). Citizens of Barcelona burned churches, monasteries, convents, and religious schools; they attacked trains and trams; graves were desecrated, and corpses were paraded through the streets.

The anarchists were blamed, jailed, and in some cases, executed.[16] The week ended in three thousand arrests, over one hundred deaths, thousands forced into exile, and seventeen death sentences, of which five were executed, such as Francisco Ferrer, founder of the first anarchist school in Spain, Escuela Moderna (the Modern School).[17] By the end of the week, just under half of the city's religious establishments were damaged or destroyed. The incident was ultimately a failure, because it did not end the war in Morocco, but rather invigorated the military's control. King Alfonso XIII forced Prime Minister Antonio Maura to resign, but no other major political changes resulted from this show of violence. It was also a disappointment for those on the left, who saw the Tragic Week as a poorly executed way to topple the regime. The violence discouraged conservative Catalanists from opposing the government, while the military and police reinforced repression. Other repercussions of the Tragic Week included the extension of martial law, the banning of all organizations to the left of center, and the closing of over 150 lay schools and progressive institutions in the greater community of Barcelona, as well as numerous centers and clubs focused around Catalan culture.[18] The world looked on as Spain burned and bled, just one decade after their loss to the United States in the Spanish-American War of 1898. As a result of the violence that reigned in Barcelona, it became known internationally as the "Rose of Fire" and the "City of Bombs." Unfortunately, the Tragic Week was only the beginning of the violence and injustice that characterize early twentieth-century Spain.

Caped in violence, the people of Barcelona forged ahead with their vision of modernity. The restoration of the once crown jewel of the Mediterranean was an idea born of great minds and major events of the previous century, like the architect Antoni Gaudí and the International World Fair of 1888, as well as the new ideas promoted by *modernisme* and *noucentisme*. The local government had big plans to modernize the city, known as the *reforma* (reform), consisting of considerable urban projects. By opening a major road, the Via Laietana, eighty streets disappeared, more than two thousand buildings were destroyed, and approximately one thousand people were forced to relocate (1908).[19] Barcelona's makeover went beyond the physical. The city council overhauled the social infrastructure of the capital by creating cultural and educational programs and institutions for the future of the nation (e.g., Estudis Universitaris Catalans, Institut d'Estudis Catalans, Escola Industrial, Escola d'Administració Local).

Considering that almost 60 percent of Spain's population was illiterate at the turn of the century, many Catalans and Spaniards believed that the future success of the nation depended on improving its education system. One of the goals of educators like Alberto Jiménez Fraud, director of the Residencia de Estudiantes in Madrid (founded in 1910), was to eradicate illiteracy and direct Spain toward a more liberal and tolerant state. This private boarding school, for instance, was designed to be free from any political or religious affiliations. Modeled on the colleges of Oxford and Cambridge in England, it was primarily a dormitory, but also offered classes. It was the first school in Spain to have co-educational classes, even though the female students had their separate quarters (Residencia de Señoritas). It was also the place where the Catalan Salvador Dalí, the Aragonese Luis Buñuel, and the Andalusian Federico García Lorca would meet for the first time. Centered in Madrid, the Residencia promoted progress and modernity through its tri-annual publication (*Residencia* [1926–34]), lecture series, publications, conferences, and relationships with foreign institutions. In Catalonia, in addition to the various educational institutions backed by the ideals of *noucentisme* mentioned above, Spain's anarchist trade union, CNT (Confederación Nacional de Trabajo), founded in Barcelona in 1910, also played a part in educational reform. The CNT established free cultural centers where members could meet, hold conferences, take classes, and read. They also disseminated information through newspapers like *Tierra y Libertad* (Land and Liberty), *Solidaridad Obrera* (Workers' Solidarity) and other periodicals.

At the beginning of the First World War, half of Spain's population was employed in agriculture. Exports boomed, since neutrally positioned Spain supplied much of Europe during the war. Economic growth stimulated banking and commerce, converting Spain's deficit into a surplus, which in turn caused severe inflation.[20] The economic excess resulted in a reduction in wages and an increase in layoffs, leading to union strikes, food riots, popular uprisings, and other demonstrations. According to Balfour's research, the number of strikes in Spain rose from approximately two hundred annually during the war to over one thousand in 1920; the number of workers on strike during this period also rose fivefold.[21] In Barcelona, violence peaked from 1919 to 1923. The reality of everyday life has been described as being downright hostile. Catalan employers unionized, organized lockouts, and mobilized vigilante squads. Anarchists formed armed gangs, resulting in assassinations such as that of the conservative Prime Minister Eduardo Dato (1921); and private businessmen in Barcelona created a private militia (Somatén).

The chaos in this Mediterranean city at the beginning of the twentieth century brought quick changes. In the span of a decade, Catalonia went from being dependent on the central state of Spain to achieving a significant degree of political autonomy. The Mancomunitat proposal was approved, then constituted, and finally established (1913), with Enric Prat de la Riba elected as president. By the end of this decade, the Mancomunitat approved a Statute of Autonomy. Progress on the normalization of the Catalan language also continued through the efforts of Pompeu Fabra (*Normes Ortogràfiques* [1913]; *Diccionari Ortogràfic* [1914]; *Gramatica Catalana* [1918]). Many of the variations in the Catalan language found a place to work themselves out in the daily press of Barcelona; namely *Revista de Catalunya* (1912–34), *Revista Nova* (1914–16), *Vell i Nou* (1915–21), and *La Nau* (1917). In the same vein as the preceding decade, schools focused on the future of Catalonia continued to be established, such as the Escola Català d'Art Dramàtic (Catalan School of Dramatic Arts) (1913), Escola Superior dels Bells Oficis (Superior School of Fine Arts) (1914), as well as the National Library of Catalonia (1914). As a result of these fast and furious changes, the political, cultural, economic, and social gap dividing Barcelona and Madrid widened, and tensions between the two cities increased.

The Avant-Garde Revolution

During the First World War, many artists escaped Paris in search of a more peaceful place to practice their art. Some of them came to Spain and brought new ideas that fall under the general umbrella of the Avant-Garde. In Barcelona, the movement found expression in a variety of small periodicals that voiced these radically new ideas. Within the pages of these publications, experimental poetry, new art, and manifestos proliferated. Cutting-edge art galleries, especially the one owned by Josep Dalmau, also opened their minds and doors to this movement.[22] These new ideas from abroad also infiltrated Madrid. Some of the exiles who participated in the European Avant-Garde movement and made their home in Madrid included the French painters Sonia and Robert Delaunay, the Mexican painter and muralist Diego Rivera, the Lithuanian sculptor Jacques Lipchitz, the Chilean poet Vicente Huidobro, and the Argentinean writer Jorge Luis Borges and his sister, the artist Norah Borges. Ramón Gómez de la Serna could be considered the counterpart of Josep Dalmau in Madrid in the sense that his weekly *tertulia*, or literary gathering, at Café Pombo, established in 1915, functioned as the gathering place for intellectuals, including avant-garde artists and writers. He was the first in Spain to translate and publish the Italian futurist manifesto in his father's periodical (1909), *Prometeo* (1908–12), and he was the inventor of a new poetic form influenced by the Avant-Garde spirit, known as the *greguería*. At the start of the Great War, he published a book with the eponymous title of *Greguerías* that collects a series of them.

A recent exhibition at the Metropolitan Museum of Art in New York City, "Barcelona and Modernity," considers Pablo Picasso's trips to Catalonia in 1909 and 1910 (Barcelona, Horta de Sant Joan, and Cadaqués), along with the sculptor Pablo Gargallo's early cutout metal sculptures (1907–15), as the first indicators of artistic avant-garde activity in Spain. Interestingly, neither one of these artists is Catalan (Picasso is from Andalusia and Gargallo from Aragon). Yet, some historians often adopt Picasso and Gargallo as Catalans, since they both lived in Barcelona. Along these lines, the Metropolitan exhibit classifies Joaquín Torres-García and Rafael Barradas as the first avant-garde practitioners who came after Picasso and Gargallo. Once again, neither one of these two artists is Catalan. Both of them emigrated from Uruguay and arrived in Spain as young adults. In the case of Barradas, his work was very influenced by an avant-garde movement in Madrid (*Ultraísmo*) that is barely mentioned in the exhibit or catalog.

The spark of the Avant-Garde revolution in the troubled Mediterranean city was quick to catch fire. Barcelona had already prepared its public by establishing an infrastructure for the business, teaching, and practice of art, due in large part to the success of two major art-centered movements: *modernisme* and *noucentisme*. The Avant-Garde in Barcelona emerges from a very specific political and cultural context that differs significantly from Madrid's. The differences in the reality of daily life help explain why the Avant-Garde in Barcelona and Madrid took on two very different shapes that are usually kept separate, even though they form part of the same puzzle.

An alphabet soup of isms—from cubism to surrealism—emerged in Spain during the first three decades of the twentieth century. In the case of Barcelona and Madrid, some artists and writers who were influenced by these imported aesthetic and literary movements appropriated them as their own and, in turn, invented their own styles. For example, in Barcelona, Italian futurism was adopted by a small group of Catalan poets led by Joan Salvat-Papasseit. Inspired by the Italian futurists, Salvat-Papasseit developed a brand of futurism that was distinctly Catalan. He explored futurism in his two first books of poetry: *Poemes en ondes hertzianes* (1919) and *L'irradiador del port i les gavines* (1921); he penned a Catalan futurist manifesto, *Contra els poetes amb minuscula: primer manifest català futurista* (Against Poets Who Write Their Names in Lowercase Letters: First Catalan Futurist Manifesto) (1920); and he founded literary magazines in which he and his friends practiced the lessons of futurism, such as *Un enemic del Poble* (An Enemy of the People) (1917–18) and *Arc-Voltaic* (Voltaic Arc) (1918). One of the only poets of Madrid who collaborated with Joan Salvat-Papasseit was Ramón Gómez de la Serna, precisely the person who first informed his peers in Madrid of this new Italian poetic style when it was first defined by Marinetti in 1909. The common link between these two pioneers, one from Barcelona (Joan Salvat-Papasseit) and the other from Madrid (Ramón Gómez de la Serna), was a blind faith in the power and impact that a literary movement, like Italian futurism, could have on a troubled society.

In contrast to Barcelona, there were no cultural publications in Madrid that were strictly devoted to futurism. Indeed, there were reports of Italian futurism in the Madrid press, but there was not a significant interest on behalf of the writers there. Instead, the experimental poets of Madrid were more intrigued by the Chilean poet Vicente Huidobro, who promoted an ism of his own: *creacionismo* (creationism). In Madrid, Huidobro's style of writing poetry and being a poet competed with the more popular *Ultraísmo* style. Articulated in 1919 in the form of a manifesto, ten years after the first news of Italian futurism, *Ultraísmo* included the influences of many foreign styles, including Italian futurism, but also those of Jorge Luis and Noah Borges (Argentina), Rafael and Carmen Barradas (Uruguay), Robert and Sonia Delaunay (France), Wladyslaw Jahl (Poland), and many others. *Ultraísmo* was like the paella of worldwide avant-garde styles, and it makes sense that it blossomed and came to life in Madrid, where so many different kinds of people from all over the world congregated. So long as their work expressed some sort of faith in the spirit of the Avant-Garde, the *Ultraístas* welcomed, promoted, and published their work. Notably, *Ultraísmo* never took root in Barcelona as it did in other cities of Spain, like Seville, for example.

The financial stability and political influence of cultural centers like the Residencia de Estudiantes in Madrid attracted a diverse and critical mass of writers and artists representing every corner of Spain, usually from well-to-do families. Despite their regional or national differences, a diverse group of writers and artists discovered one another by the early 1920s. They developed personal relationships and formed clusters of friends. Together, they attended cultural events, organized informal gatherings, participated in art shows, and contributed to periodicals such as *Alfar* (A Coruña, 1920–54) and *Ultra* (Madrid, 1921–22). They found that even though they spoke different languages and lived in cities with widely differing political situations, they all had something in common. They shared a belief in the radical renovation of art, literature, and society. Their similar faith in the ideas of rupture and renewal contrasted sharply with all the other efforts mentioned up until this point (i.e., *modernisme, noucentisme*, regenerationism). Naturally, individuals will always have their differences, but for the most part, there was a significant amount of communication taking place between avant-garde actors representing Barcelona and Madrid. This contact occurred through letter writing, art shows, the press, and friendships. Most importantly, believers in the Avant-Garde from both Barcelona and Madrid dialogued through and against the dictatorship of General Primo de Rivera as best they could.

Once the initial excitement of *Ultraísmo* in Madrid fizzled, and with the early death of Salvat-Papasseit of Barcelona, the presence of a literary avant-garde in both cities seems to disappear almost completely until the arrival of surrealism at the end of the 1920s in Spain. This trend is clearly evident when studying patterns in the production of cultural periodicals in Barcelona and Madrid. The interruption in the development of the Avant-Garde in Spain, especially its literary component, corresponds directly with the years of the dictatorship of Miguel Primo de Rivera, also during the 1920s. The last ism to make its grand entrance in Spain was surrealism. This movement was baptized with the screening of the short, silent, experimental film, *Un chien andalou* (An Andalusian Dog), co-written by Salvador Dalí and Luis Buñuel in 1929.[23] Surrealism had already been defined in a manifesto written by André Breton in Paris in 1924, and it was a subject of discussion in the small-circulation press, but it was not fully understood by most Spaniards. News of the scandalous reactions to Dalí and Buñuel's film screening in Barcelona spread quickly to Madrid, resulting in a peak of interest in this latest avant-garde style. During the early 1930s, an understanding of surrealism was promoted by several avant-garde periodicals, but without much success. The beginning of the Civil War in 1936, followed by the establishment of another military dictatorship, and the subsequent imprisonment, assassination, and exile of many avant-garde writers and artists, quickly extinguished the flame of the Avant-Garde spirit. It also stunted the human development of understanding difference, as promoted and practiced by circles of friends, or networks, connecting Barcelona and Madrid.

The violence with which the new millennium began persisted. In 1921, there were twenty-one assassinations in Barcelona in thirty-six hours. The war in Morocco continued as the number of casualties grew, especially after the Battle of Annual that same year, resulting in over ten thousand deaths. The political response involved a clear shift in the balance of power from parliamentary rule toward military enforcements. In order to resolve Spain's political and social chaos, a solution was found in an authoritarian regime similar to that of neighboring Italy, where Benito Mussolini marched into power in Rome. In the words of Raymond Carr, the megalomaniacal General Miguel Primo de Rivera "seems to have believed he had come to power to kill Catalanism."[24] Before he overthrew the government, he was captain general of Barcelona. He knew the city well, and according to documents from the period in which he describes his rise to power, he explains that what bothered him most about the city was not so much the constant violence, but Catalan "separatism."[25] Much as King Philip V crushed the flowering Catalan cultural renaissance with the establishment of the Nueva Planta decree in the early eighteenth century, Primo de Rivera attempted to do something similar. All of Spain's attempts to achieve greater unity, peace, stability, and democracy during the growing pains of the Restoration period (1875–23) ended when Primo de Rivera overthrew the struggling Spanish government (September 14, 1923).

King Alfonso XIII made the executive decision to allow the captain general of Barcelona, General Miguel Primo de Rivera, to resolve the violence that characterized his rule and was only worsening. Without consulting Parliament, the Bourbon monarch shattered the hope of all those who had made strides in achieving some sort of democratic progress in Spain. Thus, with Primo de Rivera's sudden imposition of a military dictatorship, modeled on Benito Mussolini's takeover in neighboring Italy, and his elimination of Parliament the year before (1922), the period of constitutional monarchy in Spain came to an abrupt halt. In my readings about Primo de Rivera and his dictatorship, there are two main reasons that are most often given to explain this sudden overthrow: (1) to cover up the military disaster in Morocco, where Spanish forces were battling the Moroccan Rif and Jibala tribes; and (2) to put an end to Catalan separatism. One of the reasons why Primo de Rivera initiated the coup when he did was because the current government was about to release a report about the war in Morocco that the people of Spain had been demanding. That report would have blamed the Spanish military for a myriad of errors in the handling of the war, also known as the War in Melilla (1919–26). The Battle of Annual was a major military defeat suffered by the Spanish army on July 22, 1921, leading to five additional years of sporadic, and what many considered to be senseless, warfare in northern Africa.

As far as the second point is concerned, the military dictator moved quickly to eradicate what he considered to be Catalan separatism. Besides censoring the press, he banned the Catalan flag and the use of Catalan in official places, like street signs, as well as in official documents. Primo de Rivera also banned the *sardana*, the national dance of Catalonia that, as Picasso once said, was much more than a dance. It also functions as an expression of the Catalan identity, a symbol of Catalan nationalism. Selling products with foreign names was also prohibited.[26] Even seasonal art shows in Barcelona were banned.[27] Primo de Rivera suspended all activities at intellectual centers throughout Spain known as *ateneos*, and disbanded the Catalan governing body, the Mancomunitat (1926). This same year he established the Civil Directory, a military unit charged with eradicating Catalan separatism, and his version of the Somatén, based on a Catalan model of law enforcement, which used severe measures to repress regionalist and separatist demonstrations.

In an archival document titled "Repression of Separatism" (September 18, 1923), General Primo de Rivera makes clear the consequences of failing to obey his rules.[28] For example, flying any national flag other than Spain's resulted in six months of jail and a fine of five hundred to five thousand *pesetas*; or for any written or spoken evidence of separatism, the punishment involved six to twelve months in prison and a fine of five hundred to five thousand *pesetas*; distribution of separatist ideas in schools resulted in two years in prison; holding public or private demonstrations resulted in three to twelve years in prison for the leader and three to six years for others; public resistance in the form of a political party resulted in the death penalty or six to twelve years in prison; communicating or writing in languages or dialects, as well as songs, dances, customs, and traditional costumes were permitted, but in official acts of international or national character, all representatives were required to use Castilian. All books and registers in local and regional corporations also had to be printed in Castilian.[29]

As part of his reform, Primo de Rivera also established a centralized political party, *Unión Patriótica* (established April 1924). The function of this entity was to define a Spanish nationalism that enforced doctrines of anti-separatism, anti-liberalism, anti-parliamentarianism, anti-individualism, and anti-Bolshevism. Primo de Rivera strongly believed that peace and the unity of a central state would be achieved through the fusion of the church and monarchy. Many wealthy business people and intellectuals were benevolent to his regime (e.g., Ortega y Gasset, Eugeni D'Ors, Ramiro de Maetzu), while others defied its oppression (e.g., Ramón Pérez de Ayala, Antonio Machado), even to the point of exile (e.g., Unamuno). Seven years after the overthrow, in 1930, King Alfonso XIII forced Primo de Rivera to resign. Spain was bankrupt. In the next municipal elections (April 1931), the majority of people in Spain voted for a Second Republic (the first being in 1873 at the beginning of the Restoration period). With the declaration of this new government, King Alfonso XIII and Primo de Rivera fled into exile. Curiously, Primo de Rivera met his death six days after fleeing the country. Spain's troubles would not end here. After the death of the dictator came the struggles of the Second Spanish Republic, the Spanish Civil War, and the Second World War, all of which ended in a second, much more oppressive dictatorship that finally provided Spain with the stability it so deeply desired for so long.

Notes

1. Sometimes the European Avant-Garde that corresponds to the beginning of the twentieth century is called the "Historical Avant-Garde." The adjective "historical" is used to distinguish this Avant-Garde from later ones (circa 1950s to today) that were and have been inspired by those of the first half of the twentieth century. Since the qualifier "historical" is problematic for some, and confusing to most, I omit it. The Avant-Garde that is the subject of this book takes place during the first half of the twentieth century in Europe, mostly in Spain and particularly in Barcelona and Madrid.

2. Considering that Spain's American colonies began to claim their independence (1819–24) at about the same time as Spain's victory against France in the War of Independence, a "myth of Spanish identity" began to take shape at this time. See Jo Labanyi, *Constructing Identity in Contemporary Spain: Theoretical Debates and Cultural Practice* (Oxford: Oxford University Press, 2002), 5. The image and illusion of a unified Spanish state was carried out by the absolutist regime of Ferdinand VII from the Bourbon dynasty. This king is remembered for reinstating the Inquisition and refusing to abide by Spain's Constitution of 1812.

3. Deep political divisions burrowed their way into the makeup of the land, causing much more than the family feuds depicted in literary works like those of the writer Benito Pérez Galdós, such as *Doña Perfecta* (1826). In this novel, which is representative of Spain's nascent realism movement, the liberal nephew from Madrid travels to the invented provincial town of Orbajosa to marry his young, virgin cousin. In the courtship process, a civil war breaks out. One lover is executed, while the other is sent away to a madhouse.

4. To hear the Catalan national anthem, "Els Segadors," and learn more about the Reapers' War, please visit the Web site for the Museu d'Història de Catalunya (accessed on July 10, 2011): http://www.en.mhcat.net/the_mhc_offers/permanent_exhibition/on_the_edge_of_the_empire/the_reapers_war.

5. One clear example of the period's medievalism can be seen in Catalonia's national anthem, "Els Segadors" (The Reapers). Please see note 4.

6. In 1886, only 2 percent of Spain's population voted. See Joaquín Valle-Inclán, *Luces de Bohemia* (Madrid: Espasa Calpe, 2006), 218.

7. Raymond Carr, *Modern Spain 1875–1980* (Oxford: Oxford University Press, 1980), 33.

8. The Disaster of 1898 caused serious setbacks for Catalan business. For example, 60 percent of Catalan exports went to Cuba. See Sandie Holguín, *Creating Spaniards: Culture and National Identity in Republican Spain* (Madison: University of Wisconsin Press, 2002), 41. Also, the fortunes of most Catalan capitalist dynasties were the result of colonial trade under the protection of the Spanish state, and in particular, from the lucrative slave trade during the nineteenth century. See Sebastian Balfour, *The End of the Spanish Empire 1898–1923* (Oxford: Oxford University Press, 1997), 140. With the loss of Cuba, Catalan industry now depended more than it wanted to on the Spanish market.

9. Balfour, *End of the Spanish Empire*, 137.

10. The Barcelona–Madrid rivalry was first played out on the soccer fields in Spain's first Copa del Rey, a soccer tournament in honor of the Spanish monarch, in 1902. The same year that the Bourbon king Alfonso XIII inherited the throne, he founded F.C. Real Madrid. By 1909 there were twelve soccer clubs in Spain, and on March 14, 1909, F.C. Barcelona played its first game in its new stadium. The first time the two professional football clubs would play against each other in a first-division game was 1929. My special thanks go to Joaquin Bueno, a longtime friend and soccer scholar, for confirming these facts.

11. The popularity of *noucentisme* among many important artists, editors, politicians, and writers may have been one reason why Alomar looked outside of Catalonia for support for his *futurisme* movement. Alomar shows clear signs of shifting his gaze toward Madrid, where he published numerous articles about his ideas about the future of Catalonia, Spain, and Europe.

12. Eugeni d'Ors (Barcelona, 1881–1954), also known by his pen name, Xènius, lived, studied, and worked in Madrid on several occasions and for extended periods of time. His first move to Madrid was in 1920. After the Disaster of 1898, he was one of the intellectuals who worked hard to pull Spain out of its funk. He made friends in Madrid and published frequently in its periodicals. We can find his byline in many publications, including *Renacimiento, España, Ultra, Revista de Occidente, Residencia*, and *La Gaceta Literaria*. His work was also published in Barcelona's daily newspaper, *La Veu de Catalunya*, as well as in *Correo de las artes y las letras, Vell i nou, Un enemic del Poble*, and *D'ací, d'allà*. Outside of Barcelona and Madrid, he also published in the following periodicals in other parts of Spain and beyond: *Hermes* (Bilbao), *La*

columna de foc (Reus), *Alfar* (La Coruña), *Horizonte* (Sevilla), *Mediodía* (Sevilla), *Sagitario* (Mexico), and *Papel de Aleluyas* (Huelva-Sevilla). See Josep Murgades, "D'Ors," accessed 2007, www.lletra.uoc.edu, and Bonet, *Diccionario*, 467.

13. The *noucentisme* movement was responsible for establishing institutions like the following: Estudis Universitaris Catalans (EUC) (1906); Institut d'Estudis Catalans (IEC) (1907); Mancomunitat (1914); Fundació Bernat Metge; Biblioteca de Catalunya; Escola Nova; Universitat Industrial; Escola Superior de Belles Artes; Escola de Treball; Escola de l'Administració Local; and Junta de Museos.

14. Julián Casanova, "Terror and Violence: The Dark Face of Spanish Anarchism," *International Labor and Working-Class History* 67 (2005): 85.

15. Spain began its military campaign in Morocco in 1859. Notably, a massacre of Spanish troops resulted from a battle in Melilla in 1893.

16. Francisco Pi y Maragall, a Barcelona native, has been credited with introducing anarchism to Spain. See Holguín, *Creating Spaniards*, 28. The anarchist movement in Barcelona reached record highs during the 1890s, when labor strikes, bombings, and police brutality took over the city. The bombing of the Gran Teatre del Liceu in 1892 (Europe's first privately built opera house, built in 1847, and a temple of bourgeois values) killed twenty people and destroyed the modernist-style structure. Bombings during a religious procession in 1896 resulted in ten deaths and provoked drastic police response in the form of torture and public executions. These medieval-style punishments are remembered by the Catalan painter Ramon Casas in his work *The Garroting* (1894), which belongs to the permanent collection of the Museo Nacional Centro de Arte Reina Sofia in Madrid. For more on anarchism at the beginning of twentieth-century Spain, see Casanova, "Terror and Violence."

17. The figures of casualties differ: Albert Balcells, *Catalan Nationalism* (New York: St. Martin's Press, 1996), 62–62; Balfour, *End of the Spanish Empire*, 124–25; Gerald Brenan, *The Spanish Labyrinth* (Cambridge: Cambridge University Press, 2000), 34–35. I have used the most recent figures per Pere Guxà, "Tras los pasos de la Setmana Tràgica," *365 Culturas*. *La Vanguardia*, June 17, 2009.

18. Balfour, *End of the Spanish Empire*, 129.

19. Alexia Domínguez Álvarez, *La Setmana Tràgica de Barcelona, 1909* (Valls, Tarragona: Cossetània, 2009), 21.

20. Balfour, *End of the Spanish Empire*, 212.

21. Ibid., 223.

22. The first art exhibition introducing cubism outside of Paris took place in Barcelona in 1912 at the gallery of an ex-artist turned entrepreneur, Josep Dalmau. Subsequently, his locale became one of the central headquarters of the Avant-Garde movement in Spain. "Can Dalmau," or "home of Josep Dalmau" in Catalan, hosted this historical exhibition, leading to press coverage of the event throughout Europe and beyond. From this point onwards, Dalmau was considered the defender and promoter of the most groundbreaking visual styles in Barcelona, as well as for the rest of Spain.

23. Surrealism was defined in a manifesto published in Paris in 1924 by André Breton. News of this radical system of expression was reported by all of the major avant-garde periodicals in Barcelona and Madrid.

24. Carr, *Modern Spain*, 568–69.

25. See Díaz-Plaja, *La preguerra española en sus documentos (1923–1936)* (Barcelona: Ediciones G.P., 1969), and Jordi Cassasas Ymbert, *La dictadura de Primo de Rivera (1923–1930)* (Barcelona: Anthropos, 1983).

26. Domínguez Álvarez, *La Setmana Tràgica*, 17.

27. Jaime Brihuega. "La *ESAI* y el arte español en el bisagra de 1925," in *La Sociedad de Artistas Ibéricos y el arte español de 1925* (Madrid: Museo Nacional Centro de Arte Reina Sofía, 1995), 23.

28. General Primo de Rivera, "Repression of Separatism," September 18, 1923.

29. Cassasas Ymbert, *La dictadura de Primo de Rivera*, 121.

CHAPTER FOUR

~

One Hundred Little Magazines

Substantial proof that members of avant-garde circles in Barcelona and Madrid were well aware of one another lies within the pages of over one hundred small-circulation periodicals, more commonly known as "little magazines." Many of these publications are art objects in and of themselves, for it was in their nature to be everything that commercial publishing was not. In Spain, they came in all shapes and sizes. Editors of the little magazines published poems alongside drawings, arranged for illustrated covers, printed on a variety of paper textures, and experimented with color printing and new fonts. Unfortunately, since many of these periodicals did not have consistent financial backing, most of them were short lived. Some editors managed to publish only one issue of their periodical. Others succeeded and were in print for years. Some little magazines were smaller than others, while others were far from little. For example, Ramón Gómez de la Serna's monthly *Prometeo* (Madrid, 1908–12), the periodical to first report the news of Italian futurism in Madrid, averaged about one hundred pages per issue.

In Catalonia, literary reviews played an important role in what Robert Davidson calls "the consolidation of Catalan culture."[1] In Barcelona, especially, there was an artistic and literary journal for every taste (e.g., *modernisme*, *noucentisme*, *futurisme*), as well as publications associated with a variety of political groups (e.g., anarchists, communists, traditionalists). The function of these Catalan publications went far beyond reporting news. As Joan Ramon Resina puts it, they "took the ostensible public role of modernizing culture."[2] Writing about the little magazines in 1930, Ezra Pound believed that the history of contemporary literature is contained within the pages of these magazines. The motivation to produce and sustain these publications was a combination of creating, documenting, debating, and modernizing contemporary culture. Without these periodicals, it would be difficult to imagine how the Avant-Garde could have thrived.

Matthew Luskey notes how culture is formed within the pages of the small-press periodicals, in which social, political, material, and economic forces interconnect.[3] In the case of the periodicals directly related to the Avant-Garde, "[They] functioned as brief yet defiant public spheres, promoting vanguard movements and providing forums for their initial reception of an artist's works."[4] While Luskey refers to the Avant-Garde in the United States, the same can be said for the movement in Catalonia and in the rest of Spain. The homepage for the Little Magazine Collection at the Memorial Library at the University of Wisconsin offers another reason why these texts are so fundamental for the study of early twentieth-century culture:

> Little magazines have continuously rebelled against established literary expression and theory, demonstrating an aggressive receptivity to new authors, new ideas, and new styles . . . Little magazines have sponsored or introduced all of this century's literary trends, including imagism, dadaism, surrealism, symbolism, and the Beat generation. They were also the first to publish and discuss the artistic and literary manifestations of socialism, psychoanalysis, and Marxism and other social movements.[5]

Even though the collection at Madison is centered on English-language periodicals, this summary can also be used to describe the role of little magazines in Spain. In particular, the little magazines in Barcelona and Madrid were aggressively receptive to new authors, new styles, and new ideas. They were also some of the main instruments for sponsoring and introducing the century's new trends. Additionally, the majority of the little magazines from Barcelona and Madrid showed an explicit interest in connecting with other periodicals and other centers of cultural production that shared the same spirit or mission as their own publication. This final point especially supports the main argument that drives this book: the Avant-Garde as a movement in Spain functioned as a system of networks that connected people, ideas, and artifacts.

Over one hundred periodicals dedicated to art, literature, and culture from 1900 to 1936 were consulted in the periodical archives in both Barcelona and Madrid, in special libraries known as *hemerotecas*, to compile the evidence for this book. Many more periodicals pertaining to this period remain to be discovered and studied in detail. Most of them do not have facsimile editions, and many are not available in full sequence. With the progress of today's internet age, more and more of these periodicals are becoming available online and can be accessed virtually through library Web sites. Many of these documents were censored or destroyed during the Spanish Civil War and during the subsequent dictatorship of General Francisco Franco. For the most part, scholars did not have access to these texts until after Franco's death (1975). Some of the consulted periodicals for this book have been very well documented; others have rarely been considered in relation to the Avant-Garde in Spain. Given the available archival material over the last five years, this search involved discovering links between the artistic, literary, and political worlds of Barcelona and Madrid, if any.

Returning to the discipline of social networks, one could potentially create a graph or map showing how many of the little magazines of Barcelona and Madrid were related to one another. One would start by analyzing the nature of connections between nodes: editors, illustrators, journalists, advertisers, and other contributors. The relational ties connecting these nodes would reveal an elaborate network, matrix, or web. Since there were so many little magazines from the specific period in question (focused mostly in the period from 1909 to 1929), this task would be a project in and of itself. To create such a graph, chart, or map is not the intention here. Instead, the goal is to draw attention to several key periodicals from this vast editorial universe that were critical in connecting the artistic and literary avant-garde networks of Barcelona and Madrid.

It quickly became clear that the little magazines from these two cities did not exist in a vacuum. They were naturally linked to other periodicals within their own cities, and in most cases, they were connected to periodicals outside of their own city of origin. On one level, writers and artists were often the people who were most responsible for establishing these links. Going back to the Catalan art critic and avid Avant-Garde supporter, Sebastià Gasch, he started contributing to periodicals in Barcelona, then in Madrid, followed by other cities in Spain, and later in the Latin American press (e.g., *Atlántico*). The little magazine was the platform from which many friendships and relationships formed and evolved. They functioned as the heart of the literary and cultural Avant-Garde movement in Spain, and most of them, but certainly not all, were published in Barcelona and Madrid. They played a leading role in receiving and divulging avant-garde ideas in Spain and Catalonia, as well as maintaining the networks that sustained them.

The little magazines from Barcelona and Madrid share many similar qualities. They include poetry, reviews, editorials, essays, illustrations, and forums for criticism. They confront readers with new ideas that challenge tradition and the status quo. For the most part, those who contributed to the little magazines were united by a common Avant-Garde spirit, or, in the words of Ezra Pound, some sort of "binding force."[6] It is for this reason that when a periodical launched its first issue, its editors printed a statement of purpose, often adopting the kind of language and tone found in the artistic and literary manifestos so closely tied to the Avant-Garde movement; these mission statements were often located on the first page of the first issue of the periodical. Very few little magazines went to press without publishing such a declaration. Oftentimes the editor penned this mission statement, but sometimes a highly regarded member of the intellectual community, such as José Ortega y Gasset or Miguel de Unamuno, would be asked to write it. Other times, the text was anonymous, perhaps for fear of recrimination during times of censorship.

Overall, the little magazines from Barcelona and Madrid shared very similar functions. Their goal was to discover new voices that spoke to the moment and that perpetuated the Avant-Garde spirit. Usually, this voice was in the form of poetry, but it was also expressed in prose. This message was also expressed visually with illustrations or in the periodical's layout and design. The vanguard style had a distinctly modern look and new voice that clearly distinguished it from more traditional periodicals. In contrast to the immediacy of a newspaper, the weekly, bimonthly, or monthly journals called for pause and reflection. Their objective was to disseminate information about art, literature, and culture that resonated with the mission of their program, as stated in the first issue, while building a network of supporters in the process. Their function was cultural, social, intellectual, and, in some cases, political. Many of these periodicals published lesser-known writers or works that would never be considered in commercial or more conservative publications. The vanguard magazines not only introduced new literary and aesthetic theories, usually exported from abroad, but they put these new ideas to practice in the form of poetry, prose, illustrations, and the design of the overall journal. The little magazines are one of the most valuable resources for understanding the Avant-Garde movement throughout Europe, the United States, and Latin America.

In my search for understanding the kinds of relationships that connected avant-garde Barcelona and Madrid, three major patterns emerged. First, I discovered a clear intention to dialogue that predates the arrival of the Avant-Garde in Spain and Catalonia (1904–9). Second, with the arrival of the first European avant-garde movements (1909–23), there was an increase in communication and a greater emphasis placed on intercultural communication across geographical, social, and political lines. Third, a major shift occurs in the mid-twenties (1923–29), when avant-garde periodicals begin to appear mostly in areas outside of Barcelona and Madrid. This chapter deals with these three stages of development in the construction of this networking platform between Barcelona and Madrid, and how it informs our overall understanding of the Avant-Garde in Spain.

As discussed in the previous chapter, at the turn of the twentieth century, most Spanish intellectuals and politicians were preoccupied with the regeneration of Spain following the colonial Disaster of 1898. A number of periodicals from this period demonstrate a clear attempt to dialogue with one another, or have as their mission the goal of gaining greater mutual understanding between Barcelona and Madrid in particular. Some of these periodicals published in Madrid clearly state that their mission was to achieve a greater "spiritual unity" between the various regions of Spain. With the introduction of futurism in Spain in 1909, a second pattern emerges amongst the cultural press that lasts until the end of the First World War. Poets in Barcelona, inspired by Italian futurism, Swiss dadaism, and French literary cubism, experiment with these new ideas from abroad with enthusiasm. Writers in Madrid, on the other hand, were still looking inwards. It is not until a group of poets who were gathered in Madrid invented their own avant-garde style, *Ultraísmo*, in 1919, that we see the first steady signs of experimentation sparked by the European avant-garde movements within the pages of the journals published in Madrid. By this late date, the excitement of futurism, dadaism, and literary cubism had fizzled in Barcelona. By 1923, experimentation with these new poetic and artistic styles came to a sudden halt with the military takeover of General Miguel Primo de Rivera. The effects of this dictatorial regime are reflected in the small-circulation periodicals in numerous ways. This date marks the beginning of the third stage in the study of the literary and cultural press, in which direct connections between Barcelona and Madrid diminish to the point of almost disappearing. Instead, a significant number of avant-garde periodicals from other cities in Spain establish connections by circumventing or avoiding Barcelona and Madrid altogether.

Much work remains to be done in the *hemerographic* study of the Avant-Garde in Spain.[7] I am not the first to make this assertion. For one, Juan Manuel Bonet, the contemporary literary and art critic, as well as the once-director of the Museo Nacional Centro de Arte Reina Sofia (MNCARS) in Madrid, and prior to that of the Insitut Valencià d'Art Modern (IVAM) in Valencia, has already made this point. He has identified the lack of study of the little magazines as one of the most "obtrusive lacunae" preventing us from gaining a greater understanding of this cultural moment. At the beginning of the introduction to his indispensable dictionary of the Spanish Avant-Garde (1995, first edition), he admits to his lack of knowledge about the Catalan avant-garde as a major obstacle: "[C]onfieso que donde más dudas he tenido, ha sido en el ámbito catalán" (I confess that where I have had the most doubts [in compiling this dictionary], has been in the area of Catalonia).[8] Similarly, after a long career devoted to documenting the literary and cultural press of the Spanish Avant-Garde, Rafael Osuna, in his latest book, *Revistas de la vanguardia española* (2005), rallies Hispanists to continue hemerographic research of the historical Catalan press:

Mucho tememos que la fogosidad investigadora y crítica de que hoy goza la vanguardia conozca un decaimiento en el futuro, a menos que se propongan nuevas avenidas de investigación, como pueden ser las conexiones con las vanguardias francesas e italianas—no con telescopio como casi siempre hasta ahora, sino microscópicamente—, sin olvidar la catalana, ésta última por ser, no sólo muy fecunda, sino parte esencial de nuestro mundo cultural; esta ampliación de miras nos haría también redirigir un orbe más universal esos afanes localistas, regionalistas o nacionalistas que hoy se observan.

(We greatly fear that the eagerness of the research and criticism about the Avant-Garde today will experience a decline in the future, unless new avenues of investigation are proposed, like those seeking connections between the French and Italian vanguards—not with a telescope as it has been approached until now, but with a microscope—, without forgetting the Catalan avant-garde, because not only is it plentiful, but it is also essential to our cultural world. This widening of scope would also redirect our world to one that is more universal beyond the local, regional, and nationalist zeal that can be observed in the criticism and research of today.)[9]

This book serves as an initial attempt to bridge some of the blaring gaps that both Bonet and Osuna describe above in their description of the relationship between the Catalan and the non-Catalan early twentieth-century vanguard in Spain. Specifically, my focus is on defining and studying the connections between artistic, journalistic, and literary networks in Barcelona and Madrid. While I have consulted a wide array of primary sources (e.g., literary almanacs, poetic anthologies, artworks, illustrations, letters, maps, memoirs, museum exhibit catalogues, photographs, and other literary and visual texts), much of the evidence I use to describe the system of networks connecting avant-garde Barcelona and Madrid comes from small-press periodicals. After consulting these archival documents from Spain, France, Italy,

England, Switzerland, and various North and South American countries, it is abundantly clear that a relationship between Barcelona and Madrid did indeed exist—even if that means that sometimes they intentionally ignored one another.

Stage 1: Consensus (1904–9)

Renacimiento (Renaissance) (1907) was the first twentieth-century periodical printed in Madrid to regularly feature Catalan writers and artists. Although this cultural magazine predates any sort of avant-garde activity in Spain, its editor, Gregorio Martínez Sierra (Madrid, 1881–1947), would become one of the leaders in the renovation of Spanish theater in his role as playwright and director. For example, Martínez Sierra was the first director to offer the young Federico García Lorca the opportunity to stage his first play, *El maleficio de la mariposa* (The Curse of the Butterfly) (1920), at the *Teatro Eslava* in Madrid. From the earliest stages of his career, Martínez Sierra proved to have an open mind toward Catalan literature and culture, in the same way that he would be open to radical ideas proposed by the Avant-Garde.

Each issue of this monthly magazine totaled over one hundred pages. In other words, there was nothing "little" about it.[10] Under the modernist banner of "art for art's sake," or in Martínez Sierra's words, "¡Vivimos por la belleza!" (We live for the sake of beauty!), the magazine's objective, as stated on the first page of the first issue, was for readers to discover the newest modernist poetry written in Spain in any language. Besides including poems by Juan Ramón Jiménez and the Machado brothers, the inaugural issue also included work by the leader of *modernisme*, the modern Catalan poetry movement, Joan Maragall (Barcelona, 1860–1911). *Renacimiento* published one of his poems in Castilian ("La Hazaña" [The Heroic Deed]), accompanied by an article by the Spanish-speaking poet and literary critic Enrique Díez-Canedo, who was born in Badajoz, Spain, and lived in Barcelona before moving to Madrid, and who also worked as a translator.[11] The appearance of this article by Díez-Canedo, someone who lived in both Barcelona and Madrid, suggests that he is a probable link between Joan Maragall in Barcelona and Gregorio Martínez Sierra in Madrid. He also was likely the one who was able to connect what each of these two men represent—the Madrid and Barcelona cultural and intellectual elite and their respective notions of modernism. In the same issue, Martínez Sierra also published a poem written by the Catalan modernist painter Santiago Rusiñol, also in Castilian ("Cigarras y Hormigas" [Cicadas and Ants]).[12] It is important to note that *Renacimiento* had its main office in Madrid, but it also had a satellite office in Paris. Anchoring his magazine in both Madrid and Paris allowed Martínez Sierra to feasibly connect the cultural worlds of both of these cities. By reaching out to Paris, he connected with Spanish expatriates living in the French capital. It was also a likely attraction for his Catalan contributors and potential readers, who have a history of strong ties linking them to Paris. Martínez Sierra appreciated the beauty of the works by Maragall and Rusiñol, which is why he brings these two Catalan poets to light in this first issue of his Madrid and Paris-based periodical, but he made the editorial decision to print them in Spanish, rather than in their original Catalan.

After *Renacimiento* published a Spanish article by the Catalan writer Gabriel Alomar (September 1907, and continued in November 1907) titled "Futurismo" (Futurism), the periodical took a radical step. Martínez Sierra published several poems in Catalan by Alomar, Joan Maragall, José Pijoan, and Josep Carner in subsequent issues (October and November 1907). According to my research, the publication of Catalan poetry in Catalan in the Madrid press was extremely rare. After the publication of Alomar's 1907 "Futurism" article, *Renacimiento* printed texts written in Catalan without Spanish translations.

As discussed in the previous chapter, several years prior to the publication of Filippo Tommaso Marinetti's first futurist manifesto in the Parisian newspaper *Le Figaro*, Alomar gave a lecture in Barcelona's *Ateneu* entitled "*Futurisme*" (1905). He argued that Catalan autonomy and the regeneration of Catalan culture could only be achieved by adopting a forward-looking attitude, rather than reviving the past, an idea promoted by the nineteenth-century Catalan *Renaixença* movement. In response to Alomar's 1905 Barcelona lecture, the editor Ignasi Folch published the first issue of the Catalan magazine *Futurisme*, subtitled *Revista Catalana*, in Barcelona (June 1907). The future of Catalan identity, culture, and independence depended on writing, speaking, and publishing in Catalan today, in the present moment. Ignasi Folch showed his support of Alomar's futurism by publishing in Catalan.[13] Interestingly, *Renacimiento* ceased to exist after the issue in which the Catalan poems were published (December 1907). I have not found evidence to prove that the demise of *Renacimiento* is a direct result of the publication of these Catalan texts, but it is a strong possibility, given the political climate. In the journal's final issue, Martínez Sierra did not give any explanation as to why his periodical was folding. He merely stated that *Renacimiento* would merge with *La Lectura*, another literary magazine.[14] While the termination of *Renacimiento* remains a mystery, what is clear, and most important, is that the attempt made by this periodical to forge a rebirth, renaissance, and regeneration of Spanish culture included collaboration and connection with Catalan culture.

Following the futurism trail initiated by Alomar in Barcelona led me to the discovery of a small-circulation periodical that has been overlooked by most critics concerned with this movement in Spain: *España Futura* (Madrid, 1909–10). This bimonthly magazine is unique in that its contributors included a significant number of Catalan writers. Most of them were journalists or politicians, all writing in Spanish about topics as varied as science, business, agriculture, art, literature, and especially, politics. In the mission statement, the editors claim that the objective of their journal was to provide an open arena for dialogue with the common goal of achieving a brighter future for Spain. Once again, this "future Spain" is one that includes Catalonia. Specifically, the editor of this periodical from Madrid wanted to forge a Spanish national identity that was disassociated from the centrifugal powers of Madrid. The ideal readership of *España Futura* included not only those interested in art and literature, but also those involved with large industries, factories, and banks. Another way that this periodical hoped to reach a wider audience was by focusing on a different area of the country in each issue. This periodical served as a potential model for understanding between Madrid and other parts of Spain, from the point of view of business-minded people whose eyes were set on the future. Almost every issue included news from Barcelona, one of the major industrial centers of Spain, with a specific focus on its relationship to Madrid and the rest of Spain.

The wide scope of *España Futura* centered on an explicit interest in politics. For instance, in the inaugural issue, the editors published a speech by the Catalan politician Francesc Cambó, wherein he makes an argument for Catalonia's autonomy.[15] Printed alongside Cambó's text, another article by the Castilian lawyer, journalist, and writer Luis Bello cautions Madrid about the dangers of ignoring the other regions of Spain, especially Catalonia. Bello recommends that Madrid, which he believes is economically weaker than other cities in Spain, should work with the Catalans, not against them. Bello points out that up until now, one of the causes of the mutual incomprehension between Barcelona and Madrid has been that all of the communication between these two cities has been stimulated by either politicians or *caciques*, elite landowners, rather than by intellectuals or common citizens. According to Bello, politicians and the bourgeoisie are to blame for the establishment and perpetuation of a divide between Barcelona and the rest of Spain. But with the efforts of periodicals such as *España Futura*, made up of mostly common citizens rather than politicians or the wealthy, this mutual incomprehension can be minimized.

The mission of *España Futura*, as stated in the first issue, was to provide an alternative to the communication initiated by politicians and the

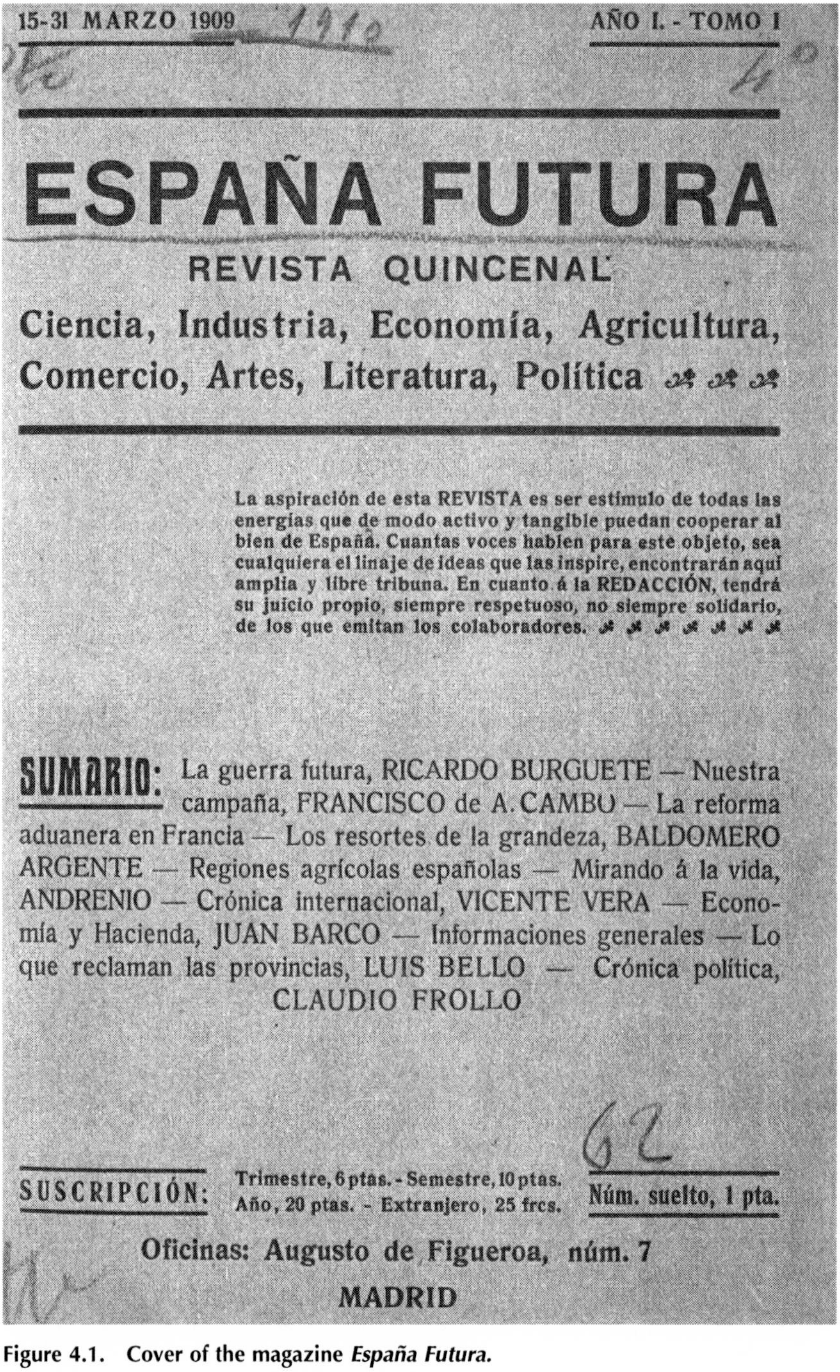

15-31 MARZO 1909 *1910*   AÑO I. - TOMO I

ESPAÑA FUTURA

REVISTA QUINCENAL

Ciencia, Industria, Economía, Agricultura, Comercio, Artes, Literatura, Política

La aspiración de esta REVISTA es ser estímulo de todas las energías que de modo activo y tangible puedan cooperar al bien de España. Cuantas voces hablen para este objeto, sea cualquiera el linaje de ideas que las inspire, encontrarán aquí amplia y libre tribuna. En cuanto á la REDACCIÓN, tendrá su juicio propio, siempre respetuoso, no siempre solidario, de los que emitan los colaboradores.

SUMARIO: La guerra futura, RICARDO BURGUETE — Nuestra campaña, FRANCISCO de A. CAMBÓ — La reforma aduanera en Francia — Los resortes de la grandeza, BALDOMERO ARGENTE — Regiones agrícolas españolas — Mirando á la vida, ANDRENIO — Crónica internacional, VICENTE VERA — Economía y Hacienda, JUAN BARCO — Informaciones generales — Lo que reclaman las provincias, LUIS BELLO — Crónica política, CLAUDIO FROLLO

SUSCRIPCIÓN: Trimestre, 6 ptas. - Semestre, 10 ptas. Año, 20 ptas. - Extranjero, 25 frcs. **Núm. suelto, 1 pta.**

Oficinas: Augusto de Figueroa, núm. 7

MADRID

Figure 4.1.   Cover of the magazine *España Futura*.

bourgeoisie by providing a more objective form of reporting for the people and by the people. The frequent news reported in this periodical about Catalans and their relationship to Madrid is noteworthy. *España Futura* reprinted an article by Cambó, who founded the Lliga Regionalista party in Catalonia, which would otherwise be almost impossible to access in Madrid. In a subsequent issue, Bello recounts a recent visit by Catalans to the Parliament in Madrid. According to the report, the purpose of their trip was to complain that the central state was halting their economic and political progress. They argued that Madrid moved at a much slower pace than Barcelona. Instead of focusing on the politics that motivated this visit to Congress, Bello suggests that non-Catalans in Madrid should use this encounter as an opportunity for them to learn about Catalans.

As is often the case, it is almost impossible to ignore politics when addressing the relationship between Barcelona and Madrid, or the Catalans and non-Catalans in Spain. The co-director of the periodical, Claudio Frollo, used *España Futura* to inform his Madrid readership about Catalonia and its potential power to build a brighter future for Spain. On several occasions, he notes that Spanish politics revolved around the axis of Catalonia, because the political influence of Catalonia was much greater than that of the rest of Spain. He argues that Catalan politics were stronger and more productive than ever, yet he insists that separatism is a mistake. His utopian vision for Spain involved the "disentanglement" of the provinces from the central powers of the state, without compromising the country's unity:

> Lo del separatismo es un error. Los catalanes todos somos fervientes españoles, y nosotros lo demostraremos con más elocuencia que nadie . . . los que protestan de nuestra conducta son los fracasados en política, los ambiciosos y los egoístas . . . nuestra política es que se entiendan unas regiones con otras para desenlazarse; que se unan, para desligarse del Poder central . . . esta es una obra de "inteligencias interregionales."

> (Separatism is an error. All Catalans are fervent Spaniards, and we will prove this with more eloquence than anybody . . . those who protest our behavior are failed politicians, the ambitious and the selfish . . . our politics is that the regions [of Spain] understand one another in order to untangle themselves; that they may unite, in order to unbind themselves from the central power . . . this is the work of the "interregional intelligence.")[16]

Frollo strongly believed that if Spaniards had a more comprehensive knowledge about the specifics of the other regions of Spain (e.g., economy, industry, agriculture, architecture, literature, history), they would agree with his utopian idea of a unified but decentralized Spain. In order to educate his Spanish-speaking readership in Madrid, *España Futura* published a myriad of charts and graphs with pages of statistics on taxes, commerce, trade, transportation, housing, debt, and loans, thereby offering readers the quantitative tools with which they could create arguments and form opinions of their own.

Ever concerned about the future of Spain, Alomar also made a contribution to *España Futura*, in which he mostly agrees with Frollo's utopian idea of a decentralized state composed of various regions. He uses the magazine based in Madrid to reassert his role as one of the first to work toward the "de-regionalization" of Catalanism, as he calls it. According to Alomar, in order to "futurize" the country, it must first be "de-regionalized." Then, Spain can consider itself more modern and less traditional, rural, and religious. This "futurization" process was necessary for the regeneration of Spain at this moment of political and economic crisis:

> Y si he tenido la pequeña gloria de improvisar esta palabra, futurismo, que ha entrado ya en nuestro léxico habitual ¿cómo no veré yo en esta revista el órgano mismo necesario al aspecto español, no ya meramente catalán, de la obra futurizante?

> (And if I have the small glory of inventing this word, futurism, that has entered in our everyday lexicon, how would I not see in this periodical the same opportunity to apply it to the Spanish case, no longer just merely a Catalan one, of the work of futurization?)[17]

As we can see, Alomar takes credit for inventing the term "futurism," which was making its way into the daily lexicon. As the inventor of the word and the ideology behind it, that of modernizing Catalonia, he was using the platform of this periodical to spread this "futurizing" concept outside of Catalonia, to modernize Spain as a whole. In other words, what began as a plan for the modernization of Catalonia was now being applied to Spain from the platform of Madrid's press.

Incidentally, Ramón Gómez de la Serna published an introduction to and translation of Marinetti's first futurist manifesto in his own periodical, *Prometeo*, of which he was editor, in the same month that Alomar published this article about the futurization of Spain in *España Futura*. Whether Alomar knew of Serna's intentions or vice versa prior to either of these publications is unknown. What is certain is that two different concepts of futurism were circulating in the Madrid press at the same exact time: one originating in Italy and centered on aesthetics, and the other in Catalonia and focused on politics. It is also worth noting that Gregorio Martínez Sierra had already published Alomar's two-part article on his brand of futurism in *Renacimiento* (September and November of 1907); also, by 1908, there were at least two other cultural periodicals in Catalonia titled *Futurisme* in tribute to Alomar and his new concept of futurizing Catalonia. This preoccupation with the future of Spain, especially after it lost its final colonies to the United States in 1898, was clearly shared by intellectuals both in Barcelona and Madrid during the first decade of the twentieth century. Based on the evidence found in both *Renacimiento* and *España Futura*, the construction of Spain's future by Catalan and non-Catalan intellectuals had to include Catalan culture, language, and identity.

The Spain of the future for Alomar is one in which political power had to be decentralized and redistributed throughout the different regions of Spain. He reiterates this vision in an article titled "Las dos capitales" (The Two Capitals), published in *España Futura*. In this text, he claims that the fundamental problem between Catalonia and the rest of Spain is the antagonism between Barcelona and Madrid. This assertion is followed by a list of differences comparing the two cities, in which Barcelona prevails over Madrid in every case. Furthermore, Alomar belittles Madrid and its people, arguing for the supremacy of Catalan culture. For one, he accuses the people of Madrid of having a "doubly provincial" spirit, unlike the Catalans, who are cosmopolitan. He argues that unlike the people of Madrid, Catalans had the great advantage of belonging to a culturally rich historic past. According to Alomar, Castilians were conformist when it came to politics, whereas Catalans were activists. The frustrated tone in this article shows how Alomar, like so many others, fell into the same trap of comparing and contrasting these two capitals. This article would be the last one published by Alomar in Frollo's periodical. Certainly, its negativity toward non-Catalans was unacceptable to the editor.

Besides working on bridging the gap between Barcelona and Madrid, *España Futura* also addressed other hot domestic topics of the day: the future of agriculture, terrorism, feminism, socialism, patriotism, nationhood, and monarchy. The periodical also reported on such international concerns as Moroccan society and politics, the cost and consequences of Spain's colonial war in Morocco, and the crisis in Germany. Reviews of literature and art stemming from both Barcelona and Madrid served to inform both Catalans and non-Catalans, so that these two groups could better understand one another and, in the words of one journalist, so that they could live in greater harmony. In the end, the magazine failed in transmitting its message, since it did not continue after the nineteenth issue. Perhaps the Madrid readership was not interested in this Catalan-centered message of unity. Maybe its staff dissolved, or the funds to keep the periodical in print were depleted. What is certain is that the publication closed less than one year after it first appeared, and, with the arrival of the First World War, the approach to bridging the Barcelona-Madrid gap from the point of view of the Madrid cultural press would take a different turn. *Renacimiento* and *España Futura* are just two examples of little magazines centered in Madrid from the post-1898 and pre-Avant-Garde era that show a shared interest among Catalan and non-Catalan intellectuals in establishing connections between Barcelona and Madrid, as seen in their content as well as in the composition and efforts of their editorial staff. Even though *España Futura* was centered in Madrid, the majority of the staff were Catalans who worked toward communicating news from and about Catalonia in Spanish. As was the case with many of the little magazines, this platform for informing readers in Madrid about Catalonia was short lived, but its seeds were planted.

Before continuing to track the evolution of the relationship between the Barcelona and Madrid vanguard networks as seen in the cultural press, I would like to address briefly the reception of Italian futurism in Spain, since the movement was such a pivotal phenomenon for the development of avant-garde attitudes and manifestations in both cities. One of the first writers in Spain to report on the publication of Marinetti's first futurist manifesto in the Parisian newspaper *Le Figaro* (February 20, 1909) was a defensive Gabriel Alomar in the Catalan periodical *El Poble Català* (Barcelona, March 9, 1909; "Spotula: El Futurisme a Paris").[18] One month after *El Poble Català* published Alomar's article, Ramón Gómez de la Serna published his translation of Marinetti's manifesto, "*Fundación y manifiesto del Futurismo*" (Foundation and Manifesto of Futurism), in *Prometeo*, the monthly magazine that his father founded.

Except for the epistolary relationship between Gómez de la Serna and Marinetti, which resulted in the "Proclama futurista a los españoles" (Futurist Proclamation to Spaniards), the news from Italy and France did not cause the same response in Madrid as in Barcelona.[19] Many studies concerning the reception of futurism in Spain have suggested that after a brief outburst in 1909 and 1910, interest in futurism dissipated in Spain until the arrival of *Ultraísmo* ten years later. Yet I have found substantial documentation in numerous magazines from Barcelona that proves that many journalists there followed the Italian movement with sustained interest and in great detail. There was also an equally enduring interest in the other new and extravagant European vanguard style—cubism. However, since the reception of Italian futurism in Spain is not the focus of this study, I will only mention a part of the report that appeared in Barcelona in order to challenge the idea that futurism completely disappeared from the radar until 1919.

First, an article in Barcelona's newspaper *La Publicidad* informed readers of a futurist disturbance in a square in Florence and announced that Barcelona's Real Círculo Artístico planned to mount an exhibit of futurist paintings in late 1912; that exhibit subsequently fell through. Another example of the reception of Italian futurism in Barcelona can be found in Josep Junoy's monthly journal *Correo de las letras & de las artes* (Barcelona, 1912). Printed entirely in Castilian, this periodical was evidently distributed and sold in Barcelona, Madrid, Florence, Berlin, London, Munich, Paris, and Buenos Aires. Although Junoy's first attempt at directing a periodical only amounted to three issues, this very understudied journal serves as yet another example of a little magazine that attempted to offer a vast forum for international debate that also includes readers from Barcelona and Madrid. Unlike *España Futura*, Junoy's periodical focused exclusively on literature and art. He announced that the magazine would be sold in five different bookstores and kiosks in Madrid. As a promoter of Italian futurism and French cubism, *Correo de las letras & las artes*'s first issue (November 1912) announced that Marinetti would be visiting Spain that summer to embark on a lecture tour (a visit that never took place).[20] It has been documented that Junoy maintained correspondence with Marinetti, as did other members of the Catalan vanguard, including the poets Joan Salvat-Papasseit, Sebastià Sànchez-Juan, and J. V. Foix. Additionally, the Italians Gino Cantarelli and Luciano Folgore, both poets who supported futurism, also maintained epistolary contacts with another Catalan poet, Joaquim Folguera.

Another Barcelona magazine that continued to report on the developments of Italian futurism and to which Junoy contributed was *Revista Nova* (1914–16). Directed by the illustrator Apa (pseudonym for Feliu Elias as illustrator; his second pseudonym was Joan Sacs, when in the role of a literary and art critic), this periodical, printed entirely in Catalan, made reference to the futurist movement, in a review of the Italian periodical *Lacerba*, as early as its first issue (April 11, 1914, p. 10). This first mention of futurism was followed by another, in the ninth issue, by Francesc Pujols, entitled "Cubisme i Futurisme" (Cubism and Futurism) (June 6, 1914, p. 6), and in the magazine's last issue, before it had to shut down temporarily at the onset of the Great War. Francisco Iribarne published a longer, more critical article, "Consideracions sobre el futurisme" (Concerning Futurism), written in Spanish despite its Catalan title. This piece is followed by fragments of two poems: one by Carlo Carrá and the other by Marinetti; both are reproduced from *Lacerba* (no. 31, November 5, 1914, pp. 4–6).

It would not be until 1916 that two other accounts of futurism appear in the Catalan cultural press. The first can be found in the little magazine *Vell i nou* (Barcelona, 1915–21), in an article by the Uruguayan artist and theorist Joaquin Torres-García, who had been living in Barcelona since 1891 and who contributed regularly to the cultural press.[21] Another mention was by the critic and poet Rafael Sala, who traveled to Florence in 1914 and befriended members of the *Lacerba* group. He offered a firsthand account of futurism in the last issue of another little magazine, *Themis* (Vilanova i la Geltrú, 1915–16), in his article "Els futuristes i el futurisme" (Futurists and Futurism) (no. 18, March 20 1916, pp. 1–5). This article was supplemented by a Catalan translation of Marinetti's manifesto of the futurist women, "Manifest de la dona futurista" (Manifesto to the Futurist Woman) (original dated March 25, 1912).[22] Besides these fleeting mentions, the first periodical from Spain to take a committed stance on Italian futurist poetry was *La Revista* (Barcelona, 1915–36), directed by the literary critic and poet Josep Maria López-Picó. This magazine was printed entirely in Catalan and functions as a textbook on the formulation of contemporary Catalan culture, while also engaging in critical dialogue with the artistic activity of World War I Barcelona. *La Revista* is also notable for its anti-Castilian stance.[23] In the case of this periodical, the editors wanted nothing to do with the centralizing forces of Madrid or its press. Unlike the other little magazines mentioned until now, *La Revista* was more interested in connecting with Italy and France than with the rest of Spain.

After nearly two years in print, without ever having mentioned the Italian futurist movement, *La Revista* published a series of Catalan translations of Italian futurist and French cubist poems, paying special attention to the experimental typography of the originals (no. 36, April 1, 1917, pp. 136–38). *La Revista* supplemented these poems with a brief introduction to this new style of poetry imported from Italy. These translations were an effort to remain true to a promise that the editorial staff had made to its readers one year prior to this issue: to report on the most innovative literary trends. The reception of Italian futurism in the press of Barcelona in *El Poble Català*, *La Publicidad*, *Correo de las Letras & las Artes*, *Revista Nova*, *Vell i Nou*, *Themis* (Vilanova i la Geltrú), and *La Revista* from 1909 to 1917 eventually led to futurist and literary cubist experiments in the more frequently referenced literary and artistic periodicals of the early Catalan vanguard years: *Troços* (Barcelona, 1916), *Un enemic del Poble* (1917), and *Arc-Voltaic* (1918). All three of these little magazines, centered in Barcelona, were printed before poets in Madrid renewed their interest in futurism with the founding of *Ultraísmo* late in the year 1918.

Troços (Barcelona, 1916–18), directed by the Catalan poet and literary critic Josep Maria Junoy, stands as the first journal in Spain and Catalonia that had as its mission the practice of avant-garde theories, namely Italian futurism, dadaism, and, above all, literary cubism. All of the contributors, aside from the illustrators, were either Catalan or French, and all of the written texts were published in Catalan. As indicated in an advertisement, the journal was sold in Barcelona, Paris, New York, and Milan, but not Madrid. Since only 101 copies of the inaugural issue were printed, the chances that this little magazine ended up in anybody's hands in 1916 Madrid are slim, but not impossible. Although I did not find any reviews of *Troços* in the periodicals of Madrid, there is a possibility that one of the daily newspapers may have reviewed it. Considering that *Troços* was first published by the Barcelona art gallery, Galeries Laietanes, and then later by another Barcelona gallery, the Dalmau Galleries, it is likely that its readers in Barcelona would have been familiar with Francis Picabia's equally innovative, subsequently published, Dada-inspired journal *391* (1917–24), which was founded in Barcelona. Both of these avant-garde periodicals were sold at the bookstore of the Galeries Laietanes, where the Catalan poet Joan Salvat-Papasseit worked and which many of the young poets and artists of Barcelona frequented on a regular basis, including J. V. Foix, who claimed to have visited there daily. Both *Troços* and *391* influenced and inspired Joan Salvat-Papasseit, who founded several avant-garde journals in Barcelona soon after these two were launched, in 1916 and 1917, respectively.

Stage 2: Revolution (1909–23)

Prior to the creation of *Troços* and *391*, two other important cultural periodicals, one from Madrid and the other from Barcelona, both established in 1915, explicitly had as one of their central missions the creation of a greater dialogue between the two cities they represented: *España* (Madrid, 1915–24) and *Iberia* (Barcelona, 1915–19). Originally directed by the philosopher José Ortega y Gasset, *España* outlasted the Great War, even though it encountered great challenges on several occasions.[24] This periodical covered an array of topics including art, poetry, theater, music, and book reviews in approximately twelve pages per issue. The magazine's main political concerns included Spain's colonial war in Morocco and the "Catalan problem." As stated on the cover of the first issue, its goal was to renew the lost faith in Spain, as felt by the editorial staff. After the Disaster of 1898 and all of the political, social, and economic turmoil that characterized the first two decades of twentieth-century Spain, the staff at *España*—and presumably its readership—had lost hope in the country's state-run institutions, especially the government.

España's mission was to renew the lost faith of Spaniards with optimism, while its editorial team worked toward uniting a fragmented nation. Their goal was "ante todo, una solidaridad" (before all else, solidarity). In order to achieve this ambitious goal, the staff members were carefully selected to represent a wide range of Spanish regions. Even though this periodical was published in Madrid, the editors aspired to create a publication that would be written by the entire nation, because for them, Madrid did not represent the "moral center" of Spain.[25] Following this mission statement, there is a long list of contributors, representing twenty different cities or regions of Spain. These locations were printed in capital letters, followed by the corresponding names of *España*'s journalists in title-case letters. Even though only three Catalans were listed as the magazine's representatives in Barcelona (Pedro Corominas, Manuel Reventós, and A. Ras), over the magazine's lifespan, reaching over four hundred issues, many other Catalans would be added to this list, including Salvador Albert, Gabriel Alomar, Salvador Dalí, Marcelino Domingo, Eugeni d'Ors, and J. J. Pérez-Domènech.

One critical contributor to the periodical who is not mentioned in this original list is the Catalan artist behind most of the cover pages of *España*, Luís Bagaría (Barcelona, 1882–Havana, 1940). As one of the most popular caricaturists among the intellectual elite of Madrid, his cartoons appeared in the newspaper *El Sol* nearly every day. Bagaría was born in Barcelona and spent most of his youth and adolescence there until his father's death in 1899, after which he accompanied his mother to Mexico, Cuba, and New York. One of the crucial discoveries he made while in Latin America was an interest in the visual arts. He and his mother returned to Barcelona, where he was taken under the wing of the *noucentista* painter Santiago Rusiñol, who was also a poet and playwright. By 1905, at the age of 25, Bagaría was showing his work in Paris. After a brief return to Cuba in 1908, he made Madrid his permanent home until the Spanish Civil War, when he moved to Paris (1938) before exiling to Cuba. While in Madrid, he was one of the founders of the Pombo *tertulia* alongside Ramón Gómez de la Serna. Bagaría's connections to the vanguard networks in Barcelona and Madrid through his work as an illustrator and journalist make him one of the central nodes of the Avant-Garde network in Spain, even though most have probably never heard of him.

In the spirit of solidarity, the number of articles in *España* that addressed some aspect of Catalan culture or politics, either briefly or in detail, is remarkable. Gabriel Alomar or Marcelino Domingo wrote most of these articles, and they were always printed in Spanish.[26] Evidently, Alomar found a new forum in Madrid after *España Futura* folded. Over the course of its history, this Madrid-based journal also published articles about Catalonia, Catalans, and Catalan culture written by non-Catalans, two exceptional examples being "El caso de Dalí" (The Case of Dalí), by the pioneering Spanish playwright Cipriano Rivas Cherif, and a review of Antoni Rovira i Virgili's book, *El nacionalismo catalán* (Catalan Nationalism), written by Nuñez de Cuevas. Much like another periodical from Madrid, *La Esfera*, *España* dedicated an entire issue to Catalonia and Catalan culture (June 1916). This special issue leads with the headline: "¿Qué es el catalanismo?" (What is Catalanism?). The author of the anonymously written article on the front page states that any liberal Spaniard interested in decentralizing the state and fostering regionalism should be interested in Catalanism. The fact that an entire issue was devoted to Catalan nationalism suggests that the editorial staff of *España* shared these views and hoped to convince their readership of the same. The following issue, one week later, published a series of reactions to this Catalan-centered feature issue. Catalans and non-Catalans quickly responded and sent letters to the editorial staff for publication. This speedy reply shows that Catalan culture and politics were controversial, as well as a subject of high interest for both the readership and the editorial staff.

Specifically, the Catalanism issue included articles by the politician Francesc Cambó (a fragment from a speech he gave to Madrid's Parliament); a definition of "nation" by another politician, president of the Mancomunitat Enric Prat de la Riba; a definition of "nationalism" by the author of *Historia dels moviments nacionalistes*, *La nacionalització de Catalunya*, and *Debats sobre el catalanisme* (The History of Nationalist Movements, The Nationalization of Catalonia, and Debates about Catalanism), Antoni Rovira i Virgili; a definition by the poet Josep Carner of "El hecho catalán" (The Catalan Fact); an anonymously written list of the demands of Catalan nationalism that included the desire for an autonomous state, as well as executive, legislative, and judicial power, in addition to freedom of speech in Catalan for all private and public events; and finally, an article about Catalonia's economy. In conjunction with these political and economic issues, art, language, and literature were also included in the definition of Catalanism. The issue ends with an article by the politician Marcelino Domingo, "¿Qué es España y qué es Cataluña?" (What is Spain and What is Catalonia?), which is a fragment of a speech he gave in Congress a few days prior to this issue's publication. In the midst of war, readers of *España* in Madrid had the opportunity to learn about Barcelona, Catalonia, and Catalan culture in Spanish and from the point of view of both Catalan and non-Catalan journalists.

The group of intellectuals that orbited around this weekly periodical created in Madrid came to be associated with the so-called Generation of 1914. This term, which was coined much later, places importance on 1914 as the year of the beginning of the Great War. This group of writers consisted of intellectuals like José Ortega y Gasset (editor of *España* in 1915), Luis Araquistain (editor of *España* from 1916–22), Manuel Azaña (editor of *España* from 1923–24), Ramón Gómez de la Serna, Gregorio Marañón, Gabriel Miró, Ramón Pérez de Ayala, and many others, including several women. Two Catalan writers who are sometimes associated with this group are Eugeni d'Ors (*noucentisme* leader) and Gabriel Alomar (*futurisme* founder). The phrase "Generation of 1914" is sometimes used interchangeably with the term "*novecentistas*," in a direct reference to the Catalan *noucentistas*. Similar to the goals of *noucentisme*, these writers focused on defining Spain's identity as a nation after the Disaster of 1898 by initiating radical and systematic changes in their vision of Spain and its role in history. "Science" was a key word for the Generation of 1914 writers, who openly promoted the "Europeanization" of Spain. The contents of *España* also imply that the Spain of the future was one that would be politically decentralized and strengthened by having its many regions work together.

The Barcelona counterpart of Madrid's weekly periodical *España* was *Iberia*. These two journals shared many characteristics. Both were weekly periodicals, were printed primarily in Spanish, and consisted of articles that expressed an overall preoccupation with the state of Spain as a whole from a cultural perspective. Unlike the Madrid-based journal, the Barcelona magazine preferred the more encompassing term of *Iberia*, which includes Portugal. Correspondingly, *Iberia* published articles in multiple languages, including Spanish, Catalan, and Portuguese. One of the most striking similarities between these two periodicals is the layout of their cover pages. Both consisted of a one-word title in the masthead, followed by a large illustration, almost always printed in color, with a few lines of commentary text underneath the image. The main illustrator for the Madrid magazine was the Catalan Lluís Bagaría, although other, non-Catalan artists were also featured. The most frequent illustrator for the Barcelona periodical was the Catalan artist Apa, but it also featured works by other Catalan artists, notably Inglada, Colom, Canals, and Aragay.

One of the main political differences between the two periodicals is that the editors of *España* insisted that their stance was neutral in relation to the Great War, while *Iberia* explicitly allied itself with France and Britain. According to the editor of the facsimile edition of *España*, the periodical received funding from private British entities on several occasions in order to stay afloat. Unlike *España*, which survived until 1924 and published over four hundred issues, *Iberia* only lasted until 1919, with half that number of issues. Another major difference between the two periodicals is that the journalists who wrote for *Iberia* did not represent as many different places in Spain as those who wrote for *España*. Very few Madrid-based reporters contributed to *Iberia*, whereas at least a handful of Catalans regularly contributed to *España*, such as the caricaturist Luis Bagaría.

Curiously enough, the editor in chief of *Iberia*, Claudi Ametlla, who had been a contributor to the Catalan subversive periodical *El Poble Català* (1906), opened the first issue with a mission statement by a non-Catalan, Miguel de Unamuno. The statement is written in Spanish, like the majority of articles in *Iberia*. In this inaugural message, Unamuno explains that this periodical was the result of an idea for a multilingual magazine that he and his "soul mate," the Catalan poet Joan Maragall, had envisioned many years earlier. The magazine they envisioned was also to have been called "Iberia," and it would have included the "literary languages" of the Iberian Peninsula, especially Spanish, Catalan, and Portuguese. In this opening statement for the inaugural issue, Unamuno states that he and Maragall discussed this project through a series of letters, some of which have been collected and are readily available. One of Maragall's propositions in this correspondence was that the periodical base itself in the city of Salamanca, both because of its proximity to Portugal and because it represented more of a neutral space in comparison to Barcelona or Madrid. For Maragall, Salamanca was an alternative cultural, intellectual, and spiritual center of Spain. Instead, this project, which finally came to fruition in 1915, was based out of Barcelona.

Similar to Ortega y Gasset's inaugural message in *España*, Unamuno stated that if people from the different regions of Spain, with their diverse languages, history, literature, and cultures, were going to understand one another better, they first had to learn about one another. Furthermore, Unamuno, much as Alomar had argued in *España*, emphasized the importance of the "spiritual proximity" between the different peoples of Spain:

> Halagábame el llegar a tener un órgano de aproximación espiritual entre los pueblos ibéricos de distintas lenguas. Aproximarse espiritualmente es conocerse cada vez mejor. Y mi ensueño y anhelo ha sido que nos conozcamos mejor, aunque sea para disentir.

> (It flattered me to one day have an instrument of spiritual approximation between the different peoples of Iberia and their different languages. To come closer spiritually is to get to know one another even more. And my dream and desire has been that we get to know one another better, even if it means to disagree.)[27]

Unamuno had been dreaming of a platform from which the different cultures and languages of the Iberian Peninsula could come together. In this process of achieving some sort of mutual understanding, it was Unamuno's vision that all of the different regions of Spain and Portugal would discover a broader Iberian spirit or identity. As he goes on to explain, that spirit would be that which differentiates Iberians from other Europeans. He emphasized that Iberians must defend that which differentiates them, just as much as that which unites them. Unamuno believed that without these differences, life was simply not worth living. Given the scenario of the World War, Unamuno feared that Europe would fall under an oppressive dictatorship in which Germany would dominate every other European country. Spaniards would become the "worker bees" of the Germans, and in the process they would lose their identity. Unamuno also predicted that this war would evoke repressed feelings of national identity. He finally urged the people of Iberia to resist the violent imposition of one language over another as in Alsace-Lorraine and Poland, because "La unidad es buena y santa, pero cuando es violentada no es unidad" (Unity is good and sacred, but when it is violent, it is not real).

Two years after the publication of the first issues of *Iberia* and *España*, Spain was in turmoil. The Russian Revolution erupted in February and the Great War continued. The social, political, and economic consequences of Spain's neutrality in the war led to a general strike in August 1917. The unrest in Barcelona, plus the influx of European avant-garde artists escaping the First World War, was the ideal breeding ground for a new kind of periodical. The Catalan poet Joan Salvat-Papasseit founded *Un enemic del Poble* (An Enemy of the People) (Barcelona, 1917–19), which, like its predecessors *Iberia* and *España*, included Catalan and non-Catalan writers in its eighteen issues. It was published on an irregular schedule, even though it was intended to be monthly. The mission statement emphatically denied association with any group or aesthetic movement, or as the painter Joaquín Torres-García put it, "Tindríem d'ésser inclassificables" (We must be unclassifiable). But the editor published several literary and artistic manifestos that defined the publication's radical ideas. In order to illustrate these points, the editor published poems that put into practice typographic experiments reminiscent of Italian futurism, Swiss dadaism, and French literary cubism. *Un enemic del Poble* is a small-circulation periodical directly related to the nascent literary avant-garde movement in Catalonia, in direct line with *Troços* and *391*. In form and content, it was the antithesis of *España* and *Iberia*. The journal itself was very small. Each issue consisted of one large folio printed on both sides.

Unlike the periodicals that worked toward unifying the spirit of Spain, like *Iberia* and *España*, as Unamuno put it, Salvat-Papasseit explicitly wrote in his mission statement that his goal was not to create any sort of col-lective spirit: "*Un enemic del Poble* no correspond per ara, a cap necessitat d'ànima collectiva. N'estem tan convençuts que [sic] sols el publiquem per satisfacció pròpia" (*Un enemic del Poble*, for the moment, does not answer to any necessity for a collective spirit. We are so positive in that respect that we are only publishing out of personal satisfaction).[28] In saying so, Salvat-Papasseit speaks directly against the philosophy of more mainstream journals like *Iberia* and *España*. Later on, the Uruguayan painter and theorist Joaquin Torres-García would further define the little magazine's role, in Catalan, as consisting of "individualismo, presentisme, internacionalisme" (individual-ism, being present, internationalism).[29] Even though there are more Catalan than Castilian texts overall in the lifespan of the avant-garde periodical, almost every other issue includes a Spanish text. Sometimes contributions in Spanish appeared on the front page, as was the case with a text written by the Madrid Avant-Garde enthusiast Ramón Gómez de la Serna.

The inclusion of Spanish in *Un enemic del Poble* made Salvat-Papasseit's "subversive paper" accessible to more readers. Even if it did not end up in anyone's hands outside of Catalonia, it sent out a message to non-Catalans in Spain that they too were welcome to participate in this cause. It also sent a political message that it was interested in including Spanish-speakers, not just Catalan-speakers, in its efforts to be individualistic, present and inter-national. *Un enemic del Poble* acted out its inclusionary politics without hav-ing to explain them in any sort of mission statement, as many of the other periodicals discussed so far did. In the case of this little magazine, there was no space to waste. There were only two pages available for each issue. Salvat-Papasseit began a literary and aesthetic movement in Barcelona through this periodical that welcomed anyone who shared his mission and was willing to collaborate, whether they spoke in Catalan, Castilian, Italian, or French—all the languages that appeared in print without translation. By openly includ-ing non-Catalans, Salvat-Papasseit spun a web of contacts for himself in Madrid. Along these same lines, his second publishing enterprise, *Arc-Voltaic* (Barcelona, 1918), expanded on this notion of all-inclusiveness toward other languages. Once again, texts were published in their original languages: Cat-alan, Italian, French, and Spanish. Unfortunately, there was only one issue of this periodical, with an illustration by the avant-garde painter Joan Miró on the cover, before it folded. It was likely because of these early contacts with Castilian writers like Ramón Gómez de la Serna in Madrid, as well as his openness toward other languages and cultures, that Salvat-Papasseit was one of the only Catalan poets published in the little magazines associated with Madrid's vanguard *Ultraísmo* movement.[30]

Ultraísmo, also referred to as Ultra, materialized toward the end of 1918 and was practiced by a group of young poets living in Madrid desperately seeking to renovate poetic language. The first Ultra manifesto was published in Madrid in January 1919. Even though it is primarily considered a poetic movement, it also made room for visual texts. Some of the most active participants of Ultra were three foreign artists in residence in Madrid: the Uruguayan Rafael Barradas, the Argentinean Norah Borges, and the Polish Wladyslaw Jahl. Generally speaking, *Ultraísmo* was a combination of the isms that preceded it, including futurism, dadaism, *creacionismo*, cubism, expressionism, vibrationism, and others. First and foremost, and in the spirit of other vanguard movements, it was created to radically oppose the *modernismo* style of poetry practiced by Latin American and Spanish poets since the late nineteenth century. Like many of the other European avant-garde movements, *Ultraísmo* spread its message through the platform of the little magazines and by organizing social events like literary clubs, banquets, and poetry recitals. Curiously, despite the diversity of *Ultraísmo*'s team of players in Madrid, who represented almost every Spanish region, the only Catalan participants were Salvat-Papasseit (poet), Sebastià Gasch (art critic), and Salvador Dalí (painter). In his latest study of the little magazines related to the Spanish Avant-Garde, Rafael Osuna makes note of the absence of Catalans in Madrid's *Ultraísmo* movement:

> Ante tanto nombre español y francés, un nombre catalán salta a la vista en la salida sexta (de la revista *Grecia*). Se trata de la reseña que se le hace a *Les absències paternals* de José María López-Picó; lo mismo se podría haber reseñado un libro húngaro, pues los catalanes, tanto novecentistas como actuales, brillan por su ausencia aquí como en casi en el resto de la hemerografía española vanguardista de la época, ignorándose ambas culturas mutuamente.

> (Among so many Spanish and French names, a Catalan name sticks out in the sixth issue [of the little magazine *Grecia*]. It is a review of a book by José María López-Picó titled *Les absències paternals* [Paternal Absences]; it might as well have been a review of a Hungarian book, since the Catalans, *noucentistas* and vanguardist, shine for their absence here just as they do in the whole Spanish Avant-Garde hemerography of the era, both cultures mutually ignoring one another.)[31]

Osuna's claim that Catalans were completely absent from the hemerography of Spain's Avant-Garde is not entirely accurate. Perhaps their periodicals were not included in the hemerographic archives in Madrid, something I found to be the case; but that does not mean that they did not exist. One must consult the Catalan magazines in the Barcelona archives in order to see that Osuna was only focusing on Madrid.[32] Just because Catalans did not participate in Madrid's *Ultraísmo* movement does not mean that they were not involved with the Avant-Garde movement. In fact, artists and poets in Barcelona were the first to experiment with European avant-garde ideas, as seen in periodicals that predate the Ultra movement, already discussed, such as *Troços* (1916), *391* (1917), *Un enemic del Poble* (1917), and *Arc-Voltaic* (1918).

Osuna oversimplifies when he claims that the Catalans and Spaniards mutually ignored one another throughout the vanguard years in Spain. The people of Barcelona and Madrid who were involved in the founding, practice, and promotion of these experimental movements—poets, painters, sculptors, illustrators, journalists, editors—were well aware of the literary and artistic news from the other city, primarily through the contents of the little magazines (e.g., book and magazine reviews), as well as through friendships and cultural events like art shows. One example can be found in a review of little magazines penned by Héctor (pseudonym for Guillermo de Torre) in the periodical *Cervantes* (Madrid, 1916–20). In this review, he demonstrates his knowledge of little magazines in Barcelona:

> Sus últimos números dejan ya insinuar el florecimiento de las nuevas direc-ciones ultraístas que al ser paralelizadas en las mismas páginas, con rescoldos líricos estrictamente novecentistas, adquieren un confrontamiento de super-ación, *Grecia* es, con algunas revistas barcelonesas, la publicación española más juvenil y sugeridora del momento.

> (Their latest issues are more forthright about the new direction of poetry as proposed by Ultra, that by being situated next to and on the same pages with embers of strictly nineteenth-century lyricism, they acquire a confrontation that supersedes this old style of poetry, *Grecia* is, along with some magazines from Barcelona, the most youthful and suggestive Spanish periodical of the moment.)[33]

Guillermo de Torre, for one, was aware of the little magazines published in Barcelona; why would his closest friends and colleagues be unaware? The majority of the literary periodicals of this time period had a section either at the beginning or at the end of the issue that reviewed other magazines and newly published books. The function of such sections was for the readers to stay on top of new publications, but also to stay connected to the newest literary and aesthetic trends outside of Madrid. Barcelona magazines were not often reviewed in Madrid's periodicals and vice versa, but it was one of the ways that the Avant-Garde practitioners from either city could be more aware of one another, as in this particular case from the periodical *Cervantes*.

Osuna is right in saying that the collaboration (or inclusion) of Catalans within the pages of Madrid's Ultra magazines was almost nonexistent. One of the reasons why it may appear that the Catalan periodicals had no role in the Spanish Avant-Garde is because the Madrid press, for the most part, did not pay close attention to it, or perhaps they chose to ignore the Catalan movement. Beginning when Guillermo de Torre published *Literaturas europeas de vanguardia* (1925), and continuing until today, as in the case of Osuna's *Revistas españolas de vanguardia* (2005), the periodicals from Catalonia are almost always left out of the picture in telling the story of the Avant-Garde movement in Spain as a whole. One Catalan magazine that has made its way over the divide into the histories of both sides of the Avant-Garde story in Spain is *L'Amic de les Arts* (The Friend of the Arts) (Sitges, 1926–29), but it was certainly not the only Catalan periodical that promoted avant-garde ideas and practices throughout this period.

One question that begs an answer is why the names of Catalans do not appear in the little magazines from Madrid but do appear in avant-garde periodicals from smaller cities in Spain and abroad, such as *Alfar* (A Coruña, 1920–54), *Ronsel* (Lugo, 1924), *Mediodía* (Sevilla, 1926–29), and *Circunvalación* (Mexico, 1928). Were the Catalans purposefully excluded from the Ultra magazines in Madrid? Were the Catalans not interested in Ultra? In a modification of his definition of Ultra, Osuna states that in fact it was not a movement that was a "mixed bag" of everything: "Todo no, en realidad, pues los catalanes ni están en España ni en Francia ni en Europa: simplemente no se les presta atención" (Not really everything, because the Catalans were not in Spain or France or Europe: they are simply ignored).[34] If the Catalans were neither in Spain, France, nor Europe, does Osuna suggest that they were only in Catalonia? And who is ignoring the Catalans—the artists, writers, and editors of magazines in Madrid, the scholars of today, or both? Were the Catalans not concerned about publishing their poetry in Madrid? Was their intention to publish only in Barcelona or Catalonia, and only in Catalan? Joan Salvat-Papasseit published several of his poems in Madrid and founded two multilingual periodicals; therefore it would be erroneous to say that the avant-garde movement in Barcelona was completely insular. It would be more accurate to say that from the introduction of Italian futurism in 1909 until the beginning of the Miguel Primo de Rivera's dictatorship in 1923, the vanguard movements in Barcelona and Madrid were out of synch, but not out of touch.

Stage 3: Retreat (1923–29)

By the time the *Ultraísmo* movement played itself out in Madrid (1923) and before surrealism picked up any steam (1929), the cultural periodicals in Spain passed through a third stage. Generally speaking, the main trend during this period was that even fewer Catalans contributed to the Madrid press and vice versa. During this post-*Ultraísmo* phase, only a few vanguard journals can be found on Madrid's cultural press radar, including *Vértices* (1923), *Tobogán* (1924), *Plural* (1925), and *Atlántico* (1929–30)—all of which were short-lived periodicals. *Tobogán* was the least avant-garde of these, while the others still show some signs of experimentation. The only Catalan names that appear in any of these little magazines were those of two critics: the Valencian ex-*Ultraísta* J. J. Pérez Domènech and the Catalan art critic Sebastià Gasch. Similarly, almost no names or mentions of Spanish poets, artists, or critics from outside of Catalonia appear printed in the pages of the vanguard periodicals of Barcelona. Instead, a group of pro-Catalan magazines formed a sort of barricade from the rest of Spain. All of the journals that were established in Barcelona during the Primo de Rivera dictatorship took a unified stance to protect the Catalan language and culture from further aggression.[35] The only non-Catalan Spaniards who contributed to any of these cultural periodicals appeared in the last issue of *L'Amic de les Arts* that was entirely masterminded by Salvador Dalí (March 1929). Dalí's friends from Madrid that contributed to this issue of *L'Amic* included Pepín Bello (Andalusian), Luis Buñuel (Aragonese), and Federico García Lorca (Andalusian). All of these men were Salvador Dalí's friends from his time at the Residencia de Estudiantes in Madrid.

Any progress that may have been made in increasing communication and awareness between the people of Barcelona and Madrid through the cultural press in the previous decade was almost completely erased during the Primo de Rivera dictatorship. During this time, both cities turned inwards, and this introspection reveals itself in the content of the magazines. Two exceptions to this rule include a periodical from Madrid, *La Gaceta Literaria* (1927–31), which is discussed at length in the final chapter of this book, and *Les Arts Catalanes* (1928–29) from Barcelona. In the case of the former, one of the periodical's main missions was, once again, to create a greater dialogue between Madrid and the rest of Spain, especially Catalonia, Portugal, and Latin America. The editor frequently printed articles in Catalan, and the magazine included several Catalans on its regular staff. In the case of the latter, *Les Arts Catalanes*, this periodical printed the lead article of every issue in four languages: Catalan, French, Castilian, and English. The journal's mission statement, which appeared in the inaugural issue (October 1928), was published in these four languages. This free, monthly magazine consisted of art, journal reviews, art exhibit reviews, and schedules of exhibits in Catalonia and also outside of Spain. This little magazine dedicated to the contemporary arts was clearly interested in taking an international stance. Since the journal only published eight issues, its impact may have been minor, but nevertheless, a seed was planted.

Outside of Madrid and Barcelona, the names of writers and artists from both cities often appeared side by side in the small-circulation periodicals located in the peripheries of Spain and Latin America. Up until this date, the only Catalans who contributed to any of these peripheral periodicals were either critics or visual artists, such as Salvador Dalí and Sebastià Gasch, not poets. By 1926 the names of several Catalans began to surface in these little magazines outside of Barcelona and Madrid. For example, *Mediodía* (Sevilla, 1926–29) published the work of Dalí and Gasch but also that of three other Catalan writers: Tomàs Garcés, Lluís Montanyà, and Eugeni d'Ors.[36] Another little magazine from the south of Spain that published works by Catalan artists like Dalí, Josep de Togores, and Apel·les Fenosa was *Litoral* (Málaga, 1926–29). Another journal from the south of Spain, *Verso y Prosa* (Murcia, 1927–28), which was also sold in Madrid, also published texts by Dalí and Gasch. Another Catalan, Eugeni d'Ors, and again Gasch, published in another little magazine from Andalusia, *Papel de Aleluyas* (Huelva/Sevilla, 1927–28). Finally, one last example of the appearance of Catalans in the little magazines from the south of Spain is *Meridiano* (Huelva, 1929–30), which published works by Dalí and Gasch.

A similar pattern can be seen in three avant-garde periodicals from Latin America: *Amauta* (Lima, 1926–32), *Sagitario* (Mexico, 1926–27), and *Circunvalación* (Mexico, 1928). Since the Latin American avant-garde magazines are not the focus of this study, I did not delve deeper into this area of the investigation, but at least in these three cases, Dalí and Gasch were included, as were Joan Miró, Eugeni d'Ors, and the literary critic Josep Maria de Sucre. The periodical *Circunvalación* is particularly interesting for the purposes of this study. First, it included the greatest number of Catalan contributors of any of this group of Latin American avant-garde periodicals, although only three issues made it to print. Notably, its mission statement, printed perpendicular to the rest of the words on the page and outlined in red, stated: "Para el diálogo y para la amistad" (In the name of dialogue and friendship). The editors of this vanguard magazine draw attention to the fact that expansive networking, effective communication, and strong friendships were critical elements of the Avant-Garde. The particular goal of this free periodical, *Circunvalación*, was to embrace all. It was created to connect people with similar interests despite their differences (e.g., geographical, national, linguistic). The binding force that united them was a shared belief in the Avant-Garde spirit, or renewal, renovation, and change.

One explanation for the participation of the Catalans in these peripheral periodicals, outside of Madrid and Barcelona, is that there simply were not many vanguard magazines published in either of these cities during the Primo de Rivera dictatorship.[37] Another possibility is that since one of the main goals of these little magazines was to connect with the larger world outside of their small circles, they extended their network to include experimental poets and artists from other Spanish cities. Many of these contacts were initiated by friends, or by connecting with friends of friends. For instance, Salvador Dalí's frequent appearance in the periodicals of Andalusia can be explained by his close friendship with Federico García Lorca. In 1928, Lorca founded his own little magazine, *Gallo*, in his hometown of Granada, with the help of two Catalan friends: one from Madrid, Dalí, and the other from Barcelona, Gasch.

From the marketing point of view, publishing notable writers and artists added value to these little magazines on the periphery. For instance, if one of the most respected art critics of Barcelona and Madrid contributed to the journal, it would make the publication more attractive. It was also another way of expanding the entire network. By publishing in Murcia (*Verso y Prosa*) or Huelva (*Papel de Aleluyas*, *Meridiano*), the overall Avant-Garde network expanded. Interestingly, periodicals on the periphery of Barcelona, but still within Catalonia, also show an interest in publishing the work of non-Catalans from Spain. First, *Ciutat* (Manresa, 1926–28) not only published the work of Federico García Lorca, but also featured an article about him in Catalan written by Josep Maria de Sucre. The avant-garde magazine *Hèlix* (Vilafranca del Penedès, 1929–30) published the greatest number of texts from non-Catalan Spaniards representative of the avant-garde style, including Gerardo Diego, Ernesto Giménez Caballero, Ramón Gómez de la Serna, Benjamín Jarnés, and Ledesma Ramos. All of their works were published in Spanish. Finally, there is the case of *L'Amic de les Arts* out of Sitges, mentioned earlier.

As seen in the pages of the cultural, artistic, and literary presses in Catalonia and Spain during the first three decades of the twentieth century, it is clear that the nature of the relationship between the avant-garde networks of Barcelona and Madrid evolves. The three stages of development are marked by severe political disruptions, such as war, dictatorship, and civil strife. In the first stage (1904–9), on the heels of the Disaster of 1898, the pre-Avant-Garde periodicals from Madrid demonstrated a clear intention to dialogue and collaborate with Barcelona and the Catalans in general. This desire to communicate is related to the colonial loss and the subsequent identity crisis experienced by Spanish intellectuals and regenerationist politicians. After the arrival of Italian futurism in Spain, and up until the end of the First World War (1909–18), a second phase developed. The desire for the Madrid press to collaborate with Catalans, fueled by the politics of regenerationism, lingered past the introduction of Italian futurism to Barcelona and Madrid in 1909, since it took a while for this literary and artistic style to have a significant effect in Madrid. After the introduction of Italian futurism, visual artists and poets in Barcelona, inspired and influenced by this style, as well as by dadaism, cubism, vibrationism, and constructivism, created their own avant-garde movement following the onset of the First World War (1916–18). It was not until after the Great War that the poets in Madrid invented the *Ultraísmo* avant-garde style. It was only then (1919) that more systematic avant-garde experimentation surfaced in the Madrid periodicals, much in the same way as it had in the Barcelona press several years earlier. Synchronicity between the experimental presses of Barcelona and Madrid, as seen in the case of the Catalan avant-garde protagonist Joan Salvat-Papasseit, was reached in 1919, but with his premature death and the sudden military dictatorship, dialogue between the vanguard presses of Barcelona and Madrid nearly terminated. As a result, the Avant-Garde movement as a whole shifted beyond these two urban centers, toward the peripheries of the peninsula, as evident in the proliferation of little magazines there, especially to the south and the northwest. Outside of Barcelona and Madrid, avant-garde networks spun off to much smaller cities, and the movement became more decentralized as a whole. During the Primo de Rivera dictatorship, Spaniards and Catalans also expanded their networks by collaborating with experimental periodicals from Latin America. For the most part, these little magazines outside of Barcelona and Madrid were highly experimental and very short lived. The exception to this shift to the peripheries was the major avant-garde periodical out of Madrid, *La Gaceta Literaria*, which is discussed in depth in the final chapter of this book.

Notes

1. Robert Davidson, "Observing the City, Mediating the Mountain: *Mirador* and the 1929 International Exposition of Barcelona," in *Visualizing Spanish Modernity*, ed. Susan Larson and Eva Woods (Oxford: Berg, 2005), 229.

2. Joan Ramon Resina, "The Catalan Avant-Garde," in *The Cambridge History of Spanish Literature*, ed. David Gies (Cambridge: Cambridge University Press, 2004), 388.

3. Matthew Luskey, "The Little Magazine 'Others' and the Renovation of Modern American Poetry (review)," in *Modernism/Modernity* 15, no. 4 (2008): 822–24.

4. Luskey, "The Little Magazine 'Others,'" 823.

5. Little Magazine Collection, University of Wisconsin, Madison (accessed September 2010), memorial.library.wisc.edu/collections/littlemags.html.

6. Ezra Pound, "Small Magazines," in *The English Journal* 19 (1930): 9.

7. I use the word "hemerographic" to refer to my study of the archival documents sourced in the *hemerotecas*, or periodical libraries, of Barcelona and Madrid.

8. Juan Manuel Bonet, *Diccionario de las vanguardias en España 1907–1936* (Madrid: Alianza, 1995). The *Museo Nacional Centro de Arte Reina Sofía* replaced the *Museo Español de Arte Contemporáneo* (MEAC) in Madrid in 1988. It was established as a national museum of modern and contemporary Spanish art. Juan Manuel Bonet was its fourth director, from May 2000 until he resigned in June 2004. During his tenure, Bonet organized many exhibits related to Spain's Avant-Garde.

9. Rafael Osuna, *Revistas de la vanguardia española* (Sevilla: Renacimiento, 2005), 12.

10. The contents of each issue of the periodical *Renacimiento* are so extensive that the cover page is a table of contents. Printing an index on the cover page made the periodical's content easily accessible to potential buyers perusing street-side kiosks and bookstores. Unfortunately, however, the copy at the *Biblioteca Nacional* in Madrid, which I consulted in 2005, has been bound in such a way that the front page of each issue—except for the first—has been eliminated. Consequently, it is nearly impossible to determine when one issue ends and the next begins. Also, since there is no general index available, the only option for a reader is to browse the tomes one page at a time.

11. In addition to his work as a journalist with *Renacimiento*, Enrique Díez-Canedo (Badajoz, 1879–Cuernavaca, Mexico, 1944) also contributed to a number of other newspapers and magazines in Spain, including *España, El Sol, Índice*, and *Prometeo*.

12. Other texts in *Renacimiento* authored by Catalans would also be published in Castilian, including Gabriel Alomar's essay on Don Quijote (*"Sobre 'El Quijote'"*); Victor Català (pseudonym for Caterina Alberti Paradís); Eduardo Marquina; and some of the *glosaris*, or glossaries, by Eugeni d'Ors, who first published these texts in the Barcelona newspaper *La Veu de Catalunya* in 1906. It was primarily through these journalistic texts that he shaped and defined the *noucentisme* movement in Catalonia. Readers of *Renacimiento* could have learned about *noucentisme*, because some of D'Ors's glossaries were reprinted in this periodical that was published and distributed in Madrid.

13. The periodical in Barcelona that was inspired by Alomar's proposal, *Futurisme*, was printed entirely in Catalan. Each issue was approximately twenty-five pages in length, but only three issues made it to press. Even though *Futurisme* was short

lived, two cities outside Barcelona published periodicals also titled *Futurisme*: one in Tarrasa (1908) and the other in Vilafranca del Penedés (1910). News of Alomar's brand of futurism reached Paris by December 1908, as reported by Marcel Robin in the Parisian newspaper *Le Mercure de France*. Alomar's ideas could have also been transmitted to Paris through the Madrid periodical *Renacimiento*, since this periodical was sold in Paris. For further discussion on Alomar's futurism, please see Juan Cano Ballesta, *Literatura y tecnología*. *Las letras españolas ante la revolución industrial, 1900–1933* (Madrid: Editorial Origenes, 1981), 67–70; Manfred Lentzen, "Marinetti y el futurismo en España," in *Actas del IX Congreso de la Asociación Internacional de Hispanistas* (Frankfurt: Vervuert, 1989), 311; Lilly Litvak, "Alomar and Marinetti: Catalan and Italian Futurism" *Revue des Langues Vivantes* 38 (1972): 585–603; and Molas, *La literatura catalana d'avantguarda*, 24.

14. Even though his magazine only lasted ten issues, the editor managed to keep a publishing company by the same name that he established in 1908. This company stayed in business until the end of the First World War.

15. The editors of *España Futura* translated all of the names of their Catalan journalists to their Castilian equivalents. For example, Francesc Cambó appears as Francisco Cambó.

16. *España Futura*, March 15–31, 1909, 60–62.

17. *España Futura*, April 1–15, 1909, 65–68.

18. The Catalan lawyer and politician Jaume Carner founded *El Poble Català* (first a weekly paper, then, as of May 1906, a daily) in May 1904 when he broke away from the *Lliga Regionalista* political party. Besides being printed entirely in Catalan, it functioned as the main means of widespread communication for the *Centre Nacionalista Republicà*, another political party Carner helped found in 1906 and of which he was named the first president.

19. A full account of the letters exchanged between Gómez de la Serna and Marinetti is provided in Anderson, "Ramón Gómez de la Serna and F. T. Marinetti." Marinetti's manifesto written expressly for Spaniards was published in *Prometeo* (no. 20).

20. Also in 1912, Sempere, a publishing house in Valencia, translated a collection of Marinetti's manifestos into Spanish. According to the Catalan poet, J. V. Foix, this collection was read by many of the young poets who frequently visited the bookstore of the Laietanes art gallery in Barcelona. Titled *El Futurismo* (Futurism), this collection had already appeared in France in 1911. For more on J. V. Foix and the art gallery bookstore, see Ricard Mas, *Dossier Marinetti*, (Barcelona: Universitat de Barcelona, 1994), 21.

21. Torres-García's article "*El futurisme*" appeared in the February 1916 issue of *Vell i nou*, p. 8.

22. Mas, *Dossier Marinetti*, 16–19.

23. One example of the editorial staff's negative opinion of the Barcelona press that published in Spanish, instead of in Catalan, can be seen in a section of the magazine called "Dietari Espiritual." This column, which was published anonymously, functioned as a space for severe criticism: "Creiem que els diaris que es publiquen a

Catalunya escrits en castellà, no tenen dret a proclamar-se representants de cap sec-tor de la opinió catalana. Per més que facin fulles especializades, mentre les facin en castellà. I pitjor encara si fan pàgines literàries en català com una tolerància o una excepció . . . hi ha gent que no acaba de donar-se de baixa del diari castellà, perquè després ja no sabria de què donar-se de baixa el jorn que s'enfades." (We think that journals published in the Spanish language in Catalonia have no right to make themselves representatives for any section of Catalan public opinion regardless of any specialized pamphlets they may include, as long as they are issued in Spanish. Much worse, too, if they issue literary sections in Catalan as a form of tolerance or as an exception. There are people that cannot seem to make up their minds to unsub-scribe the Spanish journal, for then they would not know what to unsubscribe the day they get angry) (no. 33, February 16, 1917, p. 91). Another example also comes from the "Dietari Espiritual," this time criticizing the motives of the more innovative periodicals of the Castilian-language press: "Abans els periodistes improvisadors de la premsa castellana veníen a descobrir-nos. Ara intenten alfalgar-nos. No ens interessa cap de les dues actituds." (Some time ago, the impromptu journalists from the Span-ish press came to discover us. Now they try to flatter us. We are not interested in either attitude) (no. 47, September 1, 1917, p. 332). My warmest thanks to Rubén Fernández Asensio, a friend and specialist in Second Language Studies, for reviewing all of my Catalan-to-English translations.

24. The censorship of the press by the Primo de Rivera regime was almost imme-diate, as we can see from the stamp placed on the front page of *España*'s September 22, 1923, issue (no. 388). The following contributors to *España* were arrested and/ or jailed as a result of this censorship: Corpus Barga, Luis García Bilbao (manager), Nuñez de Arenas, Sánchez Roja, and Araquistain. *España* was not unfamiliar with censorship rules. This periodical also faced restrictions in August 1917, when censor-ship laws were established after the general strike in Spain that summer.

25. The mission statement of *España*, published in the inaugural issue, reads in part: "Se publica en Madrid nuestro semanario, pero será escrito en toda la nación. No es para nosotros Madrid el centro moral del país." (Our weekly is published in Madrid, but it will be written by those throughout the nation. For us, Madrid is not the moral center of the country) (January 29, 1915, p. 1).

26. Some key examples of longer articles in *España* that address Catalan culture include: Alomar's "El patriotismo del espíritu" (Patriotism of the Spirit), "Los sucesos de agosto. La huelga de Barcelona" (The Events of August. The Strike in Barcelona), "El socialismo en Cataluña" (Socialism in Catalonia), and "Mi catalanismo" (My Catalanism); Corominas's "Cataluña y España. La voz de los nacionalistas idealistas" (Catalonia and Spain. The Voice of Nationalistic Idealists); and Albert's "Cataluña, el estatuto de autonomía" (Catalonia, The Statute of Autonomy).

27. *Iberia*, April 10, 1915.

28. *Un enemic del Poble*, March 1917.

29. *Un enemic del Poble*, November 1917.

30. Joan Salvat-Pappaseit's name appeared in the two principle magazines of the *Ultraísmo* movement: *Grecia* (Seville/Madrid, 1918–20) and *Ultra* (Madrid, 1921–22). He published five poems in *Grecia* that were written and published in Catalan, while his single publication in *Ultra*, as was also the case with *Tableros* (Madrid, 1921–22), was in Catalan. Although his name appeared on the list of contributors to *Reflector* (Madrid, 1920), none of his texts appear to have been published in this periodical. For a discussion of how Salvat-Papasseit contributed to the *Ultraísta* movement in Madrid, please see my article in the *Catalan Review*. Besides founding three avant-garde magazines, Salvat-Pappaseit also published six books of poetry and contributed to the following periodicals: *La Columna de Foc* (Reus, 1918–20), *L'Instant* (Paris/Barcelona, 1918–19), *Justícia Social*, *La Mainada*, *Mar Vella*, *Los Miserables*, *Noucents*, *La Revista* (Barcelona, 1915–36), *Terra Mar*, and *Vida Americana*.

31. Osuna, *Revistas de la vanguardia española*, 68–69.

32. The Biblioteca de Catalunya in Barcelona has compiled a digital archive of fifty periodicals spanning several hundred years. Please see ARCA (Arxiu de revistes catalanes antigues): http://www.bnc.cat/digital/arca/index.html.

33. Guillermo de Torre, "A través de las revistas," *Cervantes*.

34. Osuna, *Revistas de vanguardia*, 71.

35. These cultural periodicals published during the Primo de Rivera dictatorship include: *Gaseta de les Arts* (1924–30), *Revista de Catalunya* (1924–34), *La Mà Trencada* (1924–25), *Revista de Poesia* (1925–27), *L'Amic de les Arts* (Sitges, 1926–29), *La Nova Revista* (1927–29), *Les Arts Catalanes* (1928–29), and *Mirador* (1929–37?). Salvador Dalí, Sebastià Gasch, and Lluís Montanyà criticized these periodicals in their Yellow Manifesto of March 1929 for being too traditional.

36. Montanyà's contribution to *Mediodía* (Seville, 1926–29; 1933; 1939) is particularly interesting: a review of the book *Gertrudis* by the Catalan avant-garde poet J. V. Foix (no. 11, pp. 15–16). *Mediodía*'s concern for staying connected with the rest of the cultural world is evident in the importance it placed on magazine and book reviews and in the space that it made for Catalan culture. This message on the importance of being connected is given even greater weight when, as of the seventh issue, the review section was moved to the cover page of the journal, when it was customary for such a section to appear toward the end of a periodical. Also, the number of magazines that were reviewed in *Mediodía* nearly doubled after this seventh issue.

37. Catalans also contributed to the avant-garde press in Galicia, the northeast corner of the peninsula. *Ronsel* (Lugo, 1924), for example, focused on the regeneration of Galician culture. It published texts in Spanish, Portuguese, and Catalan. Unfortunately the periodical did not last beyond its seventh issue. Contributors from Catalonia included the critics López-Picó and Alfons Maseras.

CHAPTER FIVE

~

The Art of Seeing:
To See and Be Seen in
Spain's Avant-Garde Art Scene

When we think of cubism, images of distorted, cube-like women, composed of thick layers of pigment patterned in bright colors, as if painted by a child, may come to mind. When we think of surrealism, we may see melting clocks, flying tigers, and other dream-like objects flash before our eyes. When asked to evoke images of cubism or surrealism, we may remember pictures, sculptures, and films created by artists from Spain such as Joan Miró, Juan Gris, Pablo Gargallo, or Luis Buñuel—how can we forget the close-up of an eyeball being sliced with a knife?—but it is more likely that we will come up with images and shapes from the two most well-known avant-garde artists from Spain, one from the south and the other from the north: Pablo Picasso and Salvador Dalí, respectively. Picasso is known as one of the founders of cubism (circa 1907), and Salvador Dalí, who was twenty-three years younger than Picasso, is considered to be one of the greatest promoters of surrealism (beginning circa 1924). While Picasso and Dalí did not correspond in age, they followed similar life paths. Sooner or later, both of them left Spain for France. Picasso (Malaga, 1881–1973) and his family traveled from the south of Spain to Barcelona in 1895, where an adolescent Pablo spent a decade of his young life before moving to Paris. About a quarter of a century later, Dalí (Figueres, 1904–89) would make a similar move, but in the opposite direction, from north to south. Dalí traveled from one of the most northeastern points of the Iberian Peninsula to the center of Spain to study at the San Fernando Academy of Fine Arts in Madrid. His father and sister dropped him off at the Residencia de Estudiantes in the Spanish capital, where Dalí lived with other gifted students from primarily well-to-do families. At different points in time, and sometimes simultaneously, Picasso and Dalí both were connected, directly and indirectly, to the vanguard art scene in Barcelona, Madrid, Paris, and New York. But it was Dalí who was most instrumental in minimizing the gap between Barcelona and Madrid.

Picasso and Dalí had their first face-to-face encounter in Paris in the spring of 1926. This visit was Dalí's first taste of Paris. The experience whetted his appetite and prepared the ground for his more permanent move there a few years later. During this two-week trip to France and Belgium with his aunt (stepmother) and sister, he used at least two of his Madrid contacts— Federico García Lorca and Luis Buñuel—to meet important members of the Avant-Garde in Paris. Lorca, Buñuel, and Dalí met and became friends in Madrid as college-aged students while living at the Residencia de Estudiantes in the early to mid-twenties. Lorca connected Dalí with his good friend from home, Manuel Ángeles Ortiz (Jaén, 1895–Paris, 1984), a painter interested in cubism and art styles that broke with traditional forms of representation, in general. Ángeles Ortiz moved to Paris in 1922, where he befriended Picasso. Through this single contact, Dalí was personally introduced to one of the leaders of the modern art movement, Picasso. It was so important for the young Dalí to meet the already-famous Picasso that Dalí went directly to Picasso's studio before visiting the Louvre. During this meeting, Picasso showed Dalí his latest work, and vice versa.[1] This exchange influenced Dalí's style and fueled his ambitions. Manuel Ángeles Ortiz introduced Dalí to other Spanish artists living in Paris, as did his friend, Luis Buñuel, who had recently moved to Paris (1925).

One month after returning from this inspirational trip to the artistic capital of the world, Dalí refused to take his final exam in Fine Art Theory at the San Fernando Academy in Madrid. A young and impertinent Dalí considered the judges of this exam, some of whom had been his professors, to be incompetent. As a result, they expelled him. Rather than stay in Madrid, Dalí immediately returned to his hometown of Figueres in the interior of northern Catalonia, where he worked feverishly without the distractions of Madrid. Less than five years after his initial trip to France, he developed a diverse portfolio of work that became his passport to Paris. By 1929, he had made enough of a name for himself in Spain and connected with just enough of the right people that Camille Goeman, art dealer and promoter of surrealism, invited Dalí to exhibit his work individually at his new gallery in Paris. Here, the founders of surrealism greeted the young Catalan artist with curiosity.

The abyss dividing the art worlds in Barcelona and Madrid during the first quarter of the twentieth century was oceanic. Barcelona's art scene boomed under the influence of *modernisme* and *noucentisme*, two cultural movements in which art played a leading role.[2] Avant-garde artists in Barcelona rejected the conservative *noucentisme* taste that filled art galleries. The environment in Barcelona was ripe for revolutionary change. The political climate was tense, and daily life had become rather violent. Barcelona's bohemia was open to the new developments brought by vanguard artists who fled their homelands during World War I. Gallery owner Josep Dalmau, especially, showed the work of these refugees and actively promoted their new, conceptual, ground-breaking styles. In Madrid—except for the few like Ramón Gómez de la Serna, who hosted a weekly gathering on Saturday nights for his cult-like followers, who rejected all poetry and painting that was outdated, realistic, or academic—the city's appetite was not yet whetted for such abstractions.[3]

Cubism was the first major avant-garde movement to infiltrate Spain's borders from abroad. It is important to note that the first cubism exhibition outside of Paris took place in Barcelona at the gallery of Josep Dalmau (1912). This show at Dalmau's gallery resisted academic art and the more conservative vein of the Catalan *noucentisme* movement, which was still in its early stages of development. Eight artists were featured in this show, including August Agero, Marcel Duchamp, Albert Gleizes, Joan Gris, Marie Laurencin, Jean Metzinger, Le Fauconnier, and Fernand Léger. This art show was covered widely in the literary and art reviews in Barcelona, with the news of this radical new art style eventually spreading throughout the press in other cities of Catalonia as well.[4]

Not long after the cubism exhibit in 1912, Barcelona welcomed another avant-garde movement: dadaism. The French painter and poet Francis Picabia introduced dadaism to Barcelona when seeking refuge in neutral Spain during World War I. His platform for voicing Dada-inspired ideas was an irregularly published periodical called *391* (Barcelona/New York/Zurich/Paris, 1917–24). One of the main purposes of this little magazine was to connect the dadaists who were scattered throughout Europe as a consequence of the war. The first issue of *391* was published in French in Barcelona. Three more issues were printed in the Catalan capital before the little magazine and its editor moved to New York City, where the publication continued.

The example of this Barcelona-born, vanguard periodical, *391*, shows how networking was crucial for the survival of the avant-garde movements. Vanguard artists are often considered to be individualists, yet if we look closely at their practices within their larger cultural context, another truth emerges. Without their supporting networks, these artists may have never reached the fame they did during or after their lifetime. Their survival and success is related, directly or indirectly, to their associations with one another. In the case of Picabia, *391* provided a direct link to the founder of the avant-garde periodical *291*, which inspired *391*: Alfred Steiglitz and his supporters in New York City. Picabia's little magazine and the small group of artists that formed around it while in Barcelona allowed him to maintain and develop his own name recognition during his exile from Paris. It also functioned as a way of making new contacts in a new city that happened to be open to change: Barcelona.

In sum, five hundred copies of *391* were printed of the first four Barcelona issues. The founder of the Dada movement, Tristan Tzara, published a list of "Dada Presidents" in the fifth issue (March 1920) of the Swiss periodical *Dada* (Zurich/Paris, 1917–20), in which he mentioned several supporters of dadaism in Spain. These included two Catalans living in Barcelona (Josep Dalmau, the gallery owner, and Josep Maria Junoy, poet and magazine editor) and three Spaniards living in Madrid (Rafael Cansinos Assens, Guillermo de Torre, and Rafael Lasso de Vega, all of whom were poets). Of these five men, Guillermo de Torre was the only one to publish a literary text in *391*—a Dada poem in French dedicated to Picabia (published in the July 1921 Paris issue, but dated in 1920). This list is useful in that it identifies the people in Spain who were connected to dadaism in 1920, and, as we can see, they were not many. Dadaism never caught on in Spain in the way that cubism and futurism did.

One reason why dadaism did not catch on in Spain the way it did in European countries like France and Germany, for example, could be that it was an art movement that responded directly to the atrocities of World War I. Since Spain was neutral during the Great War, perhaps the climate was not right for dadaism. This vanguard movement reacted to the irrationalities of war by using absurdity as one of its main forms of expression. In the case of Picabia's little magazine, *391*, absurdity took the form of printing false news. Similar to other avant-garde movements, Dada intended on combating or destroying tradition and its conventional representation. In many ways, dadaism was more extreme than cubism. Dadaism expressed an excessive loss of faith in everything that preceded it, including cubism and futurism. It was the direct product of the first modern war, and along with it came a new form of expression primarily motivated by pain, anger, frustration, fear, and violence.[5] Dadaists felt a loss of faith in language, as evident in the name of the group—*dada*—a word that resembles the sound made by a child who has yet learned how to speak.[6] Even though they questioned language, they did not give up on the importance of communication. They combated this sense of the failure of language by creating a global network of artists that was united by little magazines like Picabia's itinerant *391*. It was largely through periodicals such as these that dadaism's influence extended far beyond its place of origin in Zurich, Switzerland. Reverberations of dadaism reached Barcelona, Berlin, Cologne, Hanover, New York, and Paris.

To be true to history, Picabia was not exactly the first to introduce dadaism to Barcelona. One year prior to the publication of the first issue of *391*, Barcelona hosted a Dada performance in the form of a boxing match between an American boxing champion and a French poet in the city's central bullfighting ring (April 23, 1916). The poet, Arthur Craven, arrived at the event inebriated, resulting in a quick victory for the legendary Jack Johnson. The brevity of the fight caused ticket holders to furiously demand a refund, and the absurdity of it all pleased the Dada organizers. Beyond this sporting event and Picabia's periodical, Dada never materialized as a movement in its own right anywhere in Spain the way it did in other countries. That is not to say that its lessons in irrationality, protest, anarchy, or loss of faith in language were not remembered or influential in the work of subsequent experimental painters and poets in Spain. Dada, like the war it came out of, left an indelible mark. What is most important here is that, in Spain, as far as cubism and dadaism are concerned, up until 1920, only Barcelona was paying close attention.

Master Bridge Builder: Rafael Barradas, the Outsider

One man who was inspired by dadaism and who would greatly influence an entire generation of vanguard poets and painters in Barcelona, Madrid, and beyond, was an outsider. Rafael Barradas (1890–1929), a painter from Uruguay born to Spanish parents, invented a style while living in Barcelona in 1918 that was inspired by futurism and dadaism. His style came to be known as *vibracionismo* (vibrationism). When Barradas initially arrived in Europe on a transatlantic ship from Montevideo, Uruguay, he landed in Italy, where he experienced Italian futurism firsthand.[7] He spent time in Genoa, Milan, and Paris, where he made it a point to meet the Italian futurists and French cubists. In 1914 he moved to Barcelona. Only one year had passed since his departure from Uruguay. It was also the first year of the Great War. In the burgeoning art scene of Barcelona, Barradas was exposed to two styles that greatly influenced his work: Celso Lagar's *planismo* (planism) and Joaquín Torres-García's *constructivismo* (constructivism). Before continuing with the importance of Barradas as a major link between the avant-garde networks of Barcelona and Madrid, a few facts about these two lesser-known painters are in order.

The Castilian painter Celso Lagar (Ciudad Rodrigo, Salamanca, 1891–1966) invented a style he called *planismo* (planism), named for the particular use of planes combined with fauvist, cubist, and futurist elements. Lagar left his hometown for Madrid (1910), visited Barcelona, and then moved to Paris (1911), where he showed his work and became well versed in the newest avant-garde styles. During the First World War, he moved to Barcelona, where Josep Dalmau invited him to exhibit his planism paintings in a one-man show in 1915. Before returning definitively to Paris after the war in 1919, he exhibited his planism paintings in several other Barcelona galleries, as well as in Madrid and Bilbao. From his time in Catalonia, Lagar published drawings in several experimental journals centered in Barcelona, including *Revista Nova* (1914–17), *Troços* (1916), and *Un enemic del Poble* (1917–19); and from his period in Madrid, his illustrations are included in the books of Ramón Gómez de la Serna documenting the Café Pombo weekly gathering, which Lagar attended on several occasions.[8] Besides influencing Barradas, Celso Lagar is also an individual who connected the vanguard worlds of Madrid and Barcelona through his contributions with planism in both his paintings and drawings. But like many of the bridge figures connecting Barcelona and Madrid, Lagar moved to Paris, the art capital of the world, early on in his career, never to return to Spain.

The other great influence in Barradas's vibrationism style was Joaquín Torres-García (1874–1949), who played a leading role in the Catalan avant-garde and in *noucentisme* before it. Torres-García also invented his own vanguard style, which he defined as *constructivismo* (constructivism). He and Barradas developed a strong friendship, documented in a collection of letters compiled by Pilar García-Sedas that are full of wonderful details about the cultural milieu of these two Uruguayan artists living in Barcelona.[9]

The vibrationism style of Barradas is the result of various life experiences: living futurism firsthand in Milan; witnessing the development of planism and constructivism in Barcelona; reproducing cubist art in periodicals in his role as illustrator and art director for several little magazines; and meeting people like Sonia and Robert Delaunay in Madrid, who at the time were immersed in their philosophical color theories. One notable example of Barradas's characteristic vibrationism style is a painting titled *Atocha*. This picture depicts an exterior of Madrid's central train station of the same name and is part of the permanent collection of Madrid's Reina Sofia Museum of Modern Art. This painting demonstrates Barradas's exceptional ability to assimilate a variety of avant-garde lessons in order to create a style of his own, while simultaneously capturing the dynamic spirit of the Avant-Garde moment.

Not only was Barradas able to understand the techniques and ideas behind the avant-garde styles, he was also able to make friends with all kinds of people. For instance, his friendship with the Catalan avant-garde poet Joan Salvat-Papasseit was so intimate that critics have noted a unifying force binding their works. A contemporary literary critic has commented that looking at Barradas's paintings reminds him of reading Salvat-Papasseit's poems: "Contemplando esos cuadros caleidoscópicos, de formas esquinadas, de colores vivos, se nos vienen a la memoria fragmentos de poemas no menos dinámicos de Salvat-Papasseit" (Looking at those paintings so kaleidoscope in nature, with cubic forms, vibrant colors, they remind us of fragments of poems by Salvat-Papasseit).[10] But before Barradas and Salvat-Papasseit became really close, Barradas felt the need to leave Barcelona.

When Barradas left Barcelona to move to Madrid, he was compelled to do so on foot, as if undergoing a spiritual journey. Barradas found himself in some sort of crisis, and he was in search of direction. His pilgrimage to Madrid ended prematurely in Zaragoza due to a serious illness. A local family housed, nursed, and cured Barradas over a twelve-month period. During this time, he and his hosts' daughter fell in love. Once he regained his health, they married. His trip to Madrid would have to wait, as Barradas worked and saved money in Zaragoza to support himself and his newlywed. In this city that sits on the Ebro River, historically one of the geographic boundaries between Catalonia and the rest of Spain, he worked as the artistic director of a cultural periodical with an interest in the avant-garde, called *Paraninfo*. This job gave him access to fellow Avant-Garde faithful in other parts of Spain. One of the influential relationships he established through his experience at *Paraninfo* was with a young poet from Madrid, Guillermo de Torre, who would later serve as one of his main contacts when he eventually arrived in Madrid several years later.

After Zaragoza, and before moving to Madrid, Barradas went back to Barcelona with a newfound confidence. He arrived triumphant, with success in the capital of Aragon, a woman he loved, advanced editorial experience, and savings. He immediately landed two jobs: one at a religious bookstore, Librería Católica Pontificia, and the other as a staff member of the magazine *Revista Popular*. By the summer of 1917, Barradas had already made three critical acquaintances in Barcelona that would shape the rest of his intensely lived, short life: Joaquín Torres-García, Josep Dalmau, and Joan Salvat-Papasseit. As mentioned earlier, Torres-García was a fellow Uruguayan, who was also a painter and closely allied with the Catalan, return-to-order, *noucentisme* movement. Unlike Barradas, Torres-García was fluent in both spoken and written

Catalan. When the host of the first cubism exhibition outside of Paris, Josep Dalmau, invited the two Uruguayans to exhibit together during Christmas of 1917, it was Barradas's first big break. Almost one year after this joint exhibit with Torres-García at the Dalmau Gallery, Barradas had his first individual show featuring his *vibracionismo* paintings (Galleries Laietanes, March 1918). His success at these shows led to various publications of his drawings in all three of Salvat-Papasseit's experimental periodicals: *Un enemic del Poble* (1917–19), *Arc-Voltaic* (1918), and *Proa* (1921). As a result of his accomplishments and the expansion of his network of painters, poets, and journalists who shared the Avant-Garde spirit, Barradas's name became intimately tied to Barcelona's new literary and artistic movement.

Barradas finally moved to Madrid in 1919, five years later than he had anticipated, just when the poetic *Ultraísmo* movement was being defined. From his correspondence with Torres-García, we know that Barradas felt uncomfortable in Barcelona. He did not speak Catalan, and he had trouble learning and understanding the language. Evidence from his correspondence suggests that this language barrier was one of the main incentives for leaving Barcelona and moving to Madrid. As fate would have it, Barradas was always in the right place at the right time (Milan, Paris, Barcelona, Zaragoza, Madrid, Montevideo). In Madrid he reconnected with his friend from his Zaragoza days: the experimental poet Guillermo de Torre. Through him, his network of contacts grew exponentially. Another contact, Manuel Abril, a leading art critic from the Madrid press, introduced Barradas to the cultural elite and Avant-Garde supporters including José Francés, Martínez Sierra, Ramón Gómez de la Serna, Benjamin Jarnés, Federico García Lorca, Chabás, Ortega y Gasset, and others.[11] One of the ways Barradas managed to make so many contacts was through his active participation in two literary gatherings, or *tertulias*, that he established: one at the Café del Prado in front of the Madrid *Ateneo* where the Ultraists gathered, and later at another café near the Atocha train station where members of the cultural periodical *Alfar* (La Coruña, 1920–54) gathered.

The founder of *vibracionismo* was actively involved in Madrid's *Ultraísmo* movement. Some of his closest friends in Madrid also happened to be some of the major actors in Madrid's avant-garde network, like Ramón Gómez de la Serna, Federico García Lorca, Luis Buñuel, and Salvador Dalí. The latter documented his friendship with Barradas, Lorca, and Buñuel in his black and white watercolor *Sueños noctámbulos* (Sleepwalking Dreams) (1922), from his initial period in Madrid.[12] Barradas also maintained his professional connections and personal relationships through Gómez de la Serna's gathering place at Café Pombo, where Barradas sketched frequently. Spending time at cafés was not only a matter of leisure for Barradas; it was an opportunity to strengthen his network. Besides Pombo and Café del Prado, he is also known to have attended the *tertulias* at Café Colonial, where Gómez de la Serna's archrival, Rafael Cansinos Assens, hosted his own gatherings. There are also records of Barradas spending time at the Residencia de Estudiantes, where Dalí, Lorca, and Buñuel lived, and where informal *tertulias* would often take place.

Figure 5.1. *Sleepwalking Dreams* **by Salvador Dalí.**

The role of Barradas is fundamental in the avant-garde movements of both Barcelona and Madrid. On the one hand, he is considered one of the artists most directly involved with the *Ultraísmo* movement in Madrid. On the other hand, his vibrationism style has been considered as one of the first artistic expressions of the Catalan avant-garde. In Barcelona he contributed to Salvat-Papasseit's little magazines with the same fervor that he contributed to Madrid's avant-garde periodicals, such as *Grecia, Reflector, Tableros, Ultra,* and many others. Barradas also landed a job as the artistic director of the most important avant-garde periodical from Galicia, *Alfar,* founded in 1920. In addition to his work with the press, he also illustrated the covers of avant-garde poetry books by poets based in Madrid, including his friend Guillermo de Torre (*Hélices,* 1923), and the editor of the Ultra periodical *Grecia,* Isaac Vando Villar (*La sombrilla japonesa,* 1924).[13] Clearly, Barradas is one of the central nodes of Madrid and Barcelona's vanguard networks. His peers called him "The Apostle," and contemporary critics have referred to him as the "helmsman," "axis," "spearhead," and "epicenter" of the Avant-Garde in Spain. As one of the strongest human links between both cities and their respective vanguard movements, Barradas was neither Spanish nor Catalan, but Uruguayan with Spanish roots.[14] Perhaps it is precisely because he was an outsider to both Barcelona and Madrid and their respective cultures that had the freedom to disassociate himself from the sociopolitical rivalry that has historically divided them. Or maybe the reason why Barradas was such an effective bridge builder was because of the overall open-mindedness that often comes from traveling so frequently and living abroad in such different settings.

Joaquim Molas, one of the contemporary leading authorities on the Catalan avant-garde, states that Barradas represents such a strong link between Barcelona and Madrid not because of his direct involvement in both cities, but because of his "origins."[15] However, since he does not elaborate, it is unclear what he means. When Molas speaks of origins, is he referring to Barradas's early years in Italy and France, or does he mean his nationality as a Uruguayan? Is the Catalan scholar referring to his initial stay in Barcelona prior to his arrival in Madrid? Juan Manuel Bonet, author of the Avant-Garde Dictionary so indispensible for the writing of this book, defines Barradas as a "bridge" between two movements, because the avant-garde circles of both Barcelona and Madrid shared an interest in Barradas. One of these common interests was expressing the rhythms of the big city using the language of the avant-garde aesthetic and following its practices: publishing in cutting-edge periodicals, hosting and attending informal gatherings, crossing boundaries between art and literature, breaking with traditional forms of representation, and resisting a bourgeois model of culture.

After a few years in Madrid, Barradas decided it was time to return to Barcelona in 1925. Accompanied by his sister and wife, he stayed there until 1928, when he left Spain and Europe for good, returning indefinitely to Uruguay. Unlike many other leaders of the Avant-Garde movement from Barcelona and Madrid, who came from wealth (e.g., Dalí, Lorca), Barradas never overcame his financial straits. Since he could not afford to live in Barcelona, he lived in the blue-collar suburb of Hospitalet de Llobregat. Here, he hosted a *tertulia* (literary gathering) every Sunday for three years. The group convened at his home, or the *ateneillo* (little athenaeum), where guests discussed poetry, politics, art, and the press for hours on end. Since Barradas could no longer attend the gatherings he so much enjoyed due to poor health, the avant-garde artists and writers came to him.

There was a group of regulars who traveled to his house every Sunday from Barcelona, and sometimes they would bring other friends. The trip to Hospitalet became a pilgrimage, as Dalí once described it: taking the subway and trains of Barcelona was part of the journey, until arriving at the humble house of "The Apostle." In his introduction to the book he edited collecting Lorca's letters to friends, the Catalan art critic Sebastià Gasch described the poverty and humility with which the Barradas family lived. His picture of the small house in the poor suburbs, filled with Barradas's friends and fans, transmits a feeling of claustrophobia. Gasch completes his description with a metaphor for Barradas's life and work based on this space. Like the window that was always wide open in his small, melancholic apartment, so Barradas was always open to new ideas and people. Although Barradas was poor and his work relatively unknown beyond Barcelona and Madrid, his life was rich with friends. Slowly, he is claiming the space he deserves in literary and artistic histories as one of the major figures of Spain's Avant-Garde movement as a whole. Remembering Molas's comment about the "origins" of Barradas, perhaps one of the reasons why he has not been completely embraced in the histories of Spain's official Avant-Garde story is because he was born in Latin America and not in Spain.

When Lorca visited Montevideo in the 1930s, he lamented over how Barradas was already nearly forgotten: "¿Sabe usted en lo que pensaba mientras los fotógrafos me enfocaban y los periodistas me preguntaban . . . ? Pues en Barradas, el gran pintor, a quien uruguayos y españoles hemos dejado morir de hambre . . . Todo eso que me daban a mí, se lo negaron a él." (Do you know what I was thinking about as the photographers were focusing their cameras on me and the journalists were asking their questions...? Well, about Barradas, the great painter, whom Uruguayans and Spaniards let die of hunger . . . Everything they were living in me, they had denied him.)[16] Barradas is an exceptional figure of the Avant-Garde movement of both Barcelona and Madrid not only because he invented one of the first autochthonous avant-garde visual art styles in Spain and Catalonia (vibrationism), but also because he connected both of these culturally distant worlds though his travels, correspondence, friendships, and strong faith in the ideas and spirit of the Avant-Garde. What is fascinating about his case is that he was neither from Barcelona or Madrid; neither Catalan nor Castilian, but Uruguayan, of Spanish descent. Besides being extremely talented and devoted to the Avant-Garde, his position as an outsider may have been what allowed him to be so easily accepted as a participant in the avant-garde circles of Milan, Paris, Barcelona, Madrid, and Zaragoza. Or maybe, Barradas was simply a very talented and friendly person who happened to get along with just about everyone.

Dissonances and Resonances of Avant-Garde Art in Spain Prior To and During World War I

Avant-garde art shows functioned as pivotal moments for contact, knowledge, education, and exchange among the members of the artistic and literary vanguard networks of Barcelona and Madrid. They also speak to the similarities and differences in art-exhibiting practices, as well as the nature of the Avant-Garde as a system of social power. Several exhibitions in particular serve as central nodes in closely connecting the avant-garde networks of Barcelona and Madrid. Before discussing those major exhibitions that linked the artistic worlds of Barcelona and Madrid, the importance of the Catalan art gallery owner Josep Dalmau must be emphasized. The early introduction and subsequent development of modern and avant-garde art in Spain can be attributed in large part to this one man. He and his galleries were among the main reasons why experimental art from Europe found a home in Barcelona.[17] Dalmau opened his gallery in 1911 as an antique shop with a small selection of modern art pieces. The distinguishing characteristic of his gallery was that it functioned, in the words of Dalmau's biographer, as an importer of foreign art.[18] The Sala Parés, a competing gallery run by Santiago Segura, famous for being one of the oldest commercially owned art galleries in the world, was considered to be more conservative, as well as more financially successful. Segura's gallery was known as noucentista turf, while Dalmau's gallery was considered to be the place for vanguard art. Not long after Dalmau opened his gallery, he organized the first cubism exhibit outside of Paris, to take place in his "home," as it was called in Catalan (Can Dalmau), in 1912, as discussed earlier in this chapter.

Historically speaking, many more art exhibits took place regularly in Barcelona than in Madrid during the early years of the new century. In Barcelona, the Junta de Museos (Association of Museums) and the Corporación Municipal (Municipal Corporation) organized local art exhibitions every spring season since 1891.[19] Like Paris, Barcelona also hosted periodic exhibitions similar to the more independent Autumn and Spring Salons.[20] Smaller associations in both cities, such as Barcelona's Les Arts i els Artists (The Arts and Artists) and Madrid's Sociedad de Amigos del Arte (Society of Friends of the Arts), both of which were founded in 1910, frequently organized shows as well. Unlike in Madrid, during the late 1910s and early 1920s, many different artistic schools were founded in Barcelona, namely Els Evolucionistes (1918), Nou Ambient (1919), and Agrupació Courbet, all of which fell under the umbrella of the *noucentisme* cultural movement and corresponding classicist style.

Many artistic groups like these did their part in organizing shows that would travel to other cities in Spain. For instance, Les Arts i lels Artistes exhibited in Bilbao in November 1916 during the middle of the First World War.[21] Similarly, the Asociación de Artistas Vascos (Association of Basque Artists) set up an exhibit in Madrid in the same month and year as the Catalan show in Bilbao. Gabriel Maroto, an artist and art critic centered in Madrid, commented on the importance of viewing the work of the Galician painters in their Madrid show. His remarks offer insight into the mentality of the Madrid viewing public: "Se planteó el problema entre los pintores de ideal ajeno a nuestras tierras, y los que creían que el arte gallego había de orientarse sobre el mismo país" (The problem was posed between artists with an ideal that was foreign to ours, and those who thought that the art of Galicia had to direct itself toward Spain).[22] This art show dedicated exclusively to works produced in Galicia stirred a politically motivated debate about Madrid's lack of control in the formation of Galician identity and its disconnection with Spanish identity overall.

Another politically charged art show, also a noteworthy example of artistic activity that minimized the divide between the art scenes in Barcelona and Madrid, is the very little-studied Exposición de Legionarios (The Legionnaire Exhibit) (1917). This show was organized in honor of Spanish soldiers who voluntarily joined either the French or German armies during Word War I. A group of artists and writers, disappointed by the nation's indifference to the fact that young Spaniards were sacrificing their lives in a war that was not even theirs, organized a show of drawings in Madrid. Proceeds from the exhibit were sent to the front line as Christmas gifts. In order to reach a large audience, the show traveled to three major artistic centers in

Spain: Madrid, Barcelona, and Bilbao. This event caught the eye of the director of the Parisian newspaper *Le Journal*, who enthusiastically arranged for the participation of several Parisian illustrators, thus turning the art exhibit into an international event to raise awareness about the war.

Ministers, ambassadors, journalists, and high-society members attended the show's opening in Madrid (January 3, 1917). The works exhibited represented a diverse group of artists from Spain, including Catalans, Galicians, and Basques, as well as contributions by the French. The only artist who exhibited his work here who was blatantly experimenting with the ideas of the Avant-Garde was Celso Lagar.[23] After the Madrid opening, and upon discovery of the coetaneous publication of an anti-German manifesto in one of Madrid's most important daily newspapers, *El Liberal*, that was signed by many of the artists whose works were on display at the Legionarios exhibit, the Germans declared a submarine blockade on all those countries who declared neutrality in the Great War.[24] In addition to the blockade, the German navy sank several Spanish ships. The German government interpreted this exhibit in Madrid and the corresponding publication of the anti-German manifesto as a violation of Spain's neutrality agreements. The Legionnaire show opened in Barcelona at the Laietanes Galleries (February 1917), where it stayed open for ten days until it traveled to Bilbao, where it showed for approximately the same amount of time. This exhibition is interesting because it represents a moment of bridge building in the arts between three of Spain's modern cities, and even though the work displayed was not avant-garde per se, the act, with its corresponding manifesto, most certainly was.

Soon after the Legionnaire show in Madrid closed, and perhaps as a result of the cooperation established between the people from Madrid and Paris who were involved, a group of French artists petitioned the Barcelona government to endorse an art exhibit that had been cancelled as a result of the war. After some negotiations, the Catalan government approved the Exposició d'Arts Français (French Art Exhibition). The show opened its doors on April 23, 1917, bringing together hundreds of French artists who displayed over one thousand paintings. Madrid followed suit in 1918 by organizing a similar show. Historians like Jaime Brihuega have noted that this second show, with only 190 works, was a poor comparison to the Barcelona precedent. Furthermore, the more experimental artists who exhibited in Barcelona did not participate in the corresponding Madrid show. Brihuega very appropriately uses this exhibit to describe the vast differences in artistic attitudes, buying behaviors, and showing practices between Barcelona and Madrid during this time.

One example of these differences in artistic taste can be seen in the publication of an article about avant-garde art published in the Madrid press by a member of the Catalan avant-garde. One month after the Basque painters exhibited in Madrid (November 1916), the founder of the constructivism style, Joaquín Torres-García, the Uruguayan artist and friend of Barradas who resided in Barcelona, published an argument in defense of the artistic avant-garde in Madrid's periodical *España* (December 1916).[25] While this article represents one of the first exchanges in print of opinions about avant-garde art between Barcelona and Madrid, as well as one of the first extensive articles ever printed about avant-garde art in the Madrid press, the effect was most likely minimal, despite the periodical's popularity, since it did not generate more articles on the topic. Torres-García was addressing himself to an audience that was still quite unaware of the artistic revolution that had already made its grand entrance in Barcelona prior to World War I.

When Celso Lagar first exhibited his *planismo* paintings in Madrid several months after the publication of this article by Torres-García (March 1917), his style was ridiculed in the press. One year later Barradas had his first individual show in Madrid, introducing his vibrationism style (March 1918), followed by a second Lagar show, both of which were widely reviewed in the specialized press. Barradas's first exhibit was followed by two more in Madrid. It was not until the public was exposed to these series of Lagar and Barradas shows that the Madrid public began to see what Torres-García had been referring to two years earlier in his article in the Madrid-based journal *España*. Barradas was at the right place at the right time. By way of these three exhibits, his participation in literary gatherings, and his contributions to many periodicals in both Barcelona and Madrid and elsewhere in Spain, but also because of the friendships he made and maintained, Barradas bridged the gap between the two cities through the spirit and language of the Avant-Garde. He also prepared the terrain in Madrid for the invention and practice of the avant-garde poetic style that originated in Madrid known as *Ultraísmo*.

The Iberians: The First Major Modern Art Show in Madrid, but without the Catalans

It was not until 1925 that the artistic avant-garde networks of Barcelona and Madrid finally began to connect. Reminding us of the divide separating Barcelona and Madrid, which he considers to be "permanent," Brihuega points out that these cultural centers became more aware of one another and appeared to be in a more similar place: "A pesar de esta permanente distancia que separa ambos centros culturales, es un hecho fundamental el que, cuando raya 1925, Madrid y Barcelona han empezado a conocerse artísticamente" (Regardless of the permanent divide that separates both cultural centers, it is a fundamental fact that, when 1925 arrives, Madrid and Barcelona have begun to know one another artistically).[26] In this historic year, Madrid organized a major collective show called the Ibéricos (Iberians), with the goal of showing a wide variety of modern art styles that were being practiced throughout Spain. In the end, the Catalans were largely underrepresented at this show. The Society of Iberian Artists that organized this exhibition included only two Catalans, even though there were hundreds of Catalan painters practicing, showing, and selling modern art in Spain and beyond. Based on the historical accounts and available archives of this landmark event in Spain's modern art history, whether the Catalans pulled out of negotiations at the last second or whether they were excluded from the affair still remains unclear.

The Ibéricos was unprecedented in both Barcelona and Madrid. Later that year, Dalmau organized a national and international modern art exhibition titled Exposición de arte moderno nacional y extranjero (Exhibition of National and Foreign Modern Art) (October–November 1925), but the only "national art" represented was that created by Catalans.[27] The occasions that Spanish painters exhibited in Barcelona during the twenties were rare, and when they did, it would be as individuals rather than as part of a collective. On the other hand, in the few instances that Catalans exhibited in Madrid during the same period, they did so in groups. The circulation of art between these two cities reveals a pattern: Spanish artists showed as individuals in Barcelona, while Catalans showed collectively in Madrid. The first time a collective showing of Catalan art was planned in Madrid was for the Ibéricos show organized by the Madrid-based Sociedad de Artistas Ibéricos (SAI). In an effort to change its image from a city that was out of touch with modern art to one that was in the know, Madrid invited almost one hundred painters, some more well known than others, representing a variety of styles from all over Spain. Those with vanguard tendencies included Salvador Dalí, José Moreno Villa, Francisco Bores, Pancho Cossío, Benjamín Palencia, Rafael Barradas, Santiago Pelegrín, and Norah Borges. Even though the big names of Spanish painting—Pablo Picasso, Juan Gris, and Joan Miró—were missing from the lineup, the poet and painter José Moreno Villa felt that the "disturbing quality" and "enthusiasm" of the "beginners" justified the initiative.[28]

Over five hundred works were arranged in one of the major exhibition halls in Madrid's central park, El Retiro, in a show claiming to be inclusive of all Spanish art; Catalonia was notably underrepresented. If the Ibéricos was one of Spain's first "assertions" within the realm of the plastic arts as a whole, as José-Carlos Mainer has claimed, then perhaps it reveals something indicative of the relationship between Barcelona and Madrid.[29] First, it would be more historically accurate to say that this exhibit marks the first collective show of modern art in Madrid, since we already know that in Barcelona Dalmau and others had been organizing many major and minor modern art exhibits. Along these same lines, the organizers of the remake of this exhibit at the Museo Nacional Centro de Arte Reina Sofía in Madrid (1996) considered Ibéricos as the beginning of Spain's artistic renewal, which was abruptly cut short by the onset of the Spanish Civil War (1936–39).[30] But as we have already seen, artistic renewal in the visual arts began in Barcelona as early as 1912 with the first cubism exhibit organized outside of Paris, not to mention the Celso Lagar planism exhibit in 1915 and the Torres-García and Barradas vibrationism shows from 1917 and 1918, all of which took place in Barcelona approximately one decade prior to the Ibéricos in Madrid.

While its historical importance is indisputable, in some ways the Ibéricos failed in its very reason for being (to mount a collective show) by not exhibiting the works of any of the existing Catalan art schools, of which there were several. For the most part, contemporary critics who have studied this exhibit brush this discrepancy aside, mentioning the absence of the Catalans in passing and without giving it much importance. The Ibéricos failed in its goal of organizing a show that represented an all-encompassing society of "Iberian" artists, as indicated in the organizer's title and mission. Most critics excuse the absence of Catalan artists by claiming that the subsequent Catalan modern art exhibition hosted in Madrid seven months later at a different venue "made up" for that absence. Some historians even refer to this second show as "una especie de SAI" (a sort of SAI) or a sequel. However, if we closely compare the artists and styles represented in both of these shows hosted in Madrid, the Ibéricos and the Catalan modern art show, we can see that one of the only things the two exhibitions had in common was the participation of Salvador Dalí.

Before attempting to understand the importance of Dalí's role in both of these exhibits, separated only by a few months, more background on the formation of the Iberian Art Society (SAI) is necessary. The creation of the SAI in Madrid was sparked by an article written by the Basque art critic and Avant-Garde enthusiast, Juan de la Encina, in response to an individual exhibit by Francisco Cossío in Madrid's *Ateneo*. His review, "*La nueva generación artística*" (The New Artistic Generation), printed in the Madrid daily newspaper, *La Voz* (January 26, 1923), is one in a series of pleas authored by Encina, who had been calling for radical change in Madrid's stagnant art scene since at least 1917.[31] Only a few days after the Cossío review was published, during a banquet in honor of the Basque painter Juan de Echevarría (1875–1931) (who was concurrently exhibiting in Madrid, but at the Museum of Modern Art), the painter Gabriel García Maroto gave a speech calling for an independent salon of artists and a corresponding show in Madrid. He later sent the speech to Encina, who published it in *La Voz*. In a second article, "*Un mecenas catalán*" (A Catalan Sponsor) (February 1, 1923), Encina announced that the Catalan art collector Lluís Plandiura was willing to collaborate in the establishment of such a show by offering access to his important collection of Catalan modern (specifically *noucentista*) art.[32] In exchange, Plandiura asked that the satirical Catalan illustrator, Lluís Bagaría (1882–1940), known as Luis in Madrid, a participant in the 1917 Legionarios exhibition, be a member of the organizing committee, which already consisted of Juan de la Encina, Manuel Abril, Juan Ramón Jiménez, Juan de Echevarría, and Xavier Nogués, as indicated in the Maroto-Encina journalistic exchanges.

Plandiura's allegiance to the group nearly guaranteed the participation of the Catalans, at least those most representative of the *noucentista* camp. With Plandiura on board, Eugeni D'Ors, who wrote the prologue for the Plandiura exhibit in January 1923 commemorating the "Plandiura Contest" (January 1922) in Barcelona, became involved. At the end of the month, *La Voz* published Maroto's speech, "Carta a Juan de la Encina" (Letter to Juan de la Encina) (February 24, 1923), followed by Encina's response in "De una carta a un pintor" (From a Letter to a Painter) (February 28, 1923). The journalistic dialogue concluded with Plandiura's "Hay que crear el Salón de Independientes" (An Independent Salon Must Be Created) (July 3, 1923), in which he publicly agreed to form part of the organizing committee. After three meetings of this committee in April and May of 1923, a society of Spanish artists was finally created, as well as an accompanying manifesto that called for the creation of an Independent Autumn Salon in Madrid.

D'Ors and Plandiura's insistence that that the society should promote only a "return to classicism" style practiced primarily by the Catalan *noucentista* artists led to more disputes among the committee members. For D'Ors, the best artists in Spain aspired to a reestablishment of order. Return-to-order attitudes such as these did not sit well with the other members of the group. Their goal, on the other hand, was to create a society that would be accepting of all the different tendencies developing throughout Spain—not just the *noucentistas*. As a result of these fundamental ideological differences, the first manifesto was discarded and the committee dissolved. Besides D'Ors's publication of the manifesto in his ironically titled *Mi Salón de Otoño* (My

Autumn Salon) (1924), a text that sketches out the panorama of modern Catalan art with specific emphasis on the *noucentista* painters Joaquim Sunyer and Jose de Togores, the SAI committee froze for nearly two years.

Curiously, none of the many scholars who have spent time investigating this important exhibit comment on the society's name change from Sociedad de Artistas Españoles (Society of Spanish Artists) in 1923 to Sociedad de Artistas Ibéricos (Society of Iberian Artists) in 1925. The difference between the terms "Spanish" and "Iberian" is revealing. "Iberian" is a more encompassing term that includes Spain and Portugal. In March 1925, a much larger, more diverse committee signed the new manifesto; notably, Plandiura and D'Ors were no longer involved.[33] Now the art critic Manuel Abril and, to a certain degree, Gabriel García Maroto took on the leadership roles. The only Catalan who participated in the new committee was Joaquim Sunyer, who had just successfully ended his first individual exhibit in Madrid (January 1925), which was followed by an homage dinner in February attended by D'Ors, Abril, Lorca, Echevarría, Guillermo de Torre, Vázquez Díaz, and Gabriel Maroto. Despite his initial enthusiasm, Sunyer excused himself from the society. In the end, even though the group had agreed to use the more encompassing term of "Iberian" to describe their society, Catalonia no longer had a role in the organizing committee.

The absence of the Catalans was felt and emphasized by the organizers. The importance of Catalan art and Barcelona's role as its epicenter were some of the central issues that the new and improved manifesto stressed. Published widely in the press, this declaration appeared in all of Madrid's major newspapers. News of the exhibit also reached Barcelona, Bilbao, La Coruña, Valencia, Zaragoza, and even Buenos Aires, Argentina. Given this document's clarity in describing the relationship between Barcelona and Madrid and their differences in artistic attitudes, I have reproduced it here in its entirety:

> Somos muchos los que venimos notando, con dolor, el hecho de que la capital española no pueda estar al tanto del movimiento plástico del mundo, ni aun de la propia nación, en ocasiones, porque no se organiza en ella las Exposiciones de Arte necesarias para que conozca Madrid cuanto de interesante produce fuera de aquí, el esfuerzo de los artistas de esta época. Ello imposibilita o dificulta cualquier movimiento de cultura . . . Para elegir tendencia y adoptar posición, parece indispensable tener, siquiera un momento, ante los ojos las varias tendencias que en el mundo se disputan la superioridad en el acierto. Falta ello en Madrid y en casi todas las ciudades importantes españolas. Pero en otras, en cambio, no; y hemos pensado algunos que esta falta no proviene, por lo tanto, de dificultades positivas e insuperables—puesto que Bilbao y

Barcelona han logrado, en ocasiones, superarlas—sino solamente de que, acaso, no se hayan puesto a remediarla unos cuantos hombres de buena voluntad en el propósito. De ahí que los firmantes hayamos tratado de unirnos en sociedad a fin de tramitar, buscar y allanar cuando sea necesario para que Madrid conozca todo aquello que conocido y celebrado—o simplemente discutido—en otros lugares, queda de continuo alejado de la capital española sin razón que lo justifique . . . No nos une, pues, una bandera, ni una política: no vamos, ni en pro ni en contra de nadie.

(It is many of us who have been noticing, with pain, the fact that the Spanish capital cannot keep up with advances of the worldwide art movement, nor that of its own country, at times, because there are never any art exhibitions organized there which are necessary for Madrid to know about all the interesting things that are happening outside of here, like the great efforts of our age. This will make it impossible or very difficult for any sort of cultural movement . . . In order to choose a style and adopt a position, it seems indispensable to have, even if just for a moment, before its eyes the variety of styles that are being discussed worldwide as being superior in their representation. This is missing in Madrid and in almost all of the important cities in Spain. But in other cities, this is not the case; and some of us have been thinking that this fault is not because of positive or impossible difficulties—considering that Bilbao and Barcelona have achieved, at times, to resolve these problems—but rather, maybe, a few good men have not tried to resolve this difficulty. It is from here that we who sign this manifesto have tried to unite in the form of a society with the goal of negotiating, exploring, and filling in the blanks when it is necessary for Madrid to learn about all that has been celebrated and known—or at least discussed—in other places, it remains unjustifiable that the capital remain outside of these discussions . . . We are not united by a flag or by politics: we are not for or against anybody.) [34]

This document shows an explicit interest in the artistic renewal in Madrid and in its connection with the larger European avant-garde scene. It is no longer 1916, when Torres-García was promoting avant-garde styles from Barcelona, or 1917, when Juan de la Encina was the only critic calling for change from within the pages of the cultural magazine *Hermes*, published in Bilbao. Almost ten years had passed since then, and finally there was some understanding and consensus in Madrid about the impact of avant-garde art in Spain. It took Encina almost a decade to find enough support for his campaign in Madrid, but eventually, he achieved it.

By 1925, Spaniards in numerous cultural centers throughout Spain were more in tune with the powerful aesthetic revolution that had been sweeping Europe. The majority of Spanish intellectuals, including many influential politicians, understood the power of the main message of avant-garde art practices and theories by this time, even though the majority of Spaniards were generally unaware of the potential of this cultural uprising. Even the current dictator, General Primo de Rivera, from early on in his regime admired and depended on the support of Spanish intellectuals fluent in the aesthetic of the avant-garde movements, as will be discussed in the next chapter. The SAI document indicates that as the capital of Spain, Madrid should be hosting many more art exhibitions, as other European capitals did, and should be more open to new tendencies. Madrid was missing out. The manifesto signers believed that as the capital of Spain, Madrid needed to play more of a protagonist role in the organization and hosting of art exhibits. Spaniards, and particularly the community of Madrid, were largely unaware of the state of art on the international level. Their expertise in local and regional art in Spain was admirable, but they needed to be less provincial and more open to other ways of thinking.

One of the major organizational challenges of the SAI committee was that the diversity of styles practiced throughout the various regions of Spain could not be classified under one name. In Barcelona alone, there were at least five different schools of modern art practices, ranging from classical to radical. This diversity of style was one of the leading factors that caused the organizing committee so much division. One possible solution was to eliminate the Barcelona art scene altogether and focus, instead, on the rest of Spain. Or, perhaps, it was the Catalans who pulled out and decided to do something similar, but independently.

From as early on as the first decade of the new century, one of the frequent complaints that appear in Madrid's specialized press was that Spain's main roadblock to cultural progress was ignorance. Those who contributed to these minority periodicals were convinced that if Spaniards were more educated about their differences, they would be less hostile toward one another. The argument was that in order for any sort of regeneration, modernization, and progress to occur in post-1898 Spain, Spaniards had to first know about one another, not just themselves; thus Madrid-based periodicals like *España Futura* and *España* insisted on featuring articles describing the various regions of Spain and their cultures. In order to form opinions about modern art, the Spanish public first had to know about the variety of twentieth-century artistic schools and styles in Spain and beyond. As discussed earlier, Barcelona was more familiar with these new styles from abroad, in comparison to the Madrid readership. They were more fluent in the newest art vocabularies, as evident in their many artistic societies, frequent exhibitions, numerous galleries, talented artists, astute critics—a more dynamic art scene overall.

Despite all of these challenges, the individuals who signed the 1925 SAI manifesto—regardless of their national origin, political allegiance, age, religion, or artistic view—finally agreed to host a show in Madrid with or without the Catalans. They could not argue any longer. This show was long overdue.

The Society of Iberian Artists wanted to organize an exhibition that would be as comprehensive as possible in representing Spain's diverse tendencies in modern art. Yet there was only one painter from Catalonia (not including the illustrator Lluís Bagaría, at this time a Madrid resident, or the painter Ramón Pitxot, who had recently passed away) who participated in this show: Salvador Dalí.[35] This collective exhibit was Dalí's coming out in Madrid, where he showed ten paintings, the majority of which are representative of his early experiments with cubism. Five months later, Dalí would celebrate his first solo exhibition in Barcelona, where he showed fifteen paintings, few of which are of a cubist taste. This discrepancy in what Dalí showed in the first two important shows of his life can be explained by the fact that by 1925, cubism was a fading fashion in Barcelona, yet Madrid had barely been exposed it. What better way to draw the attention of his public than to introduce himself in Madrid vis-à-vis the language of cubism, knowing that he would be one of a handful of the participating artists adopting this style.

In the catalog for the 1996 commemorative Ibéricos exhibit held in Madrid, Javier Pérez Segura hypothesizes about the absence of Catalans. One of the explanations he gives is that the Catalan contingent refused to participate in any event hosted in the city that symbolized the General Miguel Primo de Rivera dictatorship.[36] As of September 1923, this government had prohibited the use of the Catalan flag and language, banned all nationalistic associations (including the annual spring art exhibits), and abolished the city council (Mancomunitat). For many Catalans, Madrid was the home of a dictatorship that intended to eliminate Catalan culture by means of a politics of cultural homogenization.[37] The fact that the SAI received support from the dictatorship, which granted its organizers use of the city's most distinguished exhibition space in Madrid (the Ice Palace in El Retiro Park), automatically associated this society and its show with the state.[38] However, the fact that the Catalans went ahead and organized their own exhibition at another space in Madrid soon thereafter leads me to believe that the break had more to do with disagreements within the organizing committee rather than with an outright rejection of Madrid, or else they would not have shown there at all.

Notably, only a few months before the inauguration of the Ibéricos, Francesc Macià, a representative in the Catalan Parliament, was tried by court martial on March 14, 1925, while in exile in Paris, for his written attacks against the Spanish nation. Six days later, the Primo de Rivera government abolished the

Mancomunitat. On April 23, 1925, Macià attempted to raise money for a small army composed mainly of Catalans. On May 24 of the same year, members of an activist group in conjunction with Macià's party planted a bomb in a failed attempt to kill the king. Subsequent demonstrations in Barcelona caused the closure of their Football Club stadium, as well as the Orfeó Català (a choral group founded in 1891). It was in this volatile atmosphere that the Ibéricos opened its doors in Madrid. Much to the surprise of many in the society, some of the younger, more avant-garde members distributed leaflets on opening day. This document communicated their objectives in this exhibition, as opposed to those of any organizing society. They disagreed with the manifesto that had been published in the press, which is reproduced above, as well as the SAI's deficiencies in organizing this exhibit. In full, the leaflet reads:

> The undersigned artists, all of us currently exhibiting at the Artistas Ibéricos Salon wish to state: (1) That we are stimulated by effort and deadened by the goodwill of the public (2) That we loathe official painting (3) And under-stand it perfectly. (4) That we consider Valencian painting horrible. (5) That we respect and find marvelous the painting of the great masters: Raphael, Rembrandt, Ingres, etc. (6) That it would appear that those who show most disrespect toward classical art are precisely the people at the Academy of San Fernando, since they are beginning to get all worked up about their discovery of the early French Impressionists, falsified by the incomprehension of the Valencian painters who, like Muñoz Degrain, now amaze the Academy. For our part we believe that few people have done more damage to the young than Sorolla and those who followed him. (7) That we admire our own age and the painters of our age and wish our works to be an expression of our admiration for: Derain, Picasso, Matisse, Braque, Juan Gris, Severini, Picabia, Chirico, Soffici, Lhote, Kisling, Gleizes, Léger, Ozenfant, Togores, Friesz, etc.[39]

The direct attack on the Royal Academy of San Fernando in Madrid has led many critics to believe that the author of this counter-manifesto was Dalí; it certainly sounds like him. By the time of the Ibéricos opening, Dalí had already been expelled once from the San Fernando Academy of Fine Arts in Madrid, when he allegedly led a student protest.[40] For all the sweat and tears involved organizing this exhibit, the press in Madrid mostly mocked the Ibéricos, while the press in Barcelona barely even mentioned it.

The First Modern Catalan Art Show Hosted in Madrid

Exposure to Catalan art in Madrid during the twenties was at best sporadic, if not null. Political tensions between the Catalans and the Primo de Rivera government had not improved by the time the Ibéricos opened in the summer of 1925, nor by the time of the inauguration of the Exposición de Arte Moderno Catalan (Modern Catalan Art Exhibit) that took place in Madrid six months after the Ibéricos show (January 16–February 1, 1926). In fact, the political situation had only worsened. Yet, the Ibéricos exhibit had piqued the curiosity of some art enthusiasts in Madrid, leaving them with a desire to expand their visual lexicon, as noted in the daily newspaper *El Heraldo*: "Hay en Madrid un . . . buen ánimo y deseos de comprender y ampliar el horizonte de la visión artística" (In Madrid there is a good attitude and a healthy desire to understand and widen the horizons of its artistic vision).[41] Considered by most to be a follow-up to the Ibéricos show, the modern Catalan art exhibit was organized by a newspaper in Madrid, *Heraldo de Madrid*, to which many Catalans contributed, most notably its editor, Rafael Marquina.[42] This was the first art show that the newspaper organized to introduce Madrid's public to major art movements, schools, and styles on the Iberian Peninsula.[43] Two of the key Catalans who had expected to participate in the Ibéricos but did not (Joaquim Sunyer and Ramon Casals), plus thirty-nine other Catalan artists, displayed their work at the Palacio de Villahermosa, the headquarters for the Círculo de Bellas Artes, located in the Plaza de las Cortes in the center of Madrid.

Some newspaper reports from the time indicate that the reason why this exhibit was successful was because of the collaboration of the experienced Catalan modern art merchant Josep Dalmau, even though the details of this partnership remain largely undocumented. Despite his alleged collaboration, Dalmau did not appear at the show, because he purportedly fell ill.[44] Much like the diversity of artwork displayed at the Ibéricos, several variants of modern Catalan art were presented. At least five different schools were introduced among the forty-one artists and sculptors showing seventy-seven works, including L'Agrupació Courbet (Espinal, Miró, Ricart, Rafols); Les Arts i els Artistes (Guàrdia, Mompou, Rebull, Ricart, Ráfols, Ynglada); Els Evolucionistes (Mompou, Rafols, Rebull, Sisquella, Serra, Viladomat); and Nou Ambient (Camps, Marqués, Soler). With only one exception, all of the artists participating in this show had already exhibited at least once in Dalmau's Barcelona gallery. The Catalan painters prompted accusations of boycotting the *Ibéricos* by printing a statement to this effect on the inside cover of the original exhibition catalog, which reads as follows:

Abrimos nuestra puerta sin pretensiones de exclusividad; pero con fervor de acogimiento. Hay quizá, en la agria inquietud de hoy y en nuestro ambiente artístico, como un enrarecimiento del aire. Modestamente queremos contribuir al mejor remedio . . . Sin prejuicios y sin intransigencias, nos es honroso ofrecer este conjunto magnífico del arte joven catalán.

(We open our doors without pretentions of being exclusive; but with a desire of being welcomed. There is perhaps, in the bitter worries of today and in our artistic environment, a sort of strangeness in the air. In all modesty, we would like to contribute to a better solution . . . Without prejudice and without intransigencies, it is an honor for us to offer this magnificent collection of art by young Catalans.)[45]

The goal of the "young" and not so young (like Sunyer, the oldest artist in the exhibition, at fifty-two years of age) Catalan artists was to help alleviate tensions between these two cultural centers of Spain through art.[46] According to this statement, their intention was to improve relations between Barcelona and Madrid through artistic exchange without being pretentious or exclusive. The substantial press coverage and controversy surrounding this exhibit resulted in the attendance of over two thousand people in just the first three days of the exhibit, a record number of visitors for any art show in Madrid.[47] As a result of *El Heraldo*'s aggressive publicity campaign, this show became a major cultural event. Anybody who was anybody in Madrid's high society attended.

An exclusive report of the pre-opening reception in *El Heraldo* listed all of the figures of the artistic, literary, and political world who were at the party, instead of publishing a review of the artworks displayed. The language used by the reporter in the first review of the exhibition reads more like an advertisement:

Hemos logrado plenamente lo que nos proponíamos: ofrecer a la cultura madrileña un índice, vario, rico, nutrido, de la novísima sensibilidad palpitante en la obra germinativa de la juventud artística que trabaja fervorosamente en una de las más interesantes regiones españolas.

(We have fully achieved everything we planned: to offer the culture of Madrid an index—varied, rich, and healthy—of the newest, palpitating sensibility of the germinating corpus of art by the young who work with fervor in one of the most interesting Spanish regions.)[48]

Over the course of the next two weeks, *El Heraldo* actively promoted the exhibit with overly enthusiastic observations, such as: "Éxito franco"; "El salón estuvo constantemente lleno de público"; "Gente conocida y buen público ingenuo"; "Numeroso y distinguido público" (Simply a success; The salon was constantly full of people; Famous people and a good public; numerous and distinguished guests). For the closing reception, to which "everyone" was invited, El Heraldo hosted an even bigger bash than the opening that included poetry readings, short lectures, and toasts. Ironically, this closing event took place at the Palacio de Hielo, a place associated with the Primo de Rivera regime, in addition to being the same hall where the Ibéricos exhibit was held five months earlier and that supposedly posed problems for the Catalans.

Similar to the Ibéricos coverage, the Modern Catalan Art exhibit was barely mentioned in the Barcelona press. There were a series of laudatory articles by Marquina (similar to those published in Madrid's El Heraldo) that appeared in Barcelona's daily Catalan-language newspaper La Veu de Catalunya, in addition to two not-so-congratulatory reviews in smaller Catalan periodicals. One of these can be found in Ciutat, a little magazine from the town of Manresa.[49] Without providing too many details, this review reported that several Catalan painters turned down the invitation to exhibit in Madrid, such as Joan Colom, who was more concerned with his upcoming exhibit in Paris. The reporter reminds his readers that "La pintura catalana—cal no oblidar-ho—està lligada amb l'art francès que és l'únic de tot el món actual" (Catalan painting—let us not forget—is tied to French art, which is the only art in the world today), thus boldly denying art in Spain outside of Barcelona any importance whatsoever.[50]

He also makes an ironic note that the people of Madrid were surprised to see that Catalan art did not involve stereotypical objects associated with the Catalan culture: "Han descobert molt extranyats que no pintàvem bar-retines, ni porrons. No tots el postrers artistas europeïtzants han volgut anar a Madrid— . . . alguns han refusat la invitació." (They have discovered, much to their surprise, that we did not paint Catalan caps or drinking vessels. Not every avant-garde artist in line with European art movements wanted to go to Madrid . . . some turned down the invitation.)[51] A more open review by the art critic Rafael Doménech criticized the show as being unrepresenta-tive of modern Catalan art. He strongly felt that the show was outdated ("seudointeligente," "conservadora," "inconciencia artística," "al margen del arte," "atrasados," "envejecido")) (half intelligent, conservative, art without a conscience, irrelevant, outdated, and old). He was certain that the Madrid public knew that Catalan art was much more contemporary than what was on display.[52]

Besides El Heraldo's unabashedly self-promoting publicity campaign, this exhibit created a lively discussion in the specialized press about Catalan identity. From the point of view of Madrid, one of the characteristics of that which is Catalan is the ability to be diverse and still maintain a sense of unity.[53] Marquina emphasizes the fact that Catalan art is more universal than local (*La Veu de Catalunya*), with which the Polish artist Paszkiewicz agrees: "no tiene nada de regional" (it does not have anything to do with regionalism). The Spanish playwright Rivas Cherif was strongly moved by the Catalan art show. He saw the Catalan soul expressed in these works that erased borders through their artistic genius and universal qualities. He called for Spanish art to join the "occult nations" like Catalonia that were in tune with the more global preoccupations and fashions of the time.[54]

Overall, art critics in Madrid were thrilled with the visit of the Catalans, seeing it as an opportunity to improve relations with Catalonia during the crisis of the Primo de Rivera dictatorship. One of the most prolific art critics of the time, José Francés, viewed this show as a cure for Madrid's stagnancy in the arts: "Este [arte] de los catalanes, ¡nos desquita de tantas inercias y parálisis!" (This Catalan art lifts our inertia and cures our paralysis).[55] Another critic, Cartagena, saw the exhibit as an invitation to learn about the diversity of cultures in Spain: "Habrá de redundar en una mayor afición a conocer y examinar el tesoro disperso de nuestros valores espirituales de esta hora" (We must take advantage with greater desire to learn and study the dispersed treasure of our spiritual values of our day).[56] An anonymous critic in Madrid's *ABC* newspaper found in this show a way to combat social problems: "Agrupados todos los españoles que contribuyen con su esfuerzo al desarrollo de las actividades nacionales, harán frente a los peligros que se ciernen sobre Europa, para lograr la tranquilidad y la alegría en España" (All the Spaniards that contribute with effort to the development of national activities will combat the dangers that threaten Europe, in order to achieve tranquility and happiness in Spain).[57] The Catalan Modern Art show went beyond the typical art show. Organizing such an exhibit in the nation's capital in the middle of a military dictatorship that attempted to exterminate Catalan culture was clearly a political message, but journalists had to be careful with their wording.

One of the most influential philosophers of the day, José Ortega y Gasset, saw the modern Catalan artworks as a representation of the overall European crisis: "Europa está en un momento de crisis. En arte, como en ciencia, como en política, todo está en crisis, en cuestión. Conviene orientarse, averiguar que va a ocurrir, porque—según la certera frase del Dante—'el dardo que se ve venir viene más despacio.'" (Europe is in a moment of crisis. In art, as in science, as in politics, everything is in crisis, in question. It behooves us to orient ourselves, think about what might come, because—according to this saying by Dante—"the dart that is coming our way is coming too slowly.")[58] Most critics agreed that this exhibit functioned as a window into the unknown. It was educational, it broadened horizons, it encouraged neighbors to get to know one another, it confronted old prejudices, and it demonstrated a shared spirit in the promotion of visual arts in general. For the critic Mendes Casal, the beauty of Spain was precisely in its huge range of differences, which should be celebrated rather than censored: "Que esta España tan varia muestra los matices más opuestos bellamente interesantes en vez de esa uniformidad engendradora de hastío estético que ofrecen algunas naciones europeas" (May this diverse Spain show its most beautifully interesting divergent shades, instead of this tired, false uniformity that other European nations offer.)[59] Most critics who reviewed this show in Madrid agreed that the strength of Spain was its cultural diversity. Mendes Casal, for one, was fearful to go in the direction of other European countries that were slowly becoming more culturally and linguistically homogenous, such as France and Italy.

The contributions made by the young Salvador Dalí to this exhibit—*Figure at a Window* (1925) and *Venus and Sailor (Homage to Salvat-Papasseit)* (1925)—visually sum up the discussion that developed in the newspapers and little magazines.[60] Both artworks literally and figuratively open windows. While the first, more naturalist, painting was popular among the general public and mainstream critics, the second picture, one of the largest in the show and cubist in style, stuck out like a sore thumb alongside the more realist and post-impressionist works of his fellow Catalan painters. Unlike the *Ibéricos*, no other painting in this show even remotely approached the cubist style; this contribution by Dalí was the only example. Cipriano Rivas Cherif, a playwright open to artistic change and devoted to the renewal of the Spanish stage, paid particular attention to Dalí's *Venus and Sailor* in a review in *El Heraldo* on January 21, 1926. Although Rivas Cherif preferred the more realist *Figure at a Window*, he noted the importance of the cubist *Venus*, a painting that he also considered "classic" because of its mythological theme, despite its (cubist) execution. He could read into the literary reference of the large painting, as it makes a direct reference in the subtitle to the avant-garde Catalan poet Joan Salvat-Papasseit, who had recently died from tuberculosis by the time of this exhibit. How much Rivas Cherif may have already known about Salvat-Papasseit or his poetry before he saw Dalí's painting is unknown. However, by making such a strong statement with this painting, Dalí encouraged his viewers to ask questions about the identity of this person named in its subtitle with such a unique name, especially if they were interested in unlocking the mysteries of the puzzling picture.

Dalí's *Figure at a Window* and *Venus and Sailor* share several key compositional features, namely the figure of a woman standing at an open window during daylight hours.[61] In one case, her back is turned to the viewer, while in the other she is facing (but not looking at) us. In both instances the window looks out over a body of water. In the case of the more naturalist picture (*Figure at a Window*), set in Cadaqués, the background depicts the sky, land, and sea; whereas in *Venus and Sailor*, the view out the window is only of the sea—the open Mediterranean as seen from a room in La Barceloneta port neighborhood of Barcelona. In the more realist work, the window and its view takes priority, since the subject has its back turned on us; while in the other work, the focus is on the male and female figures rather than on the window and its view. Besides representing the two opposing worlds of cubism and realism, these two canvases also suggest the opposing worlds of Cadaqués (rural Catalonia; tradition) and Barcelona (urban capital; modernity). The realist picture depicts a rural seascape and the cubist painting an urban one. Another contrast is that the female figure in *Figure*, most likely Ana María, Dalí's sister, stands alone; while in the other painting, a sailor embraces the mythological and goddess of love.

Figure at a Window functions like an "interior of an interior." Through a series of horizontal and vertical planes, the construction of space in this picture emphasizes the perspective of looking out to the sea, thus adding a great sense of depth to the image. Dalí extends the space on the canvas by painting the lines of the hard wood floors (one level of interiority), followed by the extended inner ledge of the window (second level), hundreds of lateral waves headed toward the viewer (third level), and finally, the land on the other side of the cove with at least three more planes of depth. The vertical blue lines on the figure's dress and the curtains stand in contrast to the horizontal planes. The wrinkled, white handkerchief to the left of the figure hangs precariously over the windowsill, maintaining its position both inside and outside of the pane as if the air were perfectly still. The depth of *Venus and Sailor*, on the other hand, is volumetric. Instead of the more traditional horizontal and vertical lines leading to one point in the distance, as in *Figure at a Window*, the images in the second canvas are constructed with overlaying circles, squares, and cylinders, giving the painting a different sense of depth, one that produces a feeling of closeness instead of distance. For a viewing public that was not accustomed to seeing live examples of cubism, this painting certainly must have been shocking. It also stood out among the *noucentista*-style paintings of his Catalan peers. Dalí made an impression in Madrid with this picture, which earned him bragging rights in Barcelona, where he would stage his first individual exhibit at the Dalmau Gallery only six months later.

The Last Modern Art Show of the Decade in Madrid and the Yellow Manifesto

After the success of the Modern Catalan Art show in 1926, a highly antici-pated art exhibit took place in Madrid three years later. For the first time in the history of modern Spanish art, works by Pablo Picasso, Juan Gris, and Joan Miró were shown collectively in Spain. This exhibit, titled Exposición de pinturas y esculturas de españoles residentes en París (Exhibition of Paint-ings and Sculptures by Spaniards Residing in Paris) brought together a group of artists known as the "Spanish School of Paris." These artists had been as-sociated with the French periodical Cahiers d'Art since 1926, and their iden-tity was forged as a result of their cohesion as a group and their similarity in style. The show took place in an exhibition space located in the area reserved for Spain's national botanical garden in Madrid. The show lasted only five days, from March 20 to 25, 1929. For the first time in Spain's history, this Spanish modern art collective gathered works by Picasso, Gris, and Miró, but also many other avant-garde painters, including Manuel Ángeles Ortiz, Francisco Bores, Mariano Cossío, Alfonso de Olivares, Benjamin Palencia, Joaquín Peinado, Pere Pruna, Ismael de Serna, José María Ucelay, Hernando Viñes, and Dalí, who stole the attention of the local press once again. The group of avant-garde sculptors represented was just as remarkable: Alberto Sánchez, Apel·les Fenosa, Pablo Gargallo, and Manuel Huguet. Of these artists and sculptors, four were Catalan (Dalí, Miró, Fenosa, Huguet). The organizing committee made a special exception for the three artists in the show who were not officially residents of Paris: Dalí, Alberto, and Palencia. A disclaimer in the catalog indicates that they were invited to participate because of their "ideological convictions, technical similarities and fraternal association to the others."[62]

The exhibition was organized by the Sociedad de Cursos y Conferencias (Society of Classes and Conferences), an organization associated with the Residencia de Estudiantes, where Dalí was once a resident. In addition to viewing the eighty-seven works on display, visitors could also attend two lec-tures. In the opening remarks by Corpus Bargas, he called for an elimination of all labels in the classification of modern art. He insisted that it was use-less to continue classifying works as naturalist, impressionist, cubist, futurist, or expressionist. For one, most of the Madrid viewing public could not tell the difference between these styles. If this collective was only the second in Madrid to display experimental techniques in line with avant-garde tendencies (the first being the Ibéricos), it is safe to say that the general viewing public in Madrid must have been quite illiterate in reading the languages of modern art.

Corpus Bargas reminds us that up until this point, Madrid still had not hosted an exhibition dedicated solely to cubism. Despite this absence in Madrid art shows, department stores were incorporating cubist-inspired styles into their window dressings: "*Ejerció su influencia (el cubismo) . . . sin haber sido comprendido, sin haber sido realmente vistos los cuadros cubistas*" (The influence of Cubism was making itself known . . . without having been understood, without really ever having seen cubist paintings.)[63] Madrid had fast-forwarded through the initial stages of the Avant-Garde and caught up to the rest of Europe in terms of incorporating this modern style and applying it to elements of everyday life. One-third of the works displayed at the *Ibéricos* show can be considered as representative of avant-garde art, while at the Modern Catalan Art exhibit six months later, only Dalí's *Venus and Sailor* can be considered as such. Given the minimal exposure of Madrid's public to avant-garde art, it is very unlikely that they were confident in their knowledge of expressionism, cubism, futurism, constructivism, vibrationism, dadaism, purism, surrealism, and their variants. Corpus Bargas probably also felt it was hopeless to use labels to categorize the regions of Spain where these artists were born (Catalonia, Asturias, Basque Country, Galicia, etc.), as had been done in the past. One way to avoid these labels was to choose a more generic and less political title: Spaniards Residing in Paris.

The impetus for this exhibit, as stated in the catalog's introduction, was to bring to Madrid those images and styles that had been reproduced in the artistic and literary magazines. The only Madrid residents who could have been remotely familiar with these artists and their work were those who contributed to or read these specialized periodicals. For the most part, the majority of Madrilenians were not accustomed to seeing art like that displayed in the Botanical Gardens, even as late as 1929.[64] Because this was the first time that all of these accomplished artists exhibited as a collective in Europe, the press in Madrid took note. The *Gaceta Literaria* insisted that modern art was here to stay and that state-run institutions and other governing bodies had to accept and respect this reality. This review also questions the nature of the "new politics" that would accompany the inevitable presence of this "new art" (*Gaceta Literaria*, April 1, 1929). However, the reviewer does not elaborate on this point. What politics was this journalist referring to? In Barcelona, Rafael Marquina (organizer of the Modern Catalan Art show) remarked on the show's great success in the journal *Mirador*. He pointed out that while the organizers of the exhibit expected the public to react to these works with hostility, the painters actually found themselves in the presence of buyers (*Mirador*, April 4, 1929). For Marquina, the revolution had already become conservative, since the aristocracy and bourgeoisie were purchasing paintings from a show that ten years earlier would have been scandalous.[65]

In the pages of the Mexican journal *Atlántico*, the Catalan art critic Sebastià Gasch did not have so many positive words for the works shown by his fellow Catalans (Dalí and Miró) in the Spaniards Residing in Paris show. Embedded between the lines of his overview of the state of Catalan art in 1929, he points out that neither one of these artists exhibited in Barcelona that year; instead, "Se han convencido ya de la inutilidad de ofrecer sus obras a un público desprovisto de las más elemental preparación" (They have convinced themselves already of the uselessness of presenting their works to a public that lacks the most elemental groundwork).[66] Gasch accuses both of these avant-garde artists of taking advantage of a public—both in Barcelona and Madrid—that for the most part lacked the foundation for understanding their work. Dalí took advantage of this inadequacy and preyed on the misunderstanding and insecurities of his wealthy public to sell his work. Gasch's disappointment in Dalí can be explained by the fact that exactly one year earlier, Dalí, Lluís Motanyà, and he published the Yellow Manifesto, subtitled the Anti-Artistic Catalan Manifesto (March 1928). According to Gasch, this document had the goal of exposing how far Catalonia had regressed in terms of its cultural progress. In retrospect, he wrote:

> We were more and more irritated by the absolute lack of preparation with which certain of our intellectuals treated artistic issues, the constant state of confusion and eclecticism into which they fell, their inordinate wish to reconcile what was irreconcilable, the deliquescent state of mind that reigned in some intellectual circles, and above all what we called the "pseudo-Hellenism" of a number of Catalan writers.[67]

Accordingly, the manifesto began with an attack on all those who represented and promoted contemporary Catalan bourgeois culture, especially Josep Maria Junoy's *La Nova Revista* and those at the Bernat Metge Foundation. Even under the Primo de Rivera dictatorship, this foundation continued its project of consolidating Catalan society through the translations of Greek and Latin classics into Catalan and other projects that Dalí, Gasch, and Montanyà found completely backwards. In the words of Dalí, "we can agree on absolutely NOTHING with the pigs and hairy intellectuals of Catalonia."[68]

The three authors of this infamous manifesto agreed in their disgust with the current state of the Catalan culture. Opposed to the classicism, naturalism, and realism of *noucentisme*, they insisted that the correct route toward modernization was through cinema, sports, jazz, fast cars, newspapers, and science. Similar to the pamphlet distributed prior to the Ibéricos exhibition four years earlier in Madrid—which is another reason to believe that Dalí was one of that pamphlet's authors—the Yellow Manifesto concludes with a list of authors and artists they emulated, including: Picasso, Gris, Ozenfant, Chirico, Miró, Lipchitz, Brancusi, Arp, Le Corbusier, Reverdy, Tzara, Eluard, Aragon, Desnos, Cocteau, Lorca, Stravinsky, Maritain, Raynal, Zervos, and Bretón. The artists who made both the Ibéricos (1925) and Yellow Manifesto (1929) lists were Picasso, Gris, Ozenfant, and Chirico. The Yellow Manifesto described the contemporary state of Catalan culture as "dangerous . . . fake . . . [and] adulterating" and its intellectual life in particular as "stagnating in a shrunken and putrefying atmosphere."[69]

By the end of the twenties, Dalí was on a roll. In the beach town of Sitges just outside of Barcelona, he joined a meeting of journalists from the cultural periodical *L'Amic de les Arts* to discuss the topic of avant-garde art and literature. At Sitges's recently inaugurated athenaeum, known as *El Centaure* (The Centaur), Dalí, along with Josep Carbonell, J. V. Foix, and Sebastià Gasch, gave a series of lectures. Dalí's talk (May 13, 1928), which was the most audacious by far, called for the demolition of the Gothic Quarter in Barcelona (to be replaced by architecture or reinforced concrete), the abolition of the *sardana* (Catalonia's national dance), and a rejection of anything that could be considered regional.[70] In autumn, Dalí gave another lecture, this time at the well-established Sala Parés in Barcelona, in conjunction with the third Autumn Salon on "Contemporary Catalan Art and its Relationship to the Latest Youthful Intelligence" (October 16, 1928). Again, his lecture created a considerable amount of controversy. A few days after the closing of Madrid's Botanical Gardens exhibit, Dalí's anti-artistic tantrums over the last twelve months (including abruptly ending his friendship with Lorca), culminated in the publication of the last issue of *L'Amic de les Arts* (March 31, 1929). Dalí grabbed the reins of this periodical he had conceived and to which he had regularly contributed, and used this final issue as a platform to announce his spiritual conversion to surrealism and his discovery of the subconscious. Dalí's friends, including Sebastià Gasch, Lluís Montanyà, Luis Buñuel, Pekín, and Andrés Bello, helped him complete the experimental issue by contributing various texts. With *L'Amic* in hand, Dalí traveled to Paris two weeks after the show in Madrid's Botanical Gardens closed. He was mounting his first individual art show in Paris (April) and helping his friend from the Residencia de Estudiantes in Madrid, Luis Buñuel, wrap up their first Surrealist film, *Un Chien Andalou*.[71] Now that Dalí had sufficiently burned most of his bridges in Spain, including those with his family, he was ready to seize the French capital.

Since his first trip to Paris, when he had visited Picasso in his studio, Dalí worked on making a name for himself in both the Madrid and Barcelona avant-garde networks at whatever cost. He accomplished this by contributing to as many avant-garde periodicals possible, as both a writer and illustrator; he expanded his network through linking Spanish and Catalan avant-garde circles by participating in creative collaborations, beyond painting, with like-minded individuals; he showed his paintings individually in select galleries of Barcelona and collectively in Madrid whenever he could; he authored several anti-artistic manifestos; he attended literary gatherings, even though this was not his favorite leisure activity; he gave outlandish talks at avant-garde conferences; he invited friends to his family's beach house in the breathtaking setting of Cadaqués; he emotionally conquered those whom he thought could catapult his career, including Gala, the wife of a French surrealist poet, who eventually divorced her husband, Paul Eluard, and abandoned their daughter in order to be with him. He built this road to Paris, where he would cling to the founders and foundations of French surrealism until he no longer had any use for them. He is known to have said that when he left his home in Spain, he no longer considered himself a Catalan, but a surrealist. Leaving what he considered decrepit behind him, he marched ahead with his work and his life, leaving much destruction behind him.

By the end of the twenties, most of the leaders of the artistic and literary avant-garde movement in Barcelona and Madrid had left Spain or prematurely passed away, including Pablo Picasso, Joan Miró, Juan Gris, Pablo Gargallo, Joaquín Torres-García, Rafael Barradas, Joan Salvat-Papasseit, Guillermo de Torre, Luis Buñuel, and Lorca (who temporarily moved to New York City in 1929). The only two major nodes of the Barcelona and Madrid avant-garde networks who remained in Spain were Ramón Gómez de la Serna and Ernesto Giménez Caballero. The Primo de Rivera dictatorship was reaching its end (1930) and the Second Spanish Republic (1931–36) would soon provide a much more open environment for radical ideas to flourish throughout Spain and Catalonia, like universal suffrage (including women's right to vote), divorce laws, civil marriage, the dissolution of the monarchy, the establishment of a secular state, and agrarian reform. These drastic changes that came about in Spain during the early 1930s did not materialize overnight. They were the result of the tense and volatile sociopolitical climate that characterized Spain for quite some time. Whether it was the chicken or the egg, the culture of the Avant-Garde was fundamental in preparing society, individually and collectively, for the major changes that would come about with the Second Spanish Republic.

More recently, an art exhibit dedicated to "Barcelona and Modernity" that showed in Cleveland and New York City made a point of distinguishing modern Catalan art from that of the rest of Spain by emphasizing its unique history. Much in the same way that Dalí's work was so unlike that of the other modern Catalan and "Iberian" artists in the collective shows of Madrid (1925, 1926), his paintings also stood out alongside those of his fellow Catalans in this contemporary show. The distinction that the curators of Barcelona and Modernity made between the modern and avant-garde artists was very clear. Modernism is a much more general term that encompasses a variety of styles—including those of the Avant-Garde, like cubism, futurism, dadaism, and surrealism—but also *noucentisme* and *modernisme*. The point they made was an important one: Dalí's paintings made more sense when they were placed in the context of other non-Catalan artists living in Barcelona, like Torres-García, Barradas, Picabia, Picasso, and Pablo Gargallo, because they all practiced avant-garde art. To place Dalí in the context of other Catalan artists living in Barcelona would have been to repeat the Modern Catalan Art show in Madrid almost a century before. The problem, however, lies in the curators' naming of the exhibit area. In the large room dedicated exclusively to "Catalan Avant-Garde Art," the only Catalan-born artists displayed were Dalí and Joan Miró. What remains to be seen is an art exhibition about the Avant-Garde as a whole in Spain; one that has progressed from the initial idea of the Society of Iberian Artists in Madrid almost one century ago; one that does not divide the art or the artists based on their nationality or their place of birth, but that is focused on the different avant-garde styles (including cubism, futurism, Dadaism, constructivism, planism, vibrationism, Ultraism, and surrealism) that so enriched Spain's—and the world's—visual legacy through the contribution of artists from all over Spain and the world. In this way, all may see that cubism was much more than just Picasso and surrealism more than Dalí. Others could see that the Avant-Garde in Spain was much more dynamic, interconnected, and stylistically diverse than what has been shown so far.

Notes

1. Dalí showed Picasso two of his paintings during his first trip to Paris: *Girl from Figueres* and *Departure (Homage to Fox Newsreel)*. For more details on this first encounter between Picasso and Dalí, please see Michael Raeburn, *Salvador Dalí: The*

Early Years (London: Thames and Hudson, 1994), 43; and Fèlix Fanés, *Salvador Dalí: The Construction of the Image 1925–1930* (New Haven and London: Yale University Press, 2007), 48–54.

2. *Noucentisme* was a Catalan cultural, political, and ideological movement that disagreed with the extravagance of Barcelona's *modernisme* fin-de-siècle movement (1888–1911), which is best exemplified in the architectural works of Antoni Gaudí.

3. A sincere concern for the overall state of the nation (whether Spain or Catalonia) can be found in literature throughout the first few decades of the twentieth century in all parts of Spain. Notably, the writers who form the group known as the Generation of '98 agonized about the present and future of Spain; they were often filled with nostalgia for a once-glorious, if illusory, past. Those involved with *noucentisme* in Barcelona also looked to the past for answers. On the other hand, the young and spirited avant-garde poets and painters in both Barcelona and Madrid were anything but nostalgic.

4. Reports of cubism in the Barcelona press can be found in journals and newspapers from 1912 through 1918. Some of these periodicals include: *Revista Nova, Trossos, La Veu de Catalunya,* and *El Día Gráfico.*

5. The cover illustration of the first issue of Picabia's *391* periodical published in Barcelona combines word and image to communicate a puzzling message. The image was created and signed by Picabia, "the saint of saints." His use of religious vocabulary to identify himself as a leader of the Dada movement in Barcelona suggests that for Picabia, Dada was more than a fad; it was a spiritual calling. The words included in the image spell out "girlfriend" in Spanish, followed by a French subtitle stating: "The first occupant." The bilingual title, however, is not followed by an image of a traditional female figure. Instead, the object is a mechanized body consisting of several wheels and rods, imitating a pulley system. The rupture of this image occurs between the signifier and the signified. We expect to see a traditional female figure after reading the title, but instead there is an image of a machine. This break in meaning suggests that life had become so industrialized, hostile, and cold that even humans had turned into machines, and their relationships were mechanical.

6. Hugo Ball wrote in his diary: "Dada is 'yes, yes' in Romanian, 'rocking horse or hobby horse' in French. For Germans it is a sign of foolish naiveté, joy in procreation and love of the baby carriage." As stated in the catalog for a recent Dada exhibit in the United States, the Dadaists delighted in the multiple meanings of the movement's name as it crossed linguistic boundaries of the nations at war. "Dada. Zurich, Berlin, Cologne, Hanover, New York, Paris," February 19 to May 14, 2006, the National Gallery of Art, Washington, D.C.; the Centre Pompidou, Paris; and the Museum of Modern Art, New York, 2.

7. For a detailed account of the contact between Barradas and the futurists in Italy, such as his meeting with Marinetti, please see Molas, *Literatura catalana,* 91.

8. http://www.fundaciontelefonica.com/en/arteytecnologia/colecciones_de_arte/cubismo/lagar.htm

9. Joaquín Torres-García describes his friendship with Rafael Barradas in his autobiography: Joaquín Torres-García, *Historia de mi vida* (Barcelona: Paidós, 1939).

10. Willards Bohn, *The Aesthetics of Visual Poetry 1914–1928* (Cambridge: Cambridge University Press, 1986), 16.

11. Santos Torroella, 1965, 206.

12. The friends represented in Dalí's *Sueños noctábulos* (1922) include Barradas, Luis Buñuel, Pepín Bello, Maruja Mallo, and Dalí himself.

13. Barradas illustrated several other *ultraísta* books of poetry, such as *Rompecabezas* (1921) by Luis Mosquera and *Bazar* (1922) by Francisco Luis Bernárdez; see Bonet, *Diccionario*, 88.

14. We should not forget that Barradas also had a sister, Carmen, an accomplished pianist who also performed in both Barcelona and Madrid and was very well regarded by her brother's peers.

15. Molas, *Literatura Catalana*, 16.

16. Recently a drawing by Lorca and Barradas has been discovered and purchased by a private collector. For more information on the picture and the image, see "El País digital," which was also the source of the Lorca quotation (accessed February 2011): http://www.elpais.com.uy/Suple/DS/08/03/30/sds_337982.asp.

17. The birth of modern art can be explained in part by the establishment of an alternative system in opposition to the Academy, as was the case with the private galleries and art merchants. This system placed rules on art and created hierarchies. It normalized art and controlled the production and sharing of art up until the French Revolution. As was the case in Paris with its Salons, the Academy in Spain possessed a monopoly on the organization of periodical exhibitions as one of the most effective methods for the diffusion of art. Independent groups went to great lengths to avoid this control. The Academy was associated with an absolute centralism, as well as a rigid, dogmatic monopoly on artistic creation. In a way, with the onset of the Industrial Era, art dealers and their galleries arise as the new cultural agents in opposition to the Academy offering an alternative to the establishment.

18. Vidal i Oliveras organizes Dalmau's career into four stages: (1) importer of foreign art (1911–13); (2) promoter of innovative local art (1911–15); (3) promoter of innovative, local art, especially by young Catalan artists, as well as avant-garde artists displaced during the First World War (1915–17); and (4) promoter of young artists and of innovative Catalan art outside of Catalonia (1918–23).

19. These exhibitions occurred regularly in Barcelona, with two exceptions. The first was in 1898, after the fourth exhibition, starting up again in 1907 with the fifth. The second break took place in 1923 after the *Exposición Municipal* in June, as a result of Primo de Rivera's new rules. These exhibits would not resume until 1932 with the arrival of the Second Republic.

20. An extension of the Asociació d'Amics de les Arts hosted its first Saló Tardor (Autumn Salon) in 1918. Other salons include the Saló of Els Noucentistse, which began in 1922; the Conreadors de les Arts (1924); and the Saló Tardor organized by the Sala Parés (1926).

21. One year later, in January 1917, the Asociación de Artistas Vascos traveled to Barcelona. These were some of the first instances that artists in Barcelona and Bilbao

witnessed the great diversity of new schools that were developing simultaneously all over Spain.

22. Gabriel Maroto, *El año artístico* (Madrid: José Fernández Arias, 1913), 101.

23. Some of the artists who exhibited their works were Andreu, Apa, Arteta, Bagaría, Bilbao, Canals, Clará, Echevarría, Lagar, Lhardy, Llimona, Riba, Romero de Torres, Zubiaurre, and Zuloaga. French illustrators like Forain, Faivre, Herman, Leandre, Paul, and Jean Weber also showed their work.

24. In addition to the artists already listed, a group of writers and intellectuals from Spain also signed the anti-Germany manifesto, including: Luis Araquistáin, Manuel Azaña, Miguel Blay, Pérez Galdos, and Miguel Unamuno ("Los antigermanófilos. Manifesto," *El Liberal*. Madrid. January 7, 1917.)

25. José Ortega y Gasset founded *España* in January 1915. Its regular contributors included journalists from various areas of Spain, including Luis Araquistáin, Manuel Azaña, Eugenio d'Ors, Ramiro de Maetzu, and Ramón del Valle-Inclán. In 1916 Luis Araquistáin, who was actively involved in drafting the anti-German-sympathizer manifesto, took over the magazine's direction. After the publication of said manifesto, *España* became one of the leading voices for those opposed to Germany during World War I.

26. Brihuega, *Las vanguardias artísticas*, 250.

27. The artists who participated in this exhibition were H. Arp, T. Arp, Blaire, Cochet, Cupera, Clergé, Charchoune, van Doesburg, Eusel Rozier, Freundlich, L. Fernandez, Helion, Jouglar, Lhote André, Marembert, Nilbauer, Mondrian, van Rees, Vantongerloo, O. Weber, Xceron, Basiana, Biosca, Creixams, Carbonell, Casanova, Corberó, Costa, Claret, Daura, Ferrer, Folquer, Garay, Guell, Grau Sala, Homs, Junyer, Lamor, Cañete, Morató Luis, J. M. Puig, Pablo Planas, J. Papiol, Angel Planell, Reig, Sandalinas, Sucre, Torres-García, Vidal, and Miguel Villa.

28. J. Moreno Villa, "Nuevos artistas. Primera Exposición de la Sociedad de Artistas Ibéricos," *Revista de Occidente*, July 1925, 80–81; also see Fanés, *Construction of the Image*, 12.

29. José-Carlos Mainer, *La edad de plata 1902–1931. Ensayos de interpretación de un proceso cultural* (Barcelona: Libros de la Frontera, 1975), 194.

30. The catalogue for the Museo Nacional Centro de Arte Reina Sofía's *Ibéricos* (1996) states that in 1925 this show marked an end to the "radicalismo neófito" of Spain's artistic avant-garde in the first quarter of the century. The anonymous author of the catalogue description may be referring to avant-garde artists residing in Paris (e.g., Picasso, Gris, Miró), because the only artists who were from Spain and living in Spain who were exhibiting avant-garde art in any sort of major venue until this exhibit had only shown in Barcelona.

31. Juan de la Encina (1883–1963) was the art critic for Bilbao's literary magazine *Hermes* (1917–22), known as the publication that modernized the Basque national movement (García García and Segura, 49); and in 1919 he was the curator of the *Exposición Internacional de Pintura y Escultura* (1919).

32. In February 1923, the Círculo de Bellas Artes, a private club dedicated to the arts, located in the center of Madrid, hosted an exhibit of the Sociedad Artístico Literaria de Cataluña. One month later, the Catalan art critic Plandiura announced his willingness to become part of the organizing committee of the Salón de Independientes (which, as mentioned earlier, eventually evolved into the SAI). Over the next couple of years, a slim picking of Catalan painters enjoyed individual exhibits in Madrid, including Ramón Pitxot (May 1924); Rafael Durán i Camps (December 1924); and Joaquim Sunyer (January 1925).

33. Those who signed the revised version of the SAI manifesto included José Bergamín, Rafael Bergamín, Emiliano Barral, Francisco Durrio, Joaquín Enríquez, Oscar Esplá, Manuel de Falla, Federico García Lorca, Victorio Macho, Cristóbal Ruiz, Adolfo Salazar, Ángel Sánchez Rivero, Joaquín Sunyer, Guillermo de Torre, and Daniel Vázquez Díaz.

34. See *La Sociedad de Artistas Ibericos y el arte espanol de 1925* (Madrid: Ambit, 1996).

35. As Fèlix Fanés has pointed out in *The Construction of the Image*, the works that Dalí exhibited cannot all be identified with certainty. According to the catalogue, he showed ten works at the SAI: *Portrait, Portrait of Luis Buñuel* (1924), *Bather* (1924), *Female Nude* (1924), and six *Still Lives*. Fanés has classified four of these as "naturalist" and the other six as "cubist" (Fanés, *Construction of the Image*, 17). The most problematic is the *Portrait*, which Fanés believes is what we know today as *Seated Girl from the Back*, also known in its day as *Portrait of the Artist's Sister*. However, others have argued that it is a more cubist portrait, as indicated in the appendix. Of the six still lifes that Dalí showed at the Ibéricos, only three can be identified with certainty. Fanés situates them midway between the cubist or semi-cubist tendencies of that period and the works of the Italian metaphysical painters of *Valori Plastici*. Among them is *Siphon and Bottle of Rum*, which would soon belong to the poet Federico García Lorca. The second *Still Life* (1924–25) falls into the sphere of influence of Ozenfant and Jeanneret's purism. The third work that can be identified is *Still Life with Watermelon* (1924), perhaps the most cubist of the three (see Fanés, *Construction of the Image*, 12, 14, 17). A few months later, Dalí celebrated his first one-man exhibit at the Dalmau Galleries in Barcelona (November 14–27, 1925). He showed fifteen paintings—*Seated Girl Seen from the Back, Figure at a Window, Portrait of Ramonets Montsalvatje, Portrait of My Father, Empordà Landscape with Figures, Cadaqués Landscape*, two entitled *Portrait of My Sister, Figure in Profile, Still Life, Figure on a Panel, Portrait of Maria Carbona, Venus and Sailor (Homage to Salvat-Papasseit)*, and *Pierrot and Guitar*—and five drawings: *Nude on the Beach, Portraits, Nudes* (1925), *Portrait of Puig Pujades* (1924), and *Landscape* (1925) (Raeburn, *The Early Years*, 27). Fanés classifies fourteen of these as "naturalist" and the remaining three as "cubist"; see Fanés, *Construction of the Image*, 17. In other words, Dalí placed more weight on his cubist works in Madrid in comparison to his show in Barcelona, where cubism was probably seen as *passé*.

36. Javier Pérez Segura, "Anatomía de un re-encuentro: el 'arte catalán moderno' en Madrid," in *La Sociedad de Aristas Ibéricos y el arte español de 1925* (Madrid: Ambit, 1996) and *Arte moderno, vanguardia y estado: La Sociedad de Artistas Ibéricos y la República (1931–1936)* (Madrid: Consejo Superior de Investigaciones Científicas, 2002).

37. Please see Brihuega's article in the exhibit catalogue for the 1996 *Ibéricos* commemorative show hosted in Madrid; Brihuega, "La ESAI y el arte español," in *La Sociedad de Aristas Ibéricos y el arte español de 1925* (Madrid: Ambit, 1996), 22.

38. El Palacio de Hielo was the same place where the state-run art competitions were held (such as the Exposiciones Nacionales and the Salones de Otoño) and where its winners were awarded, thus associating it even more with the dictatorship.

39. *La Sociedad de Aristas Ibéricos y el arte español de 1925* (Madrid: Ambit, 1996).

40. The protest was denouncing their failure to appoint the Basque painter Daniel Vázquez Díaz to a professorship there. Vázquez Díaz would later purchase Dalí's *Venus y marinero. Homenage a Salvat-Papasseit*—one of the two works Dalí exhibited at the Catalan Modern Art exhibit one year later.

41. See *El Heraldo*, January 18, 1926.

42. Pérez Segura notes that in 1926 the *Heraldo de Madrid* changed ownership to a Catalan business whose legal advisor was the politician Amadeo Hurtado, who was one of the paper's main "ideological inspirers." Subsequently, the new direction of the newspaper gained favor in Barcelona. See "En la vida en la corte . . ." (Anonymous, *El Día Gráfico*, Barcelona, February 21, 1926; Segura, "Anatomía de un re-encuentro," p. 79). "In Madrid, Dalí's main supporters were the Marquina family. Rafael Marquina was a journalist on *El Heraldo de Madrid* and the city's correspondent for *La Veu de Catalonia*, in which he published various articles on the Exposición de los Artistas Ibéricos. Rafael Marquina had translated d'Ors' 1911 novel *La ben plantada* (The Handsome Woman) from Catalan into Castilian" (Fanés, *Construction of the Image*, 18). Eduardo Marquina, a relative of Rafael Marquina, was a well-known playwright at the time.

43. At the closing of the exhibit, Marquina announced that the next collective art collection he would bring to Madrid would be of artists from the Asturias region of Spain.

44. See "Iniciativas de 'Heraldo de Madrid,'" in *Heraldo de Madrid*, January 18, 1926.

45. See original catalog for the exhibit, *Residentes espanoles en Paris*, March 20 to April 15, 1929, Madrid, Sociedad de Cursos y Conferencias.

46. For a list of the painters who exhibited at the Modern Catalan Art show in Madrid, please see appendix B.

47. Reports of this exhibit can be found in the following primary sources: A. Méndez Casal, "En el Círculo de Bellas Artes. Catalonia y su Arte Contemporáneo," *Blanco y Negro*, February 7, 1926; *Heraldo de Madrid*, Jan. 15, 16, 18, 19, 20, 21, 22, 23, 25, 26, 28, 29, and Feb. 1; Rafael Marquina, *La Veu de Catalonia*, Jan. 16, 23, 24, 26, 27, 29, and 31.

48. See *El Heraldo*, January 16, 1926.

49. In *La Veu de Catalonia*, Rafael Benet could not find a place for Dalí within the Catalan tradition represented in Madrid, and therefore situated the "intelligent terseness" of the painter in the orbit of the Madrid "intelligentsia"; see Rafael Benet, "Salvador Dalí," *La Veu de Catalunya*, November 27, 1925. Thus, Benet "consigned Dalí to the Madrilenian intellectual elite—a poisoned dart given Benet's conservative Catalanist views" (Fanés, *Construction of the Image*, 29).

50. *Ciutat*, 40.

51. Joan Colom, *Ciutat*, 40.

52. Rafael Doménech, "Exposiciones de arte," ABC, 8.

53. *Heraldo de Madrid*, January 22, 1926.

54. Paszkiewicz and Rivas Cherif.

55. José Francés, *Heraldo de Madrid*, January 22, 1920.

56. Cartagena.

57. ABC, "Clausura de la exposición," February 2, 1926.

58. Ortega y Gasset, "Clausura de la exposición." *El Heraldo de Madrid*, February 1, 1926.

59. Méndez Casal, "En el Círculo de Bellas Artes."

60. By the time Dalí showed *Venus and Sailor*, Salvat-Papasseit had already published three avant-garde periodicals (*Un Enemic del poble*, 1917; *Arc-Voltaic*, 1918; *Proa*, 1921); published six books of poetry (*Poemas en ondes hertzianes*, 1919; *L'irradiador del por i les gavines*, 1921; *Les conspiracions*, 1922; *La gesta dels estels*, 1922; *El poema de la rosa als llavis*, 1923; *Óssa Menor*, posthumous, 1925); and some of his poems had appeared in Madrid's Ultra movement's little magazines (*Grecia*, 1920; *Ultra*, 1922; and *Tableros*, 1922).

61. Windows (and suggestions of windows) appeared often in Dalí's early interiors from this time period (e.g., *Pierrot and Guitar*, 1925; *Still Life by Moonlight*, 1926; *Still Life by Mauve Moonlight*, 1926; *Watermelon and Mandolin*, 1926).

62. See original catalog for the exhibit, *Residentes espanoles en Paris*.

63. Corpus Bargas, *Residentes espanoles en Paris*.

64. The first showing of cubism in any sort of collective way in Madrid was a show organized by Ramón Gómez de la Serna in 1915, called Exposición de Pintores Íntegros. Unlike Dalmau's revolutionary show in 1912 (Barcelona), Ramón was only able to secure works by four artists: Luis Bagaría, whose works I have not yet seen; Agustón Choco, on whom I have not been able to find more information; María Blanchard, who was in exile from World War I at the time; and Diego Rivera, a young artist from Mexico, also living in Madrid at the time. Rivera's portrait of Ramón shown at this exhibit is worth greater consideration.

65. For instance, duchesses purchased two of Dalí's five paintings on display. The five Dalí paintings on display at the Spaniards Residing in Paris Show in Madrid (1929) included: *Apparatus in Hand*, *Cenicitas*, *Nude*, *Honey is Sweeter than Blood*, and *Masculine and Feminine Figures on Beach*. Two of his paintings were sold, both purchased by duchesses (*Honey* and *Masculine and Feminine Figures*).

66. Sebastià Gasch, "*Atlántico*," in Ernesto Giménez Caballero, *Cataluña ante España* (Madrid: La Gaceta Literaria, 1930), 107.

67. Translation by Fanés, *Construction of the Image*, 85. S. Gasch, "Un 'manifest' i un 'full groc,'" *Serra d'Or* 107 (1968): 27–30.

68. Letter from Dalí to Gasch, cited by Gasch in "Un 'manifest' i un 'full groc,'" 27–30, and in Fanés, *Construction of the Image*, 85.

69. Salvador Dalí, *Oui. The Paranoid-Critical Revolution. Writings 1927–1933*, ed. Robert Descharnes, trans. Yvonne Shafir (Boston: Exact Change, 1998), 48, 49.

70. Raeburn, *The Early Years*, 34.

71. Luis Buñuel and Dalí had met at the beginning of the year in Dalí's hometown of Figueres to co-author the script, which they completed in one week.

CHAPTER SIX

~

The Quixotic Quest of
Ernesto Giménez Caballero

The objective of this book is to pay closer attention to those who linked the avant-garde circles of Barcelona and Madrid through their professional or personal relationships. In the preceding chapters, many of the individuals involved in the creation and promotion of avant-garde activity in both of these cities have been mentioned or discussed in detail. Before concluding, let us recapitulate. So far, we have seen the following individuals affiliated with Barcelona functioning as bridges with the avant-garde network in Madrid: Rafael Barradas, Salvador Dalí, Josep Dalmau, Sebastià Gasch, Lluís Montanyà, Joan Salvat-Papasseit, Sebastià Sánchez-Juan, Josep Maria Sucre, and Joaquín Torres García. Those representing Madrid who connected with the avant-garde network of Barcelona include: Federico García Lorca, Ernesto Giménez Caballero, Ramón Gómez de la Serna, and Guillermo de Torre. In comparison, there were more promoters of the Avant-Garde in Barcelona who made contact or more actively collaborated with Madrid's network than the other way around. Be that as it may, the extraordinary efforts of one man from Madrid to connect with the avant-garde network in Barcelona are unparalleled. What follows is an account of the ways in which he, Ernesto Giménez Caballero (1899–1988), became almost obsessed with connecting Barcelona and Madrid. This final chapter also explains his motives and analyzes the results.

The Madrid native had many careers: soldier, writer, editor, novelist, and teacher. This chapter shows how all of these facets of his professional life were connected and influenced one another. Ernesto Giménez Caballero, or Géce, as he liked to be called, launched his pan-Iberian and multilingual periodical, *La Gaceta Literaria*, in January 1927. For nearly six years, he consistently published two issues of this magazine each month. Each issue consisted of eight pages, was printed on a large folio, and included black-and-white photographs and illustrations. *La Gaceta Literaria* was one of the only periodicals from Madrid dedicated to supporting and promoting avant-garde culture during the second half of the General Miguel Primo de Rivera dictatorship (1923–30).[1] This periodical was responsible for most of Madrid's cultural activities related to avant-garde happenings that year, such as contests, banquets, and art shows. When the first issue of *La Gaceta Literaria* (1927–32) appeared in Madrid, most literary journals devoted to the new poetry of writers like Federico García Lorca, Juan Larrea, and Guillermo de Torre were being published in Spanish cities outside of Barcelona and Madrid, like Sitges, Murcia, and Tenerife.[2] In Madrid, *Ultraísmo* was out of fashion, as were experiments with futurism, dadaism, and cubism in Barcelona. Like other European cities during the interwar years, Spain was experiencing a return to artistic order.

Also in 1927, Giménez Caballero launched a publishing company associated with *La Gaceta Literaria*, called the Biblioteca Iberia (Iberian Library). Its first publication was a Spanish translation of the fourth poetry book written by the Catalan poet Tomàs Garcés.[3] Giménez Caballero also published two books of his own: *Los toros, las castañuelas y la virgen* (Bulls, Castanets, and The Virgin) and *Carteles* (Posters). The first is a collection of essays about the merits of Castilian culture; the second is a series of book reviews, some of which are in visual form, as explained later in this chapter. All three of these publications coincide with Giménez Caballero's quest to define a more modern Spanish identity in line with the complexities of the new century. The publication of Garcés's book shows Giménez Caballero's determination to include Catalan culture in this new version of Spanish identity.

In a lengthy article published in *La Gaceta Literaria*, the literary critic Melchor Fernández Almagro announced the publication of Garcés's book.[4] In this article the critic introduces the Catalan author and his work to those who might be unfamiliar with this poet. He concludes by explaining that the decision that the first book published by Biblioteca Ibérica would be by a Catalan author was not just made for literary reasons. Publishing Garcés's book was also politically motivated: "El porvenir de la espiritualidad hispánica dependerá de las relaciones que acierten a mantener entre si los pueblos peninsulares" (The future of Hispanic spirituality depends on the relationships that can be maintained between the cultures of the Iberian Peninsula). On the one hand, by publishing the work of a Catalan poet, readers in Madrid could learn more about the literature of Barcelona, and thus they could become more understanding toward their neighbors to the north. On the other hand, publishing the work of a Catalan was a gesture to Barcelona, so that they too might publish more works by Spanish authors.

The critic argues that just because the Catalan press, publishing companies, and bookstores turned their backs on Spain's capital did not mean that Madrid should be shut out of Barcelona's literary world. As the last line of the review suggests, in publishing a book by a Catalan poet, Giménez Caballero was not only demonstrating a willingness to participate legitimately in Barcelona's literary movement, but he was also proving that he had the publishing capacity to do so. It was Giménez Caballero's desire to prove to the rest of Spain that Madrid was more than just "españolísimo" (super-Spanish) and that neither he nor his staff were going to accept Barcelona's disdain and disregard toward them. Moreover, they were not going to allow Barcelona to "asphyxiate" Madrid's literary movement. Fernández Almagro ends the article with a warning: the truth is that if anyone suffocates, it will be those who isolate themselves, whether in Barcelona or Madrid.

Before *La Gaceta Literaria*

Before becoming such a dominant figure in Madrid's avant-garde network, Giménez Caballero had been a soldier. Only a few months before King Alfonso XIII granted General Miguel Primo de Rivera permission to capture Spain by taking over the city of Barcelona, Giménez Caballero published a series of notes describing his combat experiences while serving in Morocco. The unpopularity of this war turned out to be Spain's greatest colonial disaster since the embarrassing loss of Cuba, the Philippines, Puerto Rico, and Guam to the United States in the Spanish-American War of 1898. Spain's humiliating defeat by Rif tribesmen resulted in the dissatisfaction of many Spaniards, which in turn became one of the main factors behind Primo de Rivera's rise to power. While in Morocco, Giménez Caballero kept a diary of his experiences, from the moment he departed from the southern port of Cádiz in 1921 until his safe return eighteen months later. Using the equipment available to him at his father's printing press, and at his father's expense, Giménez Caballero printed five hundred copies of his first book: *Notas marruecas de un soldado* (Notes by a Soldier in Morocco).

When Giménez Caballero asked the writer Azorín, a member of the Generation of '98, to pen a prologue, his former professor warned him that the book had the potential to cause Giménez Caballero serious trouble. In defiance of his teacher's warning, the young veteran published his book anyway. In February 1922 the twenty-three-year-old Giménez Caballero launched the first of many publicity campaigns in what turned out to be a long career. The young author sent his book to some of the most distinguished writers and intellectuals who supported Spain's modernist cultural movement, such as Miguel de Unamuno and Eugeni d'Ors. Less than two weeks later, the existing Spanish government, led by Prime Minister Álvaro de Figueroa y Torres, also known as the Conde de Romanones, arrested Giménez Caballero and punished him for the publication of this book with an eighteen-year prison term.

Luckily for Giménez Caballero, Primo de Rivera's overthrow of the Spanish government saved him from serving time in jail. Once in power, the dictator purportedly telephoned the young author, dropped all charges, and asked for his collaboration. Since Giménez Caballero was unwilling to enter into a partnership with the proto-fascist leader, he fled to the Alsace region of France, where he had lived before serving as a soldier. Once he was there, the University of Strasbourg rehired him as a lecturer in Spanish. What offended the government was probably the book's bold conclusion: a manifesto addressed to all of the young veterans of the Morocco war. In tune with so many other nationalist social movements throughout Europe, Giménez Caballero called veterans to unite "under the bound sheaf of grain."[5] Allegedly, at the time he wrote this epilogue, he was unaware of the parallelisms between his choice of imagery and the symbols of fascism and communism. Yet, the manifesto was dated December 1922, only a few months after a military coup had brought Benito Mussolini to power in Italy. This initial manifesto sheds light on Giménez Caballero's sociopolitical mindset five years prior to the founding of *La Gaceta Literaria*. For one, it reveals the first signs of the highly demagogical tendencies that continued to develop over the course of his life. It also sheds light on his early ideas for solving Spain's political weaknesses and negotiating its identity crisis.

The contents of this early literary text may explain why the Primo de Rivera government dismissed the charges against him. The manifesto called for the unification of all the Spanish veterans of the war in Morocco. The author pleaded with his fellow soldiers to transcend their regional differences. Douglas Foard reminds us of the strained relationship between Catalans and the rest of Spain: "Catalans, in particular, had become so disenchanted living under a government dominated by Castilian interest that they made serious representations to the Paris Peace Conference in 1919 on behalf of Catalan independence."[6] According to the manifesto's author, now that the battle in North Africa had ended, Spaniards had to find another common goal: a united Spain. Giménez Caballero feared that Basque,

Catalan, Galician, Asturian, and Castilian veterans would lose sight of the sense of national unity that is required when in war. He worried that these veterans might now only concern themselves with matters of daily life specific to their respective regions. He believed that this loss in their sense of purpose on a national and international level would result in unavoidable and deadly civil strife. Giménez Caballero feared Spain's lack of unity, and his solution to prevent Spain's total disintegration was to mount a national campaign for the unification of Iberia. Five years after he dated this manifesto, he created a platform to carry out this initiative—*La Gaceta Literaria*.

Negotiating a New Iberian Identity

The fear of a fragmented Spain, as seen through the eyes of a young soldier, can help us understand why one of the main goals of *La Gaceta Literaria* was to include other languages and literatures of the Iberian Peninsula, especially those of the Catalans, but also those of the Portuguese, Basques, Galicians, and even the Sephardic Jews. Giménez Caballero also considered Latin America to be part of Iberia, so he included this area of the world in his vision of a united Spain as well. Although he presented this totalitarian view of Iberia as one of his original ideas, several periodicals in Spain from the first decade of the century had already attempted to establish and maintain some sort of sustained dialogue with the other regions and languages of the peninsula, as mentioned in the fourth chapter of this book.[7]

Giménez Caballero's *Gaceta Literaria* is remarkable in that it was the first periodical published in Madrid that was successful in sustaining a relationship with a group of patrons and other collaborators in Barcelona. This former Spanish teacher and military-veteran-turned-magazine-editor insisted on including the Catalans not only in an effort to be innovative, or avantgarde, but primarily because he firmly believed in building a united Spain. In his mind, unity would be achieved through the cooperation and mutual understanding of Spain's distinct pluralities. In the four years between the publication of his notes from Morocco and the launching of his periodical, Giménez Caballero developed his ideas of a more united Spain through his journalism as well as through his work as a Spanish lecturer abroad. After *La Gaceta Literaria* closed, Giménez Caballero confessed in his guide book to Spain, *Trabalenguas* (Tongue Twisters) (1931), that he had always longed to expand Hispanism: "El ansia de expansión hispánica—en mí siempre constante—me llevó, a los veinte años, de profesor de español a la Universidad de Estrasburgo" (The longing for a Hispanic expansion, always constant within me, took me, at the age of twenty, to teach Spanish at the University of Strasbourg).[8] This yearning was also one of his main motivations for launching his periodical, *La Gaceta Literaria*.

As soon as Giménez Caballero was saved from his prison sentence for the publication of his Moroccan wartime memoir, he spent a second year teaching Spanish in Strasbourg. In the remaining years before the first issue of *La Gaceta Literaria* appeared, he wrote for newspapers in Madrid and made professional contacts in the avant-garde network there. In a review in *El Sol* of the literary gathering at the Pombo Café, for example, Giménez Caballero commended Ramón Gómez de la Serna for transforming Madrid into "the capital of Spain" by liberating its literary scene from its smothering provincialism. Pombo was the place where Madrid was "transfigured" into a modern city. Through his work as a journalist in Madrid, besides meeting Gómez de la Serna, Giménez Caballero also made the acquaintance of the person who would become the future secretary of his periodical, Guillermo de Torre. Giménez Caballero met him in 1925 after reviewing his *Literaturas europeas de vanguardia*.

As mentioned earlier, *Literaturas europeas de vanguardia* was the first book-length study in Spanish that presents a panoramic picture of the literary avant-garde movements throughout Europe. Notably, it omits Catalonia entirely, but includes Madrid's *Ultraísmo* movement. After this publication, the word "vanguardia" (avant-garde) came into more frequent use in Madrid, even though the term had already made its way into the vocabulary of Barcelona at least ten years earlier. In his review, Giménez Caballero celebrated modern times, especially faster and more effective ways to communicate. He saw these technological advances as fundamental to achieving the unity he desired for Spain: "¡Todos somos unos ya! ¡Viva la comunicación y el dinamismo!" (We are all one now! Long live communication and dynamism!).[9] The modern era meant improved communication; comfortable travel; youthful enthusiasm, vigor, and energy; and speed—all of which were elements for helping Giménez Caballero obtain his goal of a united Spain, as stated in the epilogue of his *Notes by a Moroccan Soldier*. Therefore, modern technology and the avant-garde culture that celebrated it became his tools for creating a less culturally divided Spain, with the ultimate objective of resolving Spain's sociopolitical crisis.

After reading and reviewing Guillermo de Torre's survey of avant-garde literature, Giménez Caballero gained a greater understanding of the ideas behind this new style of writing. And it was not long before he implemented them in strengthening his own thinking, in order to create a following and become, in a sense, the captain general of the united Spain of his dreams. In contrast to his predecessors, who had founded periodicals concerned with the "spiritual" unification of Spain (Enrique Díez Canedo, Manuel Azaña,

Cipriano Rivas Cherif, Enrique González Martínez, and others), Giménez Caballero was proposing more than just a magazine. He was mounting a major cultural project whose main goal was to unify Spain under the banner of the Avant-Garde.

Even though Giménez Caballero would say time and time again that this periodical was apolitical, the symbiotic relationship between his political and aesthetic pursuits is evident from early on. Giménez Caballero's plan to bring harmony to Spain through his magazine consisted of four main goals: (1) to be a source of news for the Iberian Peninsula and Latin America; (2) to be free of imperialisms and nationalisms; (3) to promote all of the Iberian languages; and (4) to strengthen relationships with Latin America. Concerned that those outside of Madrid would see him and his periodical as just another example of the capital's centralist policies, Giménez Caballero assured his investors that this was not the case. His pitch to financial sponsors was that even though the periodical was edited in Madrid, his magazine would avoid hegemonic behaviors. He promised to be open to the rest of Spain and to be respectful toward the local in his effort to be universal. One concrete way he would achieve these goals would be by publishing all of the peninsula's languages in their original form, without translations.

To convince his potential Catalan readers and patrons that there was no political motive behind his decision to incorporate their language in his periodical, Giménez Caballero traveled to Barcelona shortly before the first issue was printed. In December 1926, he introduced himself to Catalan intellectuals and financiers. He presented his business plan for the bimonthly journal and requested their support. According to a contemporary account by the scholar Miguel Ángel Hernando, Giménez Caballero arrived in Barcelona with a recommendation letter from Nicolás de Urgoiti, director of Spain's daily newspaper in Madrid, *El Sol*, and founder of the company Papelera Española (Spanish Paper Company).[10] This letter was addressed to Víctor Sabater, who was a Catalan printer, as well as a friend of Sebastià Gasch, Salvador Dalí, and Lluís Montanyà. In turn, Sabater organized a reception for the young entrepreneur from Madrid at a private club on the Paseo de Gracià. It was at this undisclosed location that the editor of *La Gaceta Literaria* was granted access to all of the leading figures of a certain sector of Barcelona's cultural elite associated with *noucentisme*, including Joan Esterlich, Nicolau Fabra, Carles Riba, Rovira i Virgili, Gaziel (pseudonym for Agusti Calvet Pascual), and others associated with the Bernat Metge Foundation. As mentioned earlier, one of the main enterprises of this Catalan organization was a publishing company that specialized in translating foundational Greek and Latin texts into Catalan.

The significance of Giménez Caballero's initial contact and eventual partnership with the Bernat Metge Foundation is that it compromised him politically. This organization was backed by the financial support of the politician Francesc Cambó, one of the founders and leader of the Catalan Lliga Regionalista party. This moderate and socially conservative party established by the Catalan industrial bourgeoisie dominated politics in Catalonia from its foundation in 1901 until General Primo de Rivera's overthrow in 1923.[11] One of its great institutional achievements was the establishment of the Mancomunitat in 1914. After Giménez Caballero's successful visit to Barcelona, he made a similar trip to the Basque Country, Galicia, and Portugal. He encouraged all of his new contacts and potential readers to use *La Gaceta Literaria* as a platform to project their voices in their native tongues, in defiance of the military-imposed censorship rules.

In his detailed history of Catalan imperialism, the contemporary scholar Enric Ucelay-Da Cal offers insight into Giménez Caballero's initial contact with the Catalans and their interest in collaborating with him. For example, Francesc Cambó named Joan Esterlich, a publicist from Mallorca in the Balearic Islands, who later became one of the first and most frequent contributors to *La Gaceta Literaria*, to be the president of his privately funded organization, the Bernat Metge Foundation. This organization offered resources for Catalan intellectuals, such as publishing power, that were otherwise unavailable in the public sector during the Primo de Rivera dictatorship. Based on my research, the Bernat Metge Foundation was one of the most consistent advertisers from Barcelona in *La Gaceta Literaria*. Their advertisements always occupied at least one-quarter of the page on which they were printed. This space was used to publicize their organization in general and to announce titles of newly published books in Catalan. The financial backing Giménez Caballero received from this private organization helped keep his publication in print, but it also cast a political shadow on the pages of his magazine, whether he liked to admit it or not.

Ucelay-Da Cal calls attention to the fact that in Cambó's book, *Per la Concòrdancia* (For the Sake of Harmony), he states that in order to resolve the conflicts between Spain and Catalonia, the collaboration of intellectuals from both sides is needed. Giménez Caballero's proposal for a periodical with similar goals to Cambó's resonated with the Bernat Metge Foundation. Specifically, Cambó's vision was that the intelligentsia from opposing sides would fuse into a collective project based on the promotion of all Hispanic cultures, including Catalan. The distinguishing feature of Cambó's plan was that this union would stem from Barcelona, not Madrid. Together, they would forge a vision for a future that would preserve Catalan culture while modernizing Spain's culture as a whole. As we shall soon see, Cambó's plan, funneled through Esterlich and onto the printed pages of Giménez Caballero's periodical, made La Gaceta Literaria quite controversial. Cambó's plan for Catalan cultural dominance by means of collaboration with other Hispanic intellectuals resonated with the mission of Giménez Caballero's periodical. Consequently, he was eager to join forces with Giménez Caballero. Therefore, from its inception, La Gaceta Literaria became one of the platforms from which Cambó voiced his plan, through Esterlich.

Cambó's strategy quickly materialized into the successful Catalan Book Fair in Madrid, one year after Giménez Caballero's initial introduction to the Catalan intellectual elite. In his memoirs, Cambó claims that La Gaceta Literaria was in large part protected by him and directed by Esterlich, not Giménez Caballero. Although Cambó does not go into further detail, Ucelay-Da Cal persists that Giménez Caballero found a way to address his own concern with the unity of Spain, as discussed earlier in this chapter, in the "mysticism" and ideologies of the Catalan nationalists behind the noucentisme movement.[12] Cambó's Catalanism made an impression on Giménez Caballero just as much, or even more so, than fascism would later on. It came naturally for Giménez Caballero to absorb Cambó's Catalan nationalist sentiments and incorporate them into his project for the unification of Spain through the cultural program he was constructing with La Gaceta Literaria. It must also have been very encouraging to have Cambó's financial and institutional support. During the first year La Gaceta Literaria was in print, there were large and elaborately designed Bernat Metge Foundation advertisements in almost every issue. Just as Giménez Caballero hoped to spread Hispanism throughout the world, Cambó hoped to do the same with Catalanism. By collaborating, Cambó and Giménez Caballero identified common interests stemming from two different cultural movements, noucentisme and the Avant-Garde respectively, and then used La Gaceta Literaria as an instrument for carrying them out.

One of the tangible results of this relationship between La Gaceta Literaria and Catalan businesses is that in every single issue, readers would be exposed to numerous publishing companies and bookstores in Barcelona. In general, based on my observations, it was not very common for Catalan businesses to advertise in periodicals from Madrid and vice versa. On a visual level, seeing these advertisements may have triggered thoughts of Catalonia, Catalans, and Barcelona, at least on a subconscious level. These were the ads that must have helped keep Giménez Caballero's magazine in print for so long.

This financial support guaranteed that his little magazine had a greater degree of success than all the other avant-garde periodicals that barely lasted a year before going out of business. Entering into partnership with the Catalans also must have been, in part, a self-interested business decision on Giménez Caballero's behalf. In light of the confrontations with the Catalans in the magazine's first year, as we will see shortly, perhaps the only thing that kept Giménez Caballero motivated to continue publishing articles about Catalonia and in Catalan was not necessarily faith in his romantic ideas of a united Spain, as he originally imagined, but rather a coldhearted financial calculation.

Half of the seventy-two issues that make up *La Gaceta Literaria*'s first three years in print (1927–29) included some sort of Catalan text.[13] Initially, nearly every issue included a full article printed in Catalan (nos. 1–8). Then, the frequency changed to every other issue, as the published Catalan-language content was either a poem or an article (nos. 9–20). By the end of the magazine's first three years, the only texts printed in Catalan were poems, and they appeared intermittently (nos. 21–72). Based on these numbers, Giménez Caballero exaggerated the presence of Catalan in his magazine from the moment he founded *La Gaceta Literaria* until the end of his life. For instance, in the first anniversary issue, he thanked a long list of Catalan contributors. But if we pay close attention to the header that tops the list, it reads "articles received," not "articles published," which is what most readers might expect. One might think that all forty of these individuals published articles in *La Gaceta Literaria*, but most of them did not. Giménez Caballero made it seem like he was publishing more Catalans than he was. Of the forty who allegedly sent contributions to the magazine's headquarters in Madrid, only half saw their names in print, which is not so shabby, but the editor is not being completely sincere. Over the course of his life, Giménez Caballero became very adept at this kind of false advertising, especially when it came to his relationship with Catalans and how he so faithfully promoted their language and culture.

The support of the Catalan middle class, like many of those associated with the Bernat Metge Foundation, was key to the success and survival of *La Gaceta Literaria*. This collaboration explains, in large part, why Giménez Caballero had to insist on maintaining a direct, open, and positive line of communication with Barcelona. Whether his motivations were financial, ideological, spiritual, political, or all of the above, communication, with the Catalans especially, became one of the central messages of *La Gaceta Literaria*.[14] Before the inaugural issue was printed, this goal to be communicative was represented visually on the flier that publicized the new magazine.

The Madrid-based artist and art critic Gabriel García Maroto drew the image for this flier. It consisted of several symbols that communicated the

Figure 6.1.   Advertisement for *La Gaceta Literaria*.

central mission of *La Gaceta Literaria*: a bust, a map, and a ship. A profile of a Greco-Latin bust casting a shadow is the main focus of Maroto's drawing. This neoclassical image is drawn with a formalist line that harmonizes with the renewal of this ancient tradition promoted by Catalan *noucentisme*, or with the general return to artistic order adopted by avant-garde artists throughout Europe after the First World War.

As indicated in the journal's subtitle, the goal of the journal was to be Iberian, American, and international. To communicate this idea visually, there is a map of Latin America and the Iberian Peninsula to the left of the statuesque bust. The map of the peninsula is shaped like a dialogue box, giving the impression that the bust is speaking. The map of Latin America appears as a subsequent dialogue box, as if it were a second utterance, coming out of the first dialogue box. This ordering can explain why the map of Latin America is located on top of Spain and why the two are not divided by the Atlantic Ocean, but rather are connected.

If Latin is the source of the Iberian languages—not including Basque and Judeo-Spanish—then the bust in the foreground calls to mind the Roman Empire, while its shadow represents its descendents, in this case, the Spanish Empire. The ship that travels between the Americas and the Iberian Peninsula also serves as a reminder of the empire, but also suggests the idea of exchange between these two sides of the world. This transatlantic ship functions as a visual metaphor for the imperialistic goals of *La Gaceta Literaria*. Also, the maps of the Iberian Peninsula and Latin America are superimposed on a larger, white rectangular shape similar to that of a folio-sized sheet of paper, much like the large folios of *La Gaceta Literaria* (61 x 42 cm). Overall, the idea of communication expressed in the dialogue boxes, ship, and sheet of paper can be read as ideas originating in Rome, traveling to the Iberian Peninsula, and then across the Atlantic.

The constant struggle to communicate with readers outside of Madrid, particularly with Catalans, characterized *La Gaceta Literaria* from its first issue. In his opening message, Giménez Caballero announced that one of the main objectives of this new publication was to increase understanding between Castilians and Catalans. Through *La Gaceta Literaria*, he hoped to create a sense of respect between all of the languages and cultures of Spain, but particularly with that of Catalonia. José Ortega y Gasset reinforced the mission of the magazine in one of his only contributions in the first issue. While Ortega y Gasset believed that the writers of Madrid were completely unaware of how they stood in relation to the rest of Europe, the state of their current literary movement was even less known in other cultural centers of the Hispanic world, including Barcelona and Buenos Aires. The author of seminal theoretical works like *España invertebrada* (1921) and *La deshumanización del arte* (1925), Ortega y Gasset agreed with Giménez Caballero, in that he too sensed a complete disconnect between Madrid's literary world and the rest of Spain, Latin America, and the world.

The main objective of this new, bimonthly periodical, then, was not to promote one aesthetic ideal over another, but to "exclude all exclusions."[15]

That is to say, this cultural magazine served as a model of unity based on the idea of inclusion through the acceptance of difference. In these opening remarks, Ortega y Gasset encouraged writers to take advantage of Spain's plural nature rather than ignoring it. He argued that retreating into their respective regions was an act that only "mutilates" Spanish society. The people from different areas of Spain, like vertebrae, still had not managed to come together to form a fused spinal column. For the Madrid-based philosopher, Spanish letters needed to be "cured" of its "persistent provincialism" and become more international. He called for writers to stop thinking from the point of view of their hometowns. It was urgent that they think about their writing in the context of Spain, Europe, and the rest of the world. He urged writers to shake off their old garb of provincialism and face more global horizons. In order to do so, they needed to lift their eyes from the ground and look at the rest of the world. Appropriating futurist terminology, Ortega y Gasset called for feeling and thinking in "long-wave" frequencies.

Ortega wonders whether, if Madrid, Barcelona, Lisbon, and Buenos Aires changed their mindsets and thought of themselves as "neighborhoods" within a much larger "city" of letters, they could potentially cancel out their respective provincialisms and, once and for all, live in harmony? Only if and when they were capable of thinking of themselves in this way could they function as a "universal radio." The fact that Ortega's pleas are practically the same as those from the early days of regenerationism (circa 1915) goes to show that the sociopolitical situation in Spain had not improved. In fact, the immediacy of his tone suggests that by 1927, the situation had only worsened. If we take into account the bombings, strikes, hunger, disease, poverty, low employment rate, inflation, poor sanitation, assassinations, unstable political systems, unfair judicial practices, the war in Morocco, the First World War, and the military dictatorship and its censorship laws that characterized Spain from the turn of the century until the publication of this first issue of *La Gaceta Literaria*, it is easy to see why the philosopher was so concerned about finding a solution.

In order to promote his vision of a unified Spain, one of the strategies that the editor of *La Gaceta Literaria* used was to print some texts in various languages representative of the Iberian Peninsula. The publication of Catalan texts caused an instant polemic among the readership. What surprised Giménez Caballero was that those who initially opposed the use of Catalan were not Spanish speakers or military censors, but rather a group of Catalans. The debate as to whether or not to publish in Catalan was one of the periodical's earliest and most controversial issues during its first year in print. Yet those who have already studied this important avant-garde periodical rarely mention it. If this periodical is so foundational for the avant-garde in Madrid, this discussion is critical to understanding the connections and disconnections between the avant-garde networks of Barcelona and Madrid. It is also a reflection of the political realities of Spanish and Catalan society during this time.

As early as *La Gaceta Literaria*'s second issue, Giménez Caballero reiterated his reasons for publishing in Catalan in an article titled "Por la pluridad a la unidad" (Plurality in the Name of Unity).[16] The editor maps out his vision of a unified Spain as one that is tolerant of its plurality. This article is reminiscent of the manifesto at the conclusion of his first book, *Notes by a Soldier in Morocco*, five years earlier. Now, however, he is proposing a more concrete plan to achieve his goal. In order for the different people of the various regions of Spain to accept their differences, they must communicate with one another. For Giménez Caballero, communication was humanity's fundamental problem, and language was the only "transcendental vehicle" for overcoming it. Then what would Giménez Caballero gain by publishing in Catalan, a language that only some of his readers in Madrid would fully understand?

Giménez Caballero seemed to believe that if he created a multilingual periodical, the Iberian Peninsula would come closer to resolving its fundamental problem of communication and lack of understanding.[17] Every issue of *La Gaceta Literaria* included at least one article printed in Catalan, yet rarely was there a text published in any other language from the peninsula, such as Portuguese. Some Catalan readers were aggravated by a series titled "El diálogo de las lenguas" (The Dialogue of Languages) (nos. 4, 6, and 7). The dialogue between readers and the editor in reference to this article became a heated debate that continued on the cover page of the magazine for three issues. After purportedly reading the first issues of *La Gaceta Literaria*, a journalist from a newspaper in Sabadell (Catalonia), Francesc Trabal, communicated his mistrust of the magazine's use of Catalan in a letter to the editor.

Trabal considered that not translating the Catalan articles to Spanish was as if a French newspaper had left a Romanian article without translation. He argued that Catalan is just as different from Spanish as Romanian is from French. Giménez Caballero defended his decision to leave the Catalan texts in their original form so that his Spanish readership could see that Catalan was an "easy" and "pleasant" language, one of "great transparency."[18] Such patronizing only further angered the group of Catalans represented by Trabal in Sabadell. Since the Catalan *Renaixença*, scholars, philosophers, poets, and politicians—such as Pompeu Fabra, Joan Maragall, Josep Carner, and Enric Prat de la Riba—had been working to normalize a Catalan grammar.

Catalan was not a dialect of Spanish, but its own language with its own history, different from Castilian. Yet, judging by Giménez Caballero's remarks, he did not seem to fully understand this critical distinction.

On the front page of the sixth issue of *La Gaceta Literaria*, in a font larger than any other that had been used since the magazine's first issue, the editors declared themselves to be in a state of complete disbelief. They were shocked that any Catalan would have a problem with the fact that their periodical was promoting the Catalans' language, especially given the current censorship (e.g., prohibition of the use of Catalan in schools and public assemblies as well as in official notices or announcements of any sort). Giménez Caballero wondered whether it would really be more productive if Catalan texts were translated into Spanish. He wondered: Was it "counterproductive" to publish in Catalan? Was his perspective really one that was "strictly Spanish"?

Instead of leaving it at that—a series of rhetorical questions—he aggravates the discussion by defining what he calls linguistic expansion: in order for a language to thrive, it must be confident that it will survive. To illustrate his point, Giménez Caballero makes an analogy between the current situation of the Catalan language in Spain and that of the indigenous languages of Latin America during its colonization in the sixteenth century. He states that if the Spanish colonizers had asked the indigenous to translate Spanish laws into their local languages, there would not be seventy million Spanish speakers today. Like the Spanish colonizers who did not give indigenous languages a chance to cohabitate with theirs, Catalans should not submit to those who threaten the expansion of their language by means of translation. Giménez Caballero argues that the Catalans, like the Spanish colonizers, should impose their language on those who are threatening its survival, which is why they should not be asking him to translate the Catalan articles into Spanish.

The tone of an increasingly frustrated Giménez Caballero rises as the article continues, and he concludes this debate by overtly criticizing the ungrateful Catalans. To paraphrase, he states that even though many in Catalonia have spent years complaining about Madrid's oppression, it is they—the Catalans—who are the true oppressors. His main complaint is that the entire region of Catalonia is deaf to the rest of Spain; in particular, he is upset that the Barcelona press ignores Madrid. Despite his evident anger, Giménez Caballero explains that he and his staff at *La Gaceta Literaria* were going out of their way to include the people, language, and culture of Catalonia in the pages of his bimonthly periodical. He laments that the people of Catalonia were not prepared or willing to do the same.[19] This exclusion of Spanish on behalf of Catalans was detrimental for the unity of

Spain. He complains that Barcelona's press is much more repressive toward Madrid than the other way around. Nevertheless, he assures Catalans that *La Gaceta Literaria* will keep its doors open to Catalans and anybody else that wanted access. After only three months in press, Giménez Caballero's platform for achieving a more unified Spain was open to dialogue, but only under his terms.

In a final installment of this "dialogue on languages," Francesc Trabal argued that by publishing in Catalan, readers outside of Catalonia would not understand the articles. Giménez Caballero confessed that his intention to print at least one Catalan text per issue was not so much so that they should be understood by non-Catalan speakers, but more as a sign of respect. Their purpose was to be "propaedeutic"—the articles printed in Catalan were meant to function as an introduction to a more formal future study of the language among his Spanish-speaking readership. After all, Giménez Caballero claimed to have learned Catalan and Portuguese by simply reading the articles he published in *La Gaceta Literaria*. In other words, someone who did not read the Catalan articles could find all the most important information in the Spanish articles. Giménez Caballero admits that the Catalan articles were symbolic, decorative, or served a diplomatic purpose. If he believed that a Catalan article was especially newsworthy, it would be translated and printed in Spanish, as was often the case with the essays of the Catalan art critic Sebastià Gasch. Only his first publication in *La Gaceta Literaria* was printed in Catalan; his remaining articles were in Spanish.

Giménez Caballero used this debate on language to demonstrate his commitment to tolerance toward Catalonia, yet without coming across as being very tolerant, knowledgeable, or respectful. Rather than dropping the issue, he insists. The editor in chief goes on to explain that tolerance had to be achieved dispassionately, with reason and purity, in a "surreal" way. Just like poetry was freeing itself from the constraints of academic rules, Spaniards and Catalans needed to stop distrusting and offending one another based on outdated misconceptions. In order to better understand one another, these two groups had to transcend reality, just like the surrealists. By borrowing a trendy, aesthetic term that was not yet understood by most Spaniards, he insisted on the possibility of a unified Spain, and got away with it, to some extent.

Giménez Caballero ends his plea by returning to his original point: Spain's fundamental problem was one of ineffective communication. The worst thing Spaniards could do was to continue not trying to understand one another. One solution he proposed through his periodical was that Spaniards learn how to speak, read, and understand the various languages of Spain. It was "atrocious" and "Paleolithic" for the people of Barcelona and

Madrid to continue behaving in such a tribal fashion, full of so much hate toward one another. Giménez Caballero simply could not comprehend why this particular group of Catalans could not appreciate the effort he was making to inform others about their language, literature, and culture.

By the end of this three-part series on his decision to print articles in Catalan, Giménez Caballero was so exasperated that he insisted that Catalans should be thankful that he was allowing them the opportunity to be published outside of their homeland, especially under the restrictions of the dictatorship and its censorship laws. He insists that Spaniards could not afford to remain clustered in their clans, cornered in their various regions of Spain, in a position of "tribal defense," hating one another and only aggravating the country's "permanent" domestic problem.[20] For someone who was calling for emotional detachment, this series about his decision to print in Catalan without translation was remarkably passionate. Giménez Caballero would never address this issue so openly again in his magazine.

Giménez Caballero's form of dialogue was not especially open. His idea of communication was unilateral and totalitarian; based on a very personal and imperialistic idea of what Spain should be. Even his right-hand man, Guillermo de Torre, quickly distanced himself from Giménez Caballero. Eight months after the magazine went to print, Guillermo de Torre moved to Argentina to live with his new wife, Norah Borges. It would have been more communicative, in the case of Trabal, for example, for Giménez Caballero to correspond with him directly and privately rather than attack him publicly. Giménez Caballero was making an example of Trabal on the front pages of his magazine. He was the "typical" Catalan unwilling to cooperate. Why instead did Giménez Caballero not address him more privately or conduct a survey regarding this issue, a tactic he employed when confronting other controversial issues? How exactly did he define communication?

During the first three years his magazine was in print, Giménez Caballero worked feverishly toward refining his model of unity through plurality by offering his readers the means to achieve it. The plan he was proposing was unlike any other. It was modern, rational, pure, and surreal. The means by which he and other Spaniards could achieve this unity was through "neutrality," "respect," and "dialogue . . . comprehension . . . and understanding."[21] Other terms Giménez Caballero used to define his mission included: "liberal . . . fraternal . . . intelligent . . . historical" (136), and, most repeatedly, "apolitical" (159). Furthermore, it was a matter of "duty" and "will" for Spaniards to want to attain this goal.

His efforts to incorporate Catalans did not intend to exacerbate differences, but rather to emphasize similarities. If his readers followed the example of his magazine as a "transistor of a plurality of peninsular languages," Catalans, Castilians, Portuguese, and Latin Americans would inevitably communicate with and understand one another much better.[22] Like a "communication tower," the message that Giménez Caballero transmitted from the pages of La Gaceta Literaria was one of solidarity.[23] The problem, at least symbolically if not also politically, was that this tower was centered in Madrid, the seat of power of the military dictatorship that limited Catalan laws and rights; also, the editor took an imperialistic stance toward Catalans and Latin Americans. Notably, on several occasions he identified Madrid as the intellectual center of Hispanism. His stance is exactly the type of centrifugal force that aggravated many Catalans.

In terms of the layout of the magazine, Giménez Caballero carved out a specialized section to report on the literary news of Catalonia, beginning in the ninth issue of the first year in print. Up until this point, Catalan literary news appeared under the occasional heading of "Catalan Books." For the journal's second-year anniversary, an entire page was devoted to Catalan cultural news, which was usually published entirely in Spanish, with the exception of a brief article or poem published in Catalan. News from Catalonia can also be found in sections like "Postales Ibéricas" (Iberian Postcards) and "Itinerario de Revistas" (Magazine Tour), both created as of the third issue; and "Los Raids Literarios" (Literary Raids), starting in the ninth issue, in which a journalist would "raid" a different city of Spain or Europe to report on a writer from that place.

Only a few months into the publication of La Gaceta Literaria, Giménez Caballero announced the publication of his new book, Carteles. This publication compiles his approximately one hundred previously printed literary reviews, published in one of Madrid's daily newspapers, and features his latest invention, called the "literary poster."[24] With each one of these twenty-five "posters," he takes what he might normally write in a literary review and translates it into something visual.[25] When La Gaceta Literaria celebrated its first anniversary, he commemorated the occasion by landing an exhibit at the Dalmau Galleries in Barcelona at which he displayed a selection of these literary posters (show opened January 8, 1928). Giménez Caballero must have felt honored to show his posters alongside a concurrent exhibit showing some of the most contemporary artists of the day, including Salvador Dalí and Rafael Barradas.[26]

Although it is unclear when Giménez Caballero created his first visually enhanced literary poster, the earliest mention of the publication of the book in which they appeared, Carteles, was in the fourth issue of La Gaceta Literaria, in which the book was described as just out (February 15, 1927).

Considering the time needed to put together such a large book (nearly three hundred pages), Giménez Caballero must have sent it to press well before the first issue of his magazine in January 1927. In the fifth issue, he promoted this book as "the future of literary criticism." Evidently, Giménez Caballero was not ashamed to use his own magazine to market his new book. Some of the key publicity strategies for selling his book included: announcing the book and printing a sample of these visually enhanced reviews in his journal; organizing art exhibits in Barcelona and Madrid to show these works; and finally, publishing reviews of his book and the corresponding exhibits, written by other critics, in *La Gaceta Literaria*.

The Catalan critic Guillermo Díaz-Plaja felt that Giménez Caballero's literary criticism in the form of poster was a flop. Rather than offering a panoramic vision of the development of contemporary literature or its spirit, or "evolucions espirituals" (spiritual developments), the posters only captured the personalities of the authors, instead of addressing their literary works.[27] But Díaz-Plaja was intrigued by the idea. He wondered how one could explore new avenues of literary criticism and how one could communicate these opinions to a much larger audience, not just the tiny readership of small-circulation, elite periodicals.

In another review of the literary posters shown at the Dalmau Galleries, the art critic Sebastià Gasch does not seem to be so impressed either. But since Giménez Caballero was Gasch's employer in Madrid, he is not overtly critical. In a very diplomatic fashion, the only direct comment Gasch makes about Giménez Caballero's work is a remark about his use of a wide array of media (e.g., wire, sand, ash, car paint, baby powder, glitter, oil, lacquer).[28] Their collage-like quality serves as an opportunity for him to launch into a lesson on the history of collage. Like Picasso and Braque, whose love for the local is what led them to introduce real life objects into their works, Giménez Caballero's posters attempted to be a visual condensation of the work of contemporary writers. Gasch kindly concludes his review of the posters by quoting Giménez Caballero's opening remarks at the Barcelona show regarding his intention to discover an "absolute truth" through these works. Refraining from commenting on this statement, perhaps for fear of disrespecting Giménez Caballero, but still mentioning it, probably for its controversial nature, Gasch goes ahead with the rest of article. In this final section, he comments at great length on the other much more mesmerizing works on display by Barradas and Dalí.

The Catalan literary critic Lluís Montanyà was much more critical than both Díaz-Plaja and Gasch in his commentary on Giménez Caballero's posters, but he hides it in his sophisticated Catalan prose. This review appeared in *La Gaceta Literaria* four months after the Barcelona exhibit.[29] It was unusual to see this Catalan writer's byline in the Madrid press.[30] His connection to *La Gaceta Literaria* could very well have been through his relationship with two of his friends who also contributed to Giménez Caballero's magazine: Dalí and Gasch.

In a disproportionally long introductory paragraph, he complains that there is no time for anything anymore. Following this lament, he briefly and ironically comments on Giménez Caballero's posters, "marveling" at Giménez Caballero's use of mixed media, especially the glitter. Here he abruptly concludes. Montanyà wanted to make a poster depicting the poster-maker, similar to what Giménez Caballero does with contemporary Spanish writers in his posters, but he ran out of time. This excuse seems rather ridiculous, considering the time he must have spent writing the first, disproportionately long paragraph, which has nothing to do with the posters. Montanyà's irony works on several levels. He gets away with mocking the posters by exploiting Giménez Caballero's lack of understanding when it came to the subtleties of Catalan language and the complexities of its culture.

The Catalan writer Josep Maria Sucre, a regular contributor to *La Gaceta Literaria*, also published a review of the literary posters. According to this report, Sucre also gave the introductory speech at the opening of Giménez Caballero's literary poster show at the Dalmau Galleries in Barcelona. In this review, Sucre briefly describes with bullet-like precision each of the thirty-four works.[31] According to Sucre, the first poster in this series, titled *Universe of Contemporary Spanish Literature*, is a visual attempt to explain Spain's new literary scene as if it were a map of the universe. In his short description, Sucre draws attention to the viewing instrument depicted at the bottom of the poster. He calls the tool with which the author of the poster observes this "universe" the "very new Madrilenian telescope." Sucre's review is similar to the previous reviews by Montanyà and Gasch, in that the main messages of these writers—an overall dislike of Giménez Caballero's posters—are concealed in their silences. Giménez Caballero is the editor in chief of the most stable periodical in Madrid supporting the new literary and artistic scene in Spain, which has published the work of all of these Catalans. Under these circumstances, Montanyà, Gasch, and Sucre are all careful with their wording of their reviews.

By calling the telescope "Madrilenian," Sucre comments on the tendency in Madrid to consider itself the center of the universe. In Giménez Caballero's constellation of periodicals and those who contribute to them, Spain's solar system of new Spanish literature, he only considers Madrid. He clearly neglects the rest of Spain in this poster.[32] Yet, some of today's scholars of

Spain's Silver Age consider this map one of the best summaries of the Spanish literary scene from this time. Mainer, for one, believes that it is difficult to find a better synthesis of Spanish literary history than Giménez Caballero's cosmological map.[33] After all of Giménez Caballero's ranting about how the Barcelona press constantly ignores Madrid, he blatantly excludes their periodicals and writers in the first poster of the series. Leaving Catalonia out of the picture demonstrates his own unawareness. He is out of touch with his own message. One of the goals of his magazine is to "exclude all exclusions," as already addressed in the selection of La Gaceta Literaria's articles analyzed above, yet he is committing the very sin he wants to overcome.

Bejamín Jarnés also published a review of Giménez Caballero's literary posters. He considers the current literary movement to be more concerned with publicity than quality. The creators of the new literature spent too much time worrying about what everybody else was doing. He saw the new generation of writers of this "military literature" to be a "centinela de los demás, la de pasar el tiempo atisbando la obra de los otros, es decir, vigilando la vigilancia de los otros" (sentry of the others, spending time watching out for the works written by others, that is to say, watching others watching them).[34] According to Jarnés, Spain's new literature was hyper-vigilant. Giménez Caballero and La Gaceta Literaria certainly fit this description. Within the pages of this bimonthly journal, Giménez Caballero would remark on whether the press in Barcelona would make references to La Gaceta Literaria or not. On one occasion when they did mention his journal, he published a note in La Gaceta Literaria indicating that he had noticed. Based on the comments published in both the Barcelona and Madrid press in reaction to the posters, Giménez Caballero's view of Spain's new literary movement was not the norm.

Prior to 1927, Madrid did not host any sort of expo devoted exclusively to Catalan books. In the weeks leading up to Christmas, the first-ever Catalan Book Fair took place in the exhibition galleries of Spain's National Library in Madrid. Reporting from Barcelona, the Catalan writer Josep Pla considered it the "most important spiritual event" of the winter.[35] The mastermind behind this singular event was Ernesto Giménez Caballero. It is important to note that this event was sponsored by the central government in Madrid, which was currently being run by a dictatorship. In a letter directed to León Sánchez Cuesta, one of the best-known literary agents and bookstore owners in Madrid, Giménez Caballero mentions that the Ministry of Public Instruction and Fine Arts authorized the organization of this event. That is to say, the dictatorship agreed to host the Catalan Book Fair in Madrid, and supported it as well.[36] According to the main organizer, the goal of the

Universo de la literatura española contemporánea

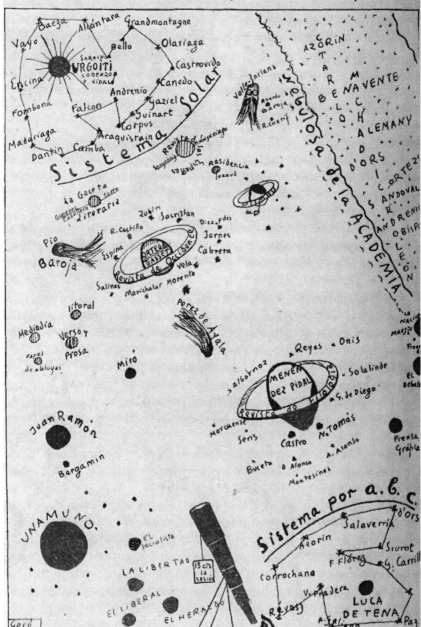

Figure 6.2. *Universe of Contemporary Spanish Literature* by Ernesto Giménez Caballero.

unprecedented exhibit was to learn about the literary and scientific progress of Catalan culture.[37] In this letter, Giménez Caballero also invited Sánchez Cuesta to be the official greeter of the Catalans. This project was much more involved than others he had coordinated in the past, and he needed all the help he could get.

According to one historian, this exhibit occurred at a time when it was nearly impossible to find Catalan books in Madrid.[38] She also reports that prior to this exhibit, the National Library of Spain in Madrid did not include any Catalan books in its holdings. In an article that Giménez Caballero published in *La Gaceta Literaria*, he elaborated on the goals of this exhibition. He explained that this event was an attempt at reconciliation with Catalonia through culture, language, and art, rather than through politics; contradicting his own words, a politician, the minister of education, gave the keynote address on opening day. For the majority of visitors, of which there were reported to be hundreds, the Catalan publishing industry came across as being very productive and lucrative. For the most part, the visitors did not realize how many books were being printed in Catalan each year. The exhibition collected more than six thousand volumes of poetry, prose, drama, science, philosophy, history, archaeology, criticism, politics, and more, all in Catalan and all published after 1900.

The Catalan book fair organizers arrived in Madrid with treasure chests filled with fine jewels: first editions of Catalan classics like Jacint Verdaguer and Joan Maragall; Catalan translations of both classic and contemporary non-Catalan authors; and hundreds of periodicals representing a wide range of themes, from philosophy to children's literature. Many Catalan authors, such as Carles Riba, Carles Soldevila, Tomàs Garcés, Joan Esterlich, and others, presented their own books in Spanish or gave lectures about a variety of topics. Two committees, one based in Madrid and the other in Barcelona, organized the event. The Madrid contingent consisted of some of the city's most influential intellectuals.[39] Many of the individuals who signed the manifesto in defense of the Catalan language addressed to General Miguel Primo de Rivera in 1924 also were involved with organizing the Catalan Book Fair.[40]

This event came after nearly five years of repression of the Catalan language and culture by the ruling regime. A collective of Castilian intellectuals in Madrid, led by a fervent supporter of the Avant-Garde, organized this event in tribute to the Catalan language and its publishing industry. For the Catalan organizing committee, this visit was like a soft cry for freedom of both language and the press. The extraordinary exhibit catalog compiled by the Barcelona committee defined their objective: to provide a general idea

about the history of the Catalan book, as well as contemporary developments.[41] Specifically, the objective was threefold: (1) to show the proliferation of genres in the Catalan letters; (2) to demonstrate the Catalan contribution to the development of general knowledge and scientific discovery;
and (3) to prove that the roots of the publishing industry in Catalonia were
deep, dating back many centuries. In order to stay out of trouble, the Catalan organizers avoided making overtly political statements. In their written
account of the Catalan book, available in the visitors' pamphlet, they apolo-
gize in advance for accidentally excluding, generalizing, and misinterpreting
anyone or anything. This exhibit was the first of its kind in Madrid, but it
was also a first for the Catalans. How does one present one's history and
culture to another without getting involved in politics?

The account of Catalan literary history at the fair begins with its
nineteenth-century Renaissance, or *Renaixença*, which came after the long
Decadència (described in the third chapter). Beginning with 1840, the
catalog provides a clear and concise, decade-by-decade description of the
development of the Catalan Renaissance. According to their version of
the history, this revival movement began with the creation of poetry inspired by the rediscovery of a medieval literary game, the Jocs Florals. This
enthusiasm spread to the creation of literary magazines and newspapers in
Barcelona, Valencia, and Mallorca.

The organizers show that as early as the 1860s, editors and printing presses
in Catalonia were extremely active, producing anthologies, novels, poetry,
calendars, periodicals, translations, and so on. The publishing industry continued to grow until the end of the century. Some of Barcelona's most important editorial companies were founded during this period.[42] If any reader of
the catalog had ever doubted the legitimacy of Catalan language, literature,
or culture, this document was designed to abruptly resolve those doubts. Written in an extremely clear fashion, the catalog also lists the names of printing
presses, cultural institutions, scholars, poets, journalists, translators, and periodicals. For over fifty years, the Catalan publishing and editorial businesses
had been thriving, and their readership had also increased dramatically to
now include the majority of the general public in Catalonia.

Some visitors to the Catalan Book Fair were more willing than others
to admit their ignorance of Catalan literature and culture. An anonymous journalist from the daily newspaper in Madrid was one of them: "No
ocultaré que mi conocimiento de vuestra lengua y vuestra literatura es
incompleta. No las conozco tan poco que no pueda entenderlas, ni tanto
que no tengan para mí algo del encanto desconocido." (It is true that what
I know of your language and literature is not exhaustive. The truth is that I

am not an expert. I know them well enough to understand them, but there is a certain delight in discovering them still.)[43] Giménez Caballero knew that this reporter was not alone. He knew that most Castilian intellectuals barely knew about the Catalan literary and cultural phenomenon that he had become acquainted with after a couple of recent trips to Barcelona. The Catalan Book Fair also became an opportunity for journalists to articulate their views on Catalan politics and culture.

For instance, Pedro Sainz Rodríguez believed that the problem Spain had with Catalonia was caused by "mutual unawareness."[44] He believed that the cause of the conflict with Catalonia went beyond the material. It was much more of a spiritual issue. This mutual unawareness, complicated by political disagreements, led to a disconnection of the spirit uniting Catalans and Spaniards. This exhibition was an opportunity to show the people of Madrid that Catalans, just like them, were "enormously lyrical and sensitive."[45] Sainz Rodríguez thought that with awareness would come the realization that their spirits were more similar than they thought. Several lectures were organized in conjunction with the exhibition in order to combat this lack of knowledge about Catalan literature and culture in Madrid. The focus of this show was to provide Spaniards in Madrid with a unique opportunity to learn more about that spirit that united them with Catalans. In this case, the spirit is a passion for literature and the culture that envelops it.

The Catalan businessman Joan Esterlich also was of the opinion that Catalans and Castilians were united by a common spirit, "Si nosotros no nos comprendiéramos, al profundizar en nuestros pensamientos, encontraríamos el punto de convergencia que existe en todos los espíritus" (If we were not able to understand one another, if we were to think hard about it, we would find a point of convergence in all of our spirits).[46] According to another report, this monumental show of Catalan culture in Madrid was a necessary first step toward mutual respect and understanding. For this writer, it was simply not true that Catalans ignored Madrid or that Spaniards ignored Catalans: "Dir que els d'ací i els d'allà es miraven sorrudament per damunt de l'espatlla… és servir al públic una imatge completament desenfocada del fet" (To say that those of us here and those over there look at each other over our backs . . . is to give the public a picture that is completely out of focus with reality).[47] These three sets of comments about the Catalan Book Fair speak to the human spirit that unites the people of Barcelona and Madrid. This spirit is one that transcends political divisions.

The publishing industry in Barcelona was so prolific that there were not enough editorial companies to publish all the books being written.[48] Besides publishing books, many of the publishing companies featured were also involved in other sociopolitical, cultural, and literary projects, such as establishing libraries and bookstores, translations, and publication of newspapers and magazines. It is important to note that many of the companies present at the Catalan Book Fair published books in Catalan, but there were also those that printed books in Spanish. Some presses, in fact, only published in Spanish (i.e., Gili, Gallach, Martin, Salvat, Montaner, Simon). The organizers felt it was necessary to bring attention to this fact, since it was a common belief that books in Spanish could not be found in Barcelona.

Just when the Catalan publishing industry's production was peaking, General Primo de Rivera came to power and attempted to repress the proliferation of the Catalan language and culture. If this industry was a profitable one for Spain, why weaken it with censorship and other unfair restrictions? Did the publication of books in Catalonia pose a serious threat to his power? What the regime may have found threatening was that this industry was producing Catalan books for a large population of readers. By reading books in Catalan, these readers were strengthening a national identity contrary to the one supported and enforced by his regime.

At the banquet honoring his Catalan guests at the Palace Hotel in Madrid, Giménez Caballero stated that this was the first time Castilians and Catalans had understood one another since the Middle Ages. He lamented the fact that while the university in Madrid offered courses in Italian, French, and German, it did not offer any of the various languages of Spain, like Catalan, Basque, or Galician. He proposed that a course on Catalan language and literature should be designed, and he suggested that the linguist Pompeu Fabra, who was at the banquet, should teach it. Giménez Caballero concluded his speech in Catalan, thanking his guests for giving all of their lectures in Spanish. According to the fragments of toasts that were given at this banquet that have been preserved, the mood at this soirée seemed to be one of mutual respect and understanding.[49]

In addition to organizing the fair and banquet, Giménez Caballero also published a book about the exhibit edited by his own publishing company, Biblioteca Ibérica. This book collects numerous newspaper articles published in both Madrid and Barcelona about the Catalan Book Fair.[50] Longer essays about the exhibit are also included. Angel Ossorio, for one, states that the greatest achievement of the show was that it renewed the topic of language diversity in Spain by moving it beyond the passionate confines of the political arena. Instead, this cultural event provided a forum of mutual respect. After twelve months of drawing attention to the Catalan situation in *La Gaceta Literaria* and all of the debates it produced, all of Giménez Caballero's efforts culminated in the unprecedented Catalan Book Fair. Yet, he still convinced leading politicians and others in Madrid to follow his lead and support him financially and otherwise. For the most part, he disagreed with the repression of Catalan culture by the Primo de Rivera dictatorship. His constant efforts to increase communication, dialogue, and cultural exchange with Catalans show that he was determined to improve relations, but all this would soon change.

After the Dictatorship

After the Catalan Book Fair in Madrid, Giménez Caballero took a trip to Italy. From this point onwards, fewer articles in languages other than Spanish appeared in *La Gaceta Literaria*. Similarly, less and less attention was paid to literary developments outside of Madrid. In 1930, Giménez Caballero only published three articles about Catalonia. By this stage, approaching the end of the Primo de Rivera regime, Giménez Caballero shifted strategies with the Catalans, but without losing hope for his ideal of a great Iberian Union. In April of that year, less than a month after the fall of the dictatorship, Barcelona staged an impressive tribute to non-Catalan intellectuals who had supported Catalans since the signing of the manifesto in defense of Catalan language in 1924. What had seemed like a cordial gesture on behalf of the Castilian intellectuals has been received with criticism.

One scholar, Ucelay-Da Cal, argues that the wrong people were congratulated at this event. He believed that those who benefited most from the propaganda of the Catalan-Castilian brotherhood were the Republicans, while those who should have been recognized were the members of the Lliga Regionalista party, such as Joan Esterlich from the Bernat Metge Foundation, and Giménez Caballero from *La Gaceta Literaria*. On several occasions in later writings, Giménez Caballero also complained that he was not given enough credit at this celebration in Barcelona. Whether or not they received the credit they deserved, the Lliga Regionalista party was at the point of dissolution. Their leader, Francesc Cambó, was diagnosed with cancer at the same time that Primo de Rivera fell from power. Cambó retired from leadership, and the party quickly lost its unity, power, and voice. The dictator's fall had grave consequences for Giménez Caballero. Many of his faithful collaborators at the magazine moved toward the left politically, as he had been shifting more and more to the right. This ideological move away from the left is very clear in the contents of *La Gaceta Literaria* and in Giménez Caballero's other writings. Feeling abandoned and realizing that his network of supporters was getting smaller, Giménez Caballero called out to the Catalans again.

He published an article in Spanish in the Barcelona-based periodical *Revista de Catalunya*, in which he approached a definition of the Catalan-Castilian divide. In this piece, he makes direct references to the book that cancer-struck Cambó had recently published, *Per la concòrdia*. Appropriating the Catalan imperialist rhetoric of both Cambó and Esterlich, Giménez Caballero called for cultural domination as a solution to the Catalan-Castilian conflict.[51] He begins making his case by referring back to the Middle Ages. He argues that there was no "peninsular problem" when Castile and Catalonia were struggling to expand their domain in areas outside of Spain. The confrontation between the two only arose when Catalonia lost its empire and maritime power, reducing its influence significantly. Catalonia turned inwards where its vision collided with Castile's, thus marking the beginning of the conflict: "un problema de recelo, de odio, de disputa por las propias entrañas . . . un problema eminente y fundamentalmente interior" (a problem of suspicion, hate, an argument centered in the gut . . . an eminently and fundamentally interior problem).[52] The only solution to resolve the Catalan-Castilian conflict was for both cultures to direct their vision outwards again as they had done in the past. Giménez Caballero believed that both Catalans and Spaniards had to focus on expanding their culture outside of Spain. After all, this was exactly what he was trying to do with *La Gaceta Literaria*.

This plea was too little too late. Only one year after Primo de Rivera's fall, the Catalan Republicans triumphed and established Spain's Second Republic. This quick and dramatic change in government put a hold on all of Giménez Caballero's imperialistic plans, while Cambó, King Alfonso XII, and many others fled into exile. Giménez Caballero suddenly found himself on the wrong side of the political fence. Desperately, he turned to the victorious Republican Catalans, specifically Francesc Macià, one of the founders of the Socialist-Communist Esquerra Republicana de Catalunya party, established in 1931. Macià had been in exile during the Primo de Rivera regime for attempting to overthrow it in 1926. With the arrival of the Second Republic, Giménez Caballero reminded his Catalan readership that he was one of their most faithful supporters and that his periodical, the events it organized, and all of its other endeavors were fundamental to the rise of their power. He writes: "Recuérdese—fundamentalmente—nuestro periódico fue la vanguardia del plurilinguismo peninsular" (Remember, fundamentally, our journal was the vanguard of peninsular multilingualism).[53] One of his motives in seeking partnership with Macià, the president of the Generalitat, was that like Giménez Caballero himself, Macià was considered by some to be a fascist. Rejected by Macià and other Catalans in power,

Giménez Caballero found shelter in Spain's Falange, a fascist political party founded by the son of the former dictator in 1933.

When the Second Spanish Republic was declared, Giménez Caballero did not want the world to forget his role as one of the major leaders of the Avant-Garde movement in Spain. Insisting on the vanguardism of his "peninsular multilingualism," he published a book using five languages. In the prologue of *Trabalenguas sobre España* (Tongue Twisters about Spain), he explains that the reason why he wrote this book using the five "capital languages of the world" (Spanish, German, Italian, French, and English) was to "suppress boundaries."[54] Once again, he felt that the way that political and national divisions could be transcended was by being multilingual. Furthermore, he considered this attitude to be avant-garde, since this movement was concerned with overcoming tradition (monolingualism) and destroying boundaries. This rhetoric is identical to that of the early days of *La Gaceta Literaria*. Written for tourists, the book is comprised of "driving tours" and "guided tours" of literary texts and historical monuments in Spain. Just as he did with his literary posters a few years earlier, he approached the literary text yet again with innovation and hope that it would sell.

The driving tour of Catalonia in his book *Tongue Twisters about Spain* is dedicated to two Catalans: (1) Antoni Maria Sbert, one of the founders of the Equerra Republicana de Catalunya party; and (2) Gustavo Gili, the publisher who purchased all of Giménez Caballero's literary posters after his show at the Dalmau Galleries in Barcelona. Giménez Caballero identifies both of these men as Catalans who helped him launch *La Gaceta Literaria*. Every mention of his periodical was another opportunity for the editor to speak about its historical importance in the cultural and literary history of Spain. He insists that the relations between the writers and intellectuals of Barcelona and Madrid are cordial because of his efforts at *La Gaceta Literaria*. To a certain extent, this statement may be true, but Giménez Caballero tends to exaggerate to make his points. For instance, he frequently insisted on the multilingual nature of his journal, when in fact, other than Catalan, very few of the other languages from the Iberian Peninsula were ever published. Another example of Giménez Caballero's tendency to exaggerate in relation to the importance of his journal is when he states that it was not until the first issue of *La Gaceta Literaria* that anyone in Madrid concerned him- or herself with the Catalan situation in a "totalizing, national, transcending manner" the way he did, rather than just in an individual and very local manner (97). He was convinced that as a direct result of his journalism, he was solely responsible for providing his readership in Madrid with a way to approach conflicts with Catalans and Catalonia in an objective, informed, and diplomatic manner.

When General Francisco Franco took his first official trip to Barcelona as the new dictator of Spain, he invited Giménez Caballero to join him. In the book Giménez Caballero published to commemorate this visit with the new dictator, *Amor a Cataluña* (*Love for Catalonia*) (1942), we get one last glimpse of his motivation for including the Catalans in *La Gaceta Literaria*. In retrospect, he describes himself as someone who, as early as 1926, had traveled to Barcelona to "conquer" that city with love by means of his cultural journal.[55] He claims that at that time, his only "weapons" were the words shaped by his pen. He explains that *La Gaceta Literaria* was meant to be the wedding band that would unite a Catalonia that rejected Spain and a Spain that was jealous and anguished because of that rejection. According to the avant-garde-leader-turned-fascist, from 1926 until 1931, Catalonia was consistent only in its lack of any desire to understand Castilian Spain. For this Catalonia, a Spain ruled by Primo de Rivera certainly could not understand the Catalan problem, soul, or language. Only the democratic, romantic, populist, liberal France could empathize with Catalonia. Giménez Caballero describes himself as a suitor that approached Barcelona to ask her hand in marriage, offering his humble magazine as an instrument of peace. He claims that he offered the people of Barcelona a forum in Madrid where they would speak, write, and be heard in Catalan. Then, just when he thought that Barcelona would finally accept his proposal, she ran off with the enemies: France, Russia, and the Spanish Republicans. It was then that Catalonia demanded a divorce from Spain.

In the last chapter of *Amor a Cataluña*, Giménez Caballero provides a final explanation for his decision to invite the participation of the Catalans in *La Gaceta Literaria*. Even though there was censorship of Catalan language and customs, by 1927, the use of Catalan language was on the rise, and Catalan book sales were at a peak. Also, Catalan political organizations were preparing a definitive assault against the rest of the peninsula. According to Giménez Caballero, beneath the apparent benevolence of Primo de Rivera's dictatorship, and particularly in 1927, Catalonia was in the final stages of planning an attack on Spain that had been incubating for a century. For Giménez Caballero, the desire for independence or separatism in Cuba was the main cause of the fall of the Spanish Empire. Separatism was the century's greatest evil, a cancer. What was even more troubling was that this desire to separate was spreading to many other regions of Spain. *La Gaceta Literaria* was his attempt to regenerate dead cells. It was the chemotherapy to cure Spain of its cancer called separatism.

Even after Franco's fall, Giménez Caballero stuck to his story. In a televised interview in the 1990s, he still described the relationship between Catalonia and the rest of Spain as one riddled by betrayal. Nearly sixty years after he shared the stage with Franco in Barcelona, Giménez Caballero insisted that his "passionate love" for Catalonia was what originally drove him to be united to her, in the same way that two lovers are joined in marriage. But once she "betrayed him" in the 1930s, he had no choice but to "kill" her, he says. Giménez Caballero confesses to "killing" her over national public radio when Franco entered Barcelona in 1939. He killed her because she could not belong to any other lover, only to him, or rather, Spain.

Given everything Giménez Caballero has written or said about Catalonia, during and after the publication of *La Gaceta Literaria*, no one has yet studied his methods and motives for including the Catalans in what is considered one of the most representative journals of documenting the cultural scene of 1920s Spain. He repeatedly denied that his periodical had any political motives. After considering his treatment of Catalonia, Catalans, and Catalanism in the magazine and its side projects over the course of this chapter, we can see how this statement is simply not true. Actions speak louder than words, and his actions state, loudly and clearly, that he had very clear political intentions regarding Catalonia and its place in his idea of Spain from very early on. It is unconvincing that his insistence on publishing so many texts in Catalan in *La Gaceta Literaria* was his way of being avant-garde. That may have been the pretext, but if we read between the lines and within a broader cultural context, it was not the case. Giménez Caballero was much more preoccupied with finding a way to unify Spain and put an end to regional separatism than exploring the avant-garde aesthetic in any sort of committed way. Little by little, most of those connected to the Barcelona and Madrid avant-garde networks abandoned him, because they saw through him. After all, his plan was purely political.

By the end of the 1930s, Giménez Caballero had lost faith that the Avant-Garde could transform Spain. Reconciliation between Catalonia and Spain seemed hopeless. Throughout the first three decades of the twentieth century, artists, intellectuals, politicians, poets, military men, and many others creatively sought solutions to end the conflicts between them once and for all. Giménez Caballero tried to resolve these differences through *La Gaceta Literaria* and all of the activities associated with this journal, but like the others, he lost hope. The people and governments of Barcelona and Madrid had been violently confronting one another off and on since at least the Reapers' War of 1640, the source of inspiration for the Catalan national anthem, with no peaceful resolution or happy compromise in sight.

As described by one former believer in the Avant-Garde, the camara-
derie intrinsic to this revolutionary movement and the shared spirit that it
created in people throughout Spain was not enough. The excitement that
connected Avant-Garde supporters in Barcelona and Madrid, engaging
them in dialogue, was inadequate. This writer notes that the "aggressive
individualism" of Spaniards and Catalans has historically taken one of two
roads: a "ferocious regionalism" or a "despotic centralism."[56] He also discerns
another pattern: during moments of cultural resurgence, it is the regions of
Spain that lead the way; while in moments of decline, centralist and imperialist politics rule. This paradigm is certainly evident when comparing the
intensity of avant-garde activity in Spain from 1909 to 1929. But Francisco
Guillén Salaya, author of this article, did not yet lose all hope. After publishing this article in *La Gaceta Literaria*, he founded a journal called *Atlántico*
(Madrid, 1929–33) that was dedicated to vanguard art and literature. Instead
of looking inwards toward Spain or even toward Europe, he directed his efforts across the Atlantic, toward Latin America. Initially an anarchist as a
youth, Guillén Salaya became an active leader in Franco's regime as one of
the founders of the union representing the Falange Party. Through his little
magazine, Guillén Salaya moved beyond the Castilian-Catalan conflict by
shifting his attention to Latin America. He focused on aesthetic issues related to the Avant-Garde and avoided controversial political matters, such
as printing in multiple languages. In doing so, he successfully collaborated
with several Catalans who contributed to this avant-garde periodical.

After the fall of Primo de Rivera, the use of multiple languages in
avant-garde journals was attempted again. This time, the Catalans tried
their hand at peninsular multilingualism. Notably, AC (Barcelona/Madrid/
San Sebastián, 1931–37), directed by two Catalans, J. L. Sert and Torres
Clavé, produced twenty-five issues trimesterly. While most of the issues
were published in Spanish, the last issue of this little magazine, inspired by
the French style of *esprit nouveau*, was trilingual: in Catalan, Spanish, and
French. Another avant-garde journal, also created in Catalonia, called *Art*
(Lleida, 1933–34) published texts in Catalan and Spanish. Reaching a total of ten issues, this little magazine devoted to the Avant-Garde included
publications by Catalans but also by non-Catalan Spaniards who were supporters of the vanguard style, such as Rafael Alberti, Vicente Aleixandre,
Federico García Lorca, and Nicolás Guillén. One last example of a little
magazine from Catalonia that took the multilingual route in its journalism
was *Quaderns de Poesia* (Barcelona, 1935–36). Even though only eight issues
were published, texts were printed in Catalan, Spanish, French, Italian, and
Portuguese, including contributions by Spanish writers like Manuel Alto-

laguirre, Federico García Lorca, José Moreno Villa, and Pedro Salinas, all of whom were connected to the avant-garde movement in Madrid.

After the Primo de Rivera dictatorship, editors of these vanguard magazines celebrated the peninsula's multilingualism. It is possible that Giménez Caballero and *La Gaceta Literaria* may have been role models for the multilingualism adopted by these three journals, two of which were explicitly avant-garde in style. But, now that the dictatorship that repressed the other peninsular languages besides Castilian, especially Catalan, was over, it may have just been a way in which the editors chose to renounce outright the repression of languages in general. Because various avant-garde magazines from Catalonia and the rest of Spain, especially Madrid, promoted multilingualism, we could say that this feature was part of being avant-garde. It was a valiant attempt, but ultimately unsuccessful in producing continued positive results.

All of Giménez Caballero's efforts to bridge the gap between Barcelona and Madrid, and all of those who came before and after him, were unable to heal centuries of injuries dividing these two cities. By adopting the avant-garde sensibility, Giménez Caballero, like so many others discussed in this book, hoped to put an end to old prejudices and to destroy politically constructed walls that divided Catalans and Spaniards. If the avant-garde as a style combated tradition, its leaders and supporters also had to resist historic rules of separation in the way that they lived out their daily lives. For Dalí, Gasch, and Montanyà, the inwardness of *noucentista* Catalan culture was decrepit. Giménez Caballero was appalled that some Catalans were offended that he published texts in Catalan in what happened to be one of the most influential cultural journals from Madrid. So many of the figures who made up the avant-garde networks of Barcelona and Madrid refused to be provincial and nationalistic. Their goal was to create a body of work and a corresponding culture that was universal, one that went beyond these politically fabricated divisions. While some searched for terms like *Iberian, pan-Iberian, Spanish,* or *Catalan,* to describe themselves, others preferred titles like *cubist, futurist, surrealist,* or simply *vanguardist.* There were even those that resisted labels all together.

What is certain is that the issue of language often got in the way. For many Catalans, Spanish represented the oppressive center of state; while for Spaniards, Catalan represented separatist desires. As we have seen in numerous examples, instead of working against each other, Avant-Garde enthusiasts throughout the first three decades of the twentieth century, representing both Barcelona and Madrid, were interested in collaborating by overcoming these pre-established misconceptions and misunderstandings.

The way they achieved this tolerance was by being interested in respecting and learning about one another with open minds and without limits. The effort was not in vain. The superior quality of art and literature created under the influence of the Avant-Garde placed Barcelona, Madrid, and Spain on the cultural map of the modern world.

Notes

1. Besides *La Gaceta Literaria*, there were two other cultural periodicals out of Madrid devoted to sustaining the Avant-Garde spirit. The first is *Nueva Revista* (1929–30). This little magazine totaled five issues, was printed entirely in Spanish, and included publications by Alberti, Bergamín, Salinas, Maruja Mallo, and students from the Faculty of Philosophy and Letters in Madrid. Unfortunately, this journal is not available at the National Library of Spain. The second periodical is *Atlántico* (1929–30), edited by Francisco Guillén Salaya. There were eighteen issues published, each of which was approximately 130 pages. This monthly journal, with a focus on cultural life in Latin America and printed entirely in Spanish, included contributions by Manuel Abril, Alberti, Francisco Ayala, Carmen Conde, Melchor Fernándes Almagro, González-Ruano, Benjamín Jarnés, Ledesma Ramos, and many others. Catalan contributors included two critics: Díaz-Plaja and Gasch.

2. Some of the little magazines in which these experimental poets and others were publishing include: *Ciutat* (Manresa, 1926–28), *L'Amic de les Arts* (Sitges/Barcelona, 1926–29), *Verso y Prosa* (Murcia, 1927–28), *Papel de Aleluyas* (Huelva/Sevilla, 1927–28), and *La rosa de los vientos* (Tenerife, 1927–28).

3. The prominent literary critic Melchor Fernández Almagro introduced readers to this little-known Catalan poet by writing the prologue to *La rosa y el laurel* (The Rose and the Laurel).

4. Melchor Fernández Almagro, *La Gaceta Literaria*, June 1, 1927, 65.

5. Ernesto Giménez Caballero, *Notas marruecas de un soldado* (Barcelona: Planeta, 1983), 6.

6. Douglas Foard, *Ernesto Giménez Caballero and the Origins of Spanish Fascism* (New York: P. Lang, 1989), 94.

7. In the first issues of *La Gaceta Literaria*, Giménez Caballero mentioned two periodicals from Spain as forerunners to his own: *La República de las Letras* (Madrid, 1905–?), directed by Benito Pérez Galdós, the realist novelist born in the Canary Islands; and the journal *España* (Madrid, 1915–24). The founder of this second periodical, José Ortega y Gasset, published his book *España invertebrada* (Invertebrate Spain) (1921), which Giménez Caballero claimed to be another source of inspiration for *La Gaceta Literaria*. Giménez Caballero writes about the influence of Ortega y Gasset's ideas on the creation of his literary journal in 1932: "Sobre esta España de Ortega yo fundé la esperanzas de mi Gaceta Literaria: es decir, el aceptar una hermandad regional de lenguas, una libertad absoluta de conciencia, un mito a ultranza

de la Cultura por la Cultura y del Arte por el Arte; una creencia central de que la salvación de España estaba en lo minoritario, sobre todo si esto de lo minoritario tenía un fundamento 'rubio', vital y 'franco.'" (It is on Ortega y Gasset's *Invertebrate Spain* that my hopes for the *Gaceta Literaria* were founded: that is to say, to accept a regional brotherhood of languages, an absolute freedom of consciousness, a total myth of Culture for Culture's Sake and Art for Art's Sake; a centralizing belief that Spain's salvation lay in the minorities, especially if this minority was blond, vital, and frank.) See José Ortega y Gasset, *Genio de España exaltaciones a una resurrección nacional y del mundo* (Barcelona: Planeta, 1983), lvi.

8. E. Giménez Caballero, *Trabalenguas sobre España* (Madrid: CIAP, 1931), 348.

9. Enrique Selva Roca de Togores, *Ernesto Giménez Caballero entre la vanguardia y el fascismo* (Valencia: Pre-Textos, 2000), 8.

10. In addition to founding *El Sol*, Nicolás María de Urgoiti (1869–1951) established a publishing company, the Compañía Anónima de Librería, Publicaciones y Ediciones (CALPE). Juan Miguel Sánchez Vigil, "Ortega y Gasset," *Revista de Estudios Orteguianos*, 10–11 (2005): 177–96. Urgoiti was a friend of Giménez Caballero's father; see Andrew Anderson, *Ernesto Giménez Caballero Caballero: The Vanguard Years (1921–1931)* (Newark: Juan de la Cuesta, 2011), 48.

11. After the Primo de Rivera overthrow, more leftist political parties emerged in Catalonia. The Lliga Regionalista was abolished during the Spanish Civil War.

12. Enric Ucelay-Da Cal. *El imperialismo catalán. Prat de la Riba, Cambó, D'Ors y la conquista moral de España* (Barcelona: Edhasa, 2003), 388.

13. Please see appendix H for a list of texts in Catalan or about Catalonia or Catalan culture that I have compiled for the first three years that *La Gaceta Literaria* was in print (1927–29).

14. In the first two years that the magazine was in print, over 50 percent of the advertisements in each issue of *La Gaceta Literaria* were paid for by bookstores and publishing houses in Barcelona. In the issue that celebrated the magazine's first anniversary, Giménez Caballero thanks his loyal patrons from Barcelona, including the Bernat Metge Foundation, as well as several publishing companies: Gustavo Gili, Montaner y Simón, Editorial Juventud, Salvat, Editorial Sopena; and two bookstores: Librería Catalonia and La Librería Francesa.

15. José Ortega y Gasset, "Sobre un periódico de las letras," *La Gaceta Literaria*, January 1, 1927, 1.

16. "Plurality in the Name of Unity," *La Gaceta Literaria*, January 15, 1927, 7.

17. Giménez Caballero's plan to achieve national unity through effective communication and an all-inclusive attitude toward difference involved modeling his magazine on those from other countries that faced similar difficulties, such as Italy, Germany, and Poland. Massimo Bomtempelli, editor of the avant-garde periodical *900: Cahiers d'Italie et d'Europe* (Rome, 1926–?), published his magazine in French, since he considered it to be the *lingua franca* of Europe. The German periodical *Ars* from Berlin published in multiple languages, as did Poland's *Polinisch Literator*.

18. Francesc Trabal, "Diálogo de las lenguas," *La Gaceta Literaria*, February 15, 1927, 21.

19. According to Giménez Caballero, news of Madrid is nowhere to be found within the pages of Catalan periodicals. *La Publicitat* (Barcelona) is a newspaper he complained about in particular and on several occasions over the course of *La Gaceta Literaria*'s first year. It bothers Giménez Caballero that it is difficult to find a book printed in Spanish in Barcelona bookstores.

20. Giménez Caballero, *La Gaceta Literaria*, 39.

21. *La Gaceta Literaria*, 45, 65, 136.

22. *La Gaceta Literaria*, 7, 151, 324.

23. *La Gaceta Literaria*, 550.

24. This conclusion is based on the assumption that these twenty-five visually enhanced literary reviews were all created in 1927. Anderson explains that most of the ninety-five text-based reviews in part one of *Carteles* are a compilation of book reviews that Giménez Caballero published in *El Sol* since 1925 (Anderson, *Ernesto Giménez Caballero*, 48).

25. For a detailed description of the contents of the book *Carteles* (1927), not to be mistaken with the posters Giménez Caballero exhibited in Barcelona and Madrid ("Carteles literarios"), see Anderson, *Ernesto Giménez Caballero*, 47–50.

26. The Dalmau Galleries showed Giménez Caballero's posters at the same time as Manifestació de Arte de Vanguardia (January 1, 1928–January 20, 1928), which included works by Barradas, Evaristo Basiana, Dalí, Magín Cassañes, Gausachs, Güell, C. Enric, Ricart, Ketterer Moya, An Guyas. For a detailed index of exhibits at the Dalmau Galleries, see Jaume Vidal i Oliveras, *Josep Dalmau. L'aventura per l'art modern* (Manresa: Fundació Caixa de Manresa, 1993), 221–33.

27. Ernesto Giménez Caballero, "Líneas autobiográficas," *Hèlix*, June 1929, 3; series ended in the February 1930 issue, p. 2.

28. Sebastià Gasch, "Arte. Madrid : Barcelona. La Exposición en Dalmau," *La Gaceta Literaria*, February 1, 1927, 168.

29. Lluís Montanyà, "Carteles," *La Gaceta Literaria*, May 1, 1928.

30. Lluís Montanyà's name appeared for the first time in Giménez Caballero's periodical in an article by another Catalan journalist, Sebastià Sánchez-Juan, titled "Lluís Montanyà. Un nou poeta català" (Lluís Montanyà. A New Catalan Poet), which was written in Catalan and accompanied by a photograph of Montanyà (no. 22, November 15, 1927, p. 131). His name also appears in an article written anonymously reporting on the *Manifest Groc* (Yellow Manifesto). This document is also known as the Catalan Anti-Art Manifesto, signed by Salvador Dalí, Montanyà, and Gasch; pamphleteered in Barcelona; and published in March 1928 (no. 31, April 1, 1928, p. 196). This manifesto is one of the most frequently referenced documents of the artistic and literary revolutionary moment. Addressed to young Catalans, it denounced the rotting state of Catalan culture and promoted the futurist, cubist, and Dadaist legacies. Montanyà's debut in *La Gaceta Literaria* was an article written in Spanish about surrealism, just prior to the launching of the Yellow Manifesto

(no. 28, February 15, 1928, p. 175). Montanyà mostly published in Catalan and contributed primarily to that press.

31. Josep Maria Sucre's review of the literary posters can be found in *La Gaceta Literaria*, March 1, 1928, 172.

32. The limits of this universe imagined by Giménez Caballero are marked by Urgoiti's liberal Madrid daily newspaper, *El Sol*, on the one hand, and Torucato Luca de Tena's conservative *ABC* competitor, on the other. Only a handful of periodicals from outside of Madrid make it onto the poster; these are *Mediodía, Litoral, Papel de Aleluyas*, and *Verso y Prosa*—all little magazines from the south of Spain.

33. José-Carlos Mainer, "Ernesto Giménez Caballero o la inoportunidad," in *Casticismo, nacionalismo y vanguardia*, ed. José-Carlos Mainer (Madrid: Fundación Santander Central Hispano, 2005), xliv.

34. Bejamín Jarnés, "El libro catalán," in *Cataluña ante España* (Madrid: La Gaceta Literaria, 1930), 90.

35. Josep Pla, "La Publicitat," in *Cataluña ante España* (Madrid: La Gaceta Literaria, 1930), 48.

36. Spain's minister of education inaugurated the show, which also had the support of the National Library's president, Francisco Rodríguez Marín, and the president of the newly restructured Real Academia Española (Spanish Royal Academy), Marcelino Menéndez Pelayo. For a list of Barcelona and Madrid organizers and collaborators of the Catalan Book Fair, see appendix C.

37. Giménez Caballero, Letter to Sánchez Cuesta, November 2, 1927. The original letter was located at the Biblioteca Transatlántica at the Residencia de Estudiantes.

38. Lucy Tandy and María Sferrazza. *Ernesto Giménez Caballero y "La Gaceta Literaria" o la Generación del 27* (Madrid: Turner, 1977), 38.

39. For a list of individuals involved with the Madrid organizing committee of the Catalan Book Fair, see appendix C, which was compiled based on my research and with the assistance of a list already available in Joaquim Ventalló, *Los intelectuales castellanos y Cataluña. Tres fechas históricas: 1924, 1927 y 1930* (Barcelona: Galba, 1976), 53.

40. The names of the "Castilian intellectuals" who signed the manifesto in defense of the Catalan language and who also were involved with the organizing of the Catalan Book Fair in Madrid were Luis Araquistáin, Azorín, Domingo Barnés, Juan de la Encina, Eduardo Gómez de Baquero, Ramón Gómez de la Serna, Luis Jiménez de Asúa, Félix Lorenzo, Gabriel Maura, Ramón Menéndez Pidal, José Ortega y Gasset, Angel Ossorio y Gallardo, Gustavo Pittaluga, Pedro Sainz Rodríguez, José Ruiz Castillo, and Fabián Vidal.

41. For a list of individuals involved with the Barcelona organizing committee of the Catalan Book Fair, see appendix C.

42. The publishing companies that were established during the Catalan Renaissance of the late nineteenth century include the following (as they appear in the catalog of the Catalan Book Fair): *La Ilustració Catalana, el Nuevo Siglo, L'Avenç,*

Biblioteca Juventut, La Revista, Editorial Catalana, Biblioteca Catalana, Biblioteca Literaria, and *Enciclopedia Catalana*.

43. *El Sol*, December 1927. I would like to give special thanks to Professor Lucia Aranda, a translation scholar from the University of Hawaii at Manoa, for assistance with this translation from Spanish to English.

44. Pedro Sainz Rodríguez, *Cataluña ante España* (Madrid: La Gaceta Literaria, 1930), 51.

45. Ibid.

46. Ibid.

47. Ibid, 83.

48. *Exposición del Libro Catalán*. Madrid (December 5–21, 1927), Catalog, 5.

49. Recorded remarks by one artist and one businessman, both residents of Madrid, document the fraternal mood of the closing banquet for the Catalan Book Fair. Luis Bagaría, a popular Catalan caricaturist working in Madrid, who had been severely persecuted by the military authorities for his drawings in the press, spoke of "patria" or homeland. For him, there were two kinds of homelands. The first is the place where one is born; the other, more abstract and universal, is made of people around the globe who share a common notion of justice and honor. A Basque native and powerful figure in Madrid's publishing industry, Nicolás María Urgoiti, spoke on a similar topic. He declared that he was an example of how Spaniards could be representatives of their place of birth but also global citizens of the world. He spoke about how people of different nationalities could come together to comprise a larger whole, whose goal must be peace and fraternity among all peoples regardless of nationality. Both of these remarks advocate for the transcendence of national identity and suggest the adoption of a more universal position as a way of resolving Spain's twentieth-century identity crisis. For more on the banquet given in honor of the Catalans at the Book Fair in Madrid, see Ventalló, *Intelectuales castellanos*, 55–60.

50. Some of the Catalan journalists who contributed to this collection of press clippings about the Catalan Book Fair are Gabriel Alomar, Gaziel, and Josep Pla; as for the Castilians, articles by Juan de la Encina, Azorín and Giménez Caballero are also available for consultation.

51. Esterlich had recently published his book *Catalonia endins* (Catalonia from within) (1930), in which he strongly argued that it was Catalonia's destiny to transform Spain.

52. Ernesto Giménez Caballero, *Revista de Catalunya*, April 14, 1931.

53. Ernesto Giménez Caballero, *La Gaceta Literaria*, no. 105.

54. Ibid.

55. Ernesto Giménez Caballero, *Amor a Cataluña* (Madrid: Ruta, 1942).

56. Francisco Guillén Salaya, *La Gaceta Literaria*, October 15, 1928, 276.

~

Conclusion

In comparison to the importance placed on the coetaneous artistic and literary movements it resisted, such as realism, naturalism, and the Generation of '98, the Avant-Garde in Spain is often treated like an annoying interruption. Most graduate students in Hispanic studies do not study this period in any depth, while undergraduates hear of it tangentially vis-à-vis Picasso, Buñuel, or Dalí, if they are lucky. The irony is that while all three of these names might be included on a list of the greatest minds that radically restructured our way of viewing the twentieth century and of finding new meaning in art, we spend very little time understanding who they were or where they came from, particularly within a much wider cultural context. For instance, many do not know that these three masterminds are actually from Spain. Many think they are French. It is true that they left their homeland in search of better opportunities in neighboring France, but all three of them were born in Spain and spent most of their formative lives here, precisely at the dawn of the Avant-Garde in Barcelona and Madrid.

What I would like to invite my readers to see is that what we remember of twentieth-century Spain, from its disastrous beginnings (e.g., the Spanish-American War, the War in Morocco, World War I, Tragic Week, the Spanish Civil War, etc.) to finally attaining a peaceful society in the form of a stable, democratic government after the fall of General Francisco Franco in 1975, is intimately tied to this alternative, artistic liberation movement. If we ignore the Avant-Garde, we conceal the freedom stories of pre-Franco Spain. This social network analysis of the Avant-Garde in Spain shows the many connections between Barcelona and Madrid on various levels. The respective avant-garde promoters of Barcelona and Madrid were interconnected and interrelated, whether they liked it or not, for it was an inherent aspect of the movement itself. We have learned about collaborations and disassociations, and also of resonances and dissonances.

If promoters of the Avant-Garde read the little magazines, attended literary gatherings, and visited modern art shows, it was impossible to be unaware of what was happening either in Barcelona or Madrid, or in other cities in Spain for that matter, like Bilbao, La Coruña, Tenerife, or Seville. One of the fundamental qualities of being avant-garde was to break boundaries, so why not move from city to city instead of staying in one place? If one could not afford to travel, avant-garde enthusiasts found other forms of traveling. One way of exploring new frontiers was by befriending foreigners, of which there were so many in Spain during the First Great War, or making friends with people from different parts of the country who were congregated in either of the two modern metropolises in question. The common bond that united all of them was a shared belief in the spirit of the Avant-Garde, one of endless possibilities.

APPENDIX A

~

The Iberians

This is a list of the artists who exhibited at the Iberians show in Madrid in 1925. Names are categorized by region in Spain or foreign nationality. Their birthplace, date of birth, and date of death are also given when available.

Basque Country:

1. Alberto Arrúe (Bilbao, 1878–1944)
2. Aurelio Arteta (Bilbao, 1879–Mexico, D.F., 1940)
3. José Benito Bikandi (Vizcaya, 1896–Buenos Aires, 1958)
4. Juan de Echevarría (Bilbao, 1875–Madrid, 1931)
5. Juan de la Encina (Bilbao–Mexico, D.F., 1963)
6. Antonio Guezala (Bilbao, 1889–1956)
7. Ernesto López Orúe (Bilbao, 1897–Pamplona, 1957)
8. Julián Tellaeche (Guipúzcoa, 1884–Lima, 1957)
9. Quintín de Torre (Bilbao, 1877–1966)
10. José María Ucelay (Vizcaya 1903–1979)
11. Jenaro Urrutia (Vizcaya, 1893–Bilbao, 1965)
12. Ramón de Zubiaurre (Vizcaya, 1882–Madrid, 1969)

Madrid:

1. Manuel Abril (Madrid, 1884–1943)
2. Francisco Bores (Madrid, 1898–Paris, 1972)

3. Roberto Fernández Balbuena (Madrid, 1891–Mexico, 1966)
4. Angel Ferrant (Madrid, 1891–1961)
5. Fernando Vargas de la Cotera (Madrid, c. 1910)
6. José Gutiérrez Solana (Madrid, 1886–1945)
7. Guillermo de Torre (Madrid, 1900–Buenos Aires, 1971)
8. Valentín de Zubiaurre (Madrid, 1879–1963)

Castile (Leon and La Mancha):

1. Emiliano Barral (Segovia, 1896–Madrid, 1936)
2. Javier Cortés (Burgos, 1890–Madrid, 1991)
3. Gabriel García Maroto (Ciudad Real, 1889–Mexico, D.F., 1969)
4. Victorio Macho (Palencia, 1887–Toledo, 1966)
5. Benjamín Palencia (Albacete, 1894–Madrid, 1980)
6. Alberto Sánchez (Toledo, 1895–Moscú, 1962)
7. Francisco Santa Cruz (Guadalajara, 1899–Madrid, 1957)

Catalonia:

1. Juan Bautista Adsuara (Castellón de la Plana, 1891–1973)
2. Luis Bagaría (Barcelona, 1882–La Habana, 1940)
3. José Capuz (Valencia, 1884–Madrid, 1964)
4. Salvador Dalí (Figueres, 1904–Púbol, 1989)
5. Ramón Pichot (Barcelona, 1870–Paris, 1925)

Andalusia:

1. José Moreno Villa (Málaga, 1887–Mexico, 1955)
2. Joaquín Peinado (Málaga, 1898–Paris, 1975)
3. José Planes (Murcia, 1891–1974)
4. Cristóbal Ruiz (Jaén, 1881–Mexico, 1962)
5. Daniel Vázquez Díaz (Huelva, 1882–Madrid, 1969)

Aragon:

1. Luis Berdejo (Teruel, 1902–Barcelona, 1980)
2. Santiago Pelegrín (Zaragoza, 1885–Madrid, 1954)

Asturias:

1. Nicanor Pinole (Gijón, 1878–1978)

Galicia:

1. José Frau (Vigo, 1898–Madrid, 1976)

Foreign:

1. Rafael Barradas (Montevideo, Uruguay, 1890–1929)
2. Norah Borges (Buenos Aires, Argentina, 1901–1998)
3. Francisco Gutiérez Cossío (Cuba, 1894–Alicante, 1970)
4. Marjan Paszkiewicz (Poland, ?–?)
5. Carlos Sáenz de Tejada (Tangier, Morocco, 1897–Madrid, 1958)
6. Pablo Zelaya (Honduras, ?–Madrid, 1933)

Unknown:

1. Fernando Arranz (?–?)
2. Irene Narezo (?–?)

APPENDIX B

~

Modern Catalan Art Show

This is an alphabetical list of artists who showed at the Modern Catalan Art Exhibition, which took place at the Círculo de Bellas Artes (Plaza de las Cortes, 4) in Madrid from January 16, 1926, to February 1, 1927.

Painters:

1. Ferran Callicó Rebull (1909–?)
2. Francesc Camps (1895–1991)
3. Ricard Canals (1876–1931)
4. Doménech Carles (1888–?)
5. Salvador Dalí (1904–1989)
6. Rafael Duran Camps (1891–?)
7. Marian Antoni Espinal (1895–?)
8. Josep Gausachs (1889–1959)
9. Ignasi Genover (?–?)
10. Jaume Guàrdia (1885–1935)
11. Manuel Humbert (1890–1975)
12. Pere Isern (1876–1946)
13. Pere Isern Alié (1876–1946)
14. Oleguer Junyent (1876–?)
15. Joan Junyner (1904–1994)
16. Labarta (?–?)
17. Marian Llavanera (1890–1927)

18. Josep María Marqués-Puig (1890–1950)
19. Jaime Mercadé (1889–?)
20. Lluís Mercadé (1898–?)
21. Joan Miró (1893–1983)
22. Josep Mompou (1888–1968)
23. Joaquim Mombrú (1892–?)
24. Jacint Olivé (1896–1967)
25. Iu Pascual (1883–1949)
26. Porcas (?–?)
27. Josep Pujol Ripoll (1904–1987)
28. Enric Ricart (1893–1960)
29. Ernest Santasusagna (1900–1964)
30. Joan Serra (1899–1970)
31. Alfred Sísquella (1900–1964)
32. Ramon (Pichot) Soler (1924–1996)
33. Joaquim Sunyer (1874–1956)
34. Pere Torné-Esquius (1879–1936)
35. Francesc Vayreda (1888–1929)

Sculptors:

1. Josep Dunyach Sala (1886–1957)
2. Josep Grené (?–?)
3. Federic Marés (1893–?)
4. Joan Rebull (1899–1981)
5. Josep Viladomat (1899–1989)

Illustrators:

1. Josep-Francesc Rafols (1889–1965)
2. Pere Ynglada (1881–1958)

APPENDIX C

~

Catalan Book Fair

The Catalan Book Fair was held at the Biblioteca Nacional in Madrid from December 5 to 21 in 1927. The following list compiles names of those who were involved in organizing it in Barcelona and in Madrid.

Organizers from Barcelona:

1. Joan Esterlich
2. Pompeu Fabra
3. Luis Bagaría
4. Rafael Vehils
5. Lluís Bertran i Pijoan
6. Jordi Rubió i Balaguer (director of the *Biblioteca de Cataluña* in Barcelona)
7. Tomás Garcés
8. Joan Givanel i Mas
9. Antoni López Llausàs
10. Anna Maria de Saavedra
11. Adela Trepay
12. Ferran Valls i Taberner
13. Carles Saldevila
14. Carles Riba
15. Miquel Ferrà
16. Felieu Elias

17. José Figuerola
18. Antonio M. Sbert
19. Cámara del Libro de Barcelona

Names of People and Groups Associated with the Catalan Book Fair in Madrid:

1. Ernesto Giménez Caballero
2. León Sánchez Cuesta
3. Eduardo Gómez de Baquero
4. Francisco Giner
5. Francisco Rodríguez Marín (director of the Biblioteca Nacional in Madrid)
6. Menéndez Pidal (president of the Real Academia Española)
7. Alvaro Alcalá Galiano
8. Feliu Eilas "Apa"
9. A. G. de Amezúa
10. Luis Araquistain
11. Azorín
12. Ricardo Baeza
13. Domingo Barnés
14. Ignacio Baüer y Landaüer
15. Luis Bello
16. Francisco Beltrán
17. Rabel Caro Raggio
18. José Castillejo
19. Américo Castro
20. Roberto Castrovido
21. The Duke of Alba
22. Juan de la Encina
23. Ramón Gómez de la Serna
24. Luis Jiménez de Asúa
25. J. Lasso de la Vega
26. Félix Lorenzo
27. Lorenzo Luzuriaga
28. Gregorio Marañon
29. Julián Matrínez Reus
30. Gabriel Maura
31. Ramón Menéndez Pidal
32. Enrique de la Mesa

33. Agustín Millares
34. Manuel G. Morente
35. José Ortega y Gasset
36. Javier de Ortueta
37. Angel Osorio y Gallardo
38. Gustavo Pittaluga
39. F. Rivera Pastor
40. Francisco Rodríguez Marín
41. The Count Rodríguez de San Pedero
42. José Ruiz Castillo
43. Pedro Sainz Rodríguez
44. José A. de Sangróniz
45. Luis Santullano
46. Nicolás M. de Urgoiti
47. Fabián Vidal
48. *La Gaceta Literaria*
49. Ministerio de Instrucción Pública y Bellas Artes

APPENDIX D

~

Spanish School in Paris

The following is a list of artists who exhibited at the Exhibition of Spanish Residents in Paris that took place in the Botanical Gardens in El Retiro Park (Pabellón Villanueva) in Madrid from March 20 to 25, 1929.

Painters:

1. Manuel Angeles Ortiz (Jaén, 1895–París, 1984)
2. Francisco Bores (Madrid, 1898–París, 1972)
3. Pancho Cossío (Cuba, 1894–Alicante, 1970)
4. Salvador Dalí (Figueres, 1904–1989)
5. Joan Gris (Madrid, 1887–Francia, 1927)
6. Ismael González de la Serna (Granada, 1898–Paris, 1968)
7. Joan Miró (Barcelona, 1893–Mallorca, 1983)
8. Alfonso de Olivares (Guipúzcoa, 1898–Madrid, 1936)
9. Benjamín Palencia (Albacete, 1894–Madrid, 1980)
10. Gabriela Pastor (?–?)
11. Joaquín Peinado (Málaga, 1898–Paris, 1975)
12. Pablo Picasso (Málaga, 1881–Francia, 1972)
13. Pere Pruna (Barcelona, 1904–1977)
14. José María Ucelay (Vizcaya, 1903–1979)
15. Hernando Viñes (París, 1904–1993)

Sculptors:

1. Luis Alberto (Valencia, 1902–1968)
2. Apel·les Fenosa (Barcelona, 1899–Paris, 1988)
3. Pablo Gargallo (Zaragoza, 1881–Reus, 1934)
4. Huguet (Manolo) (Barcelona, 1872–1945)

APPENDIX E

~

Works Displayed at the *Exposició de modernisme pictoric catala*

I have compiled a list of the works displayed in the Exposició de modernisme pictoric catala confrontada amb una selecció d'obres d'artistes d'avantguarda estrangers (Modern Catalan Painting Confronts with a Selection of Foreign Avant-Garde Artists) at the Dalmau Galleries (October 16 to November 6, 1926, Barcelona). This information was made available to me in the form of a photocopy of the original catalogue from the private archive of a friend, Miquel Visa.

Foreign Artists:

1. Frank Burty: Interior; Faubourg
2. Robert Delaunay: Joguines; Llibres
3. Raul Dufy: Notre Dame de la Chance (colored stamp); Le coq
4. Albert Gleizes: Les joueurs de football; New-York
5. Helena Grunoff: La Gruta; Natura morta; Natura morta
6. Marie Laurencin: Noia al jardí
7. Madame X: Els turistes
8. Otto Weber: Caballers al camp; Costa Catalana; Costa Catalana
9. Francis Picabia: Lampe; Manola
10. Slavi Soucek: Retrat (drawing); Impresió de carrer (watercolor)
11. Maurice Vlaminck: Paisatge

Catalan Artists:

1. Carles Albesa: Paisatge; Bodegó
2. Rafael Benet: La Boira; Fumisol
3. Rafael Barradas: Obrer; Figura en un interior; Paisatge
4. Emili Bosch Roger: Paisatge de Premiá de Mar; Paisatge Sta. Coloma de Cervelló; Dibuix
5. Francesc Camps: Noia al balcó; Oli; Gent de taberna
6. Magí A. Cassanyes: C a O; Matinal (drawing); Nocturn (drawing)
7. Salvador Dalí: Natura morta; Figura; Figura
8. Josep Dalmau: Reflexes; El gerro; Nota de color (pastel)
9. Jaume Guardia: Mediterrania; Joventut
10. Josep Gausachs: Gerro de flors; Retrat
11. Manuel Humbert: Oli
12. Manolo Hugué: Relleu
13. Joan Junyer: Oli; Oli
14. Pere Jou: Escultura
15. Joan Miró: Cap de nena; El balcó
16. Josep Mompou: Peixos; Ostres
17. Ramón Pichot: Reconet de França; La pomera; Record de la guerra
18. Enric Ricart: Coses (plafó decoratiu); La sopera
19. Joan Rebull: Dança (sculpture)
20. Joaquim Sunyer: Una noia
21. Alfred Sisquella: Bodegó
22. Joaquín Torres García; Oli

APPENDIX F

~

National and Foreign Modern Art

Provided below is a list of the artists who exhibited at the Exposición de Arte Moderno Nacional y Extranjero (National and Foreign Modern Art) (October 31 to November 15, 1929, Barcelona) at the Dalmau Galleries (Paseo de Gracia, 62). Source: Mercè Vidal, *L'Exposició d'Art Cubista de les Galeries Dalmau* (Barcelona: Universitat de Barcelona, 1996), 97.

Foreigners:

1. H. Arp
2. T. Arp
3. L. Blaire
4. G. Cochet
5. A. Clergé
6. F. Cupera
7. Charchoune
8. O. Doesburg
9. L. Fernández
10. I. Helion
11. A. Jouclar
12. A. Lhote
13. Marembert
14. Piet Mondrian
15. G. Nilbauer

16. Rees Adya Van
17. Rees Otto Van
18. Vantongerloo
19. O. Weber
20. J. Xceron

Nationals (Catalans):

1. E. Basiana
2. J. Biosca
3. A. Carbonell
4. Srta. M. Casanova
5. J. Claret
6. V. Corberó
7. A. Costa
8. P. Creixans
9. P. Daura
10. A. Ferrer
11. A. Folquer
12. L. Garay
13. F. Grau Sala
14. X. Guell
15. Srta. E. Homs
16. J. Junyer
17. López Cañete
18. Srta. M. L. Lamor
19. L. Morató
20. J. Papiol
21. P. Planas
22. J. Ma. Puig
23. R. Reig
24. J. Sandalinas
25. J. M. Sucre
26. Torres García
27. I. Vidal
28. M. Villá

APPENDIX G

~

Catalan Contributors

Ernesto Giménez Caballero listed the following Catalans as contributors during the first year of *La Gaceta Literaria*, as listed in the January 1, 1928, issue (number 25). Italicized names are those whose work was actually published (not just received) by the magazine.

1. *J. Xirau*
2. *Josep Maria de Sucre*
3. *Carles Soldevila*
4. *M. de Montoliu*
5. Josep Maria Millás
6. *Rosend Llatas (poetry)*
7. *Tomás Garcés*
8. *Juan Gutiérrez Gili*
9. *Sebastiá Gasch*
10. *Gustavo Gili*
11. *Miguel Ferrá (Mallorca) (poetry)*
12. *A. Esclasans*
13. *Joan Esterlich*
14. *A. M. Colomar*
15. Altsamora
16. *Josep Subirá*
17. *Alfons Maseras*
18. *Valls Taberner*

19. *Gaziel (poetry)*
20. Almela i Vives
21. *Ferrán i Mayoral*
22. Ortin Benedito
23. Josep Bayarri
24. S. Verdeguer
25. E. Navarro Borrás
26. F. Caballero Muñoz
27. P. Asín Lerma
28. *Sebastiá Sánchez Joan (poetry)*
29. *Lluís Montanyá*
30. Josep Carbonell
31. *Carles Riba (survey answer)*
32. Andrés Bausili
33. Millás Raurell
34. *J. M. López Picó (survey answer)*
35. *Joan Salvat-Papasseit*
36. Josep Carner
37. *L. Nicolau d'Olwer*
38. Josep Pla
39. Puig i Ferreter
40. *Salvador Dalí*

APPENDIX H

∿

Catalan Presence
in *La Gaceta Literaria*

I have compiled a list of articles written by Catalans or about Catalans, Barcelona, or Catalonia, printed in either Catalan or Castilian, that appeared in *La Gaceta Literaria*'s first three years in print (1927–29). Unless otherwise indicated, publications were printed in Castilian. Also indicated are the pages numbers on which the articles appear. This list is the first of its kind.

Number 1. January 1, 1927:

1. "Scientiste o cientifics," A. Pi Sunyer (*Catalan*) (p. 3)
2. "L. Nicolau D'Olwer: L'Expansió de Catalonia en la Mediterrania Oriental," Giménez Caballero (p. 3)

Number 2. January 15, 1927:

1. "Notes critiques sobre la nova lírica catalana," Manuel de Montoliu (*Catalan*) (p. 9)

Number 3. February 1, 1927:

1. "Postales ibéricas. Junoy," J. A. (p. 14)
2. "Poemas en mapa," "Les tres besades," Garcés (*Catalan*); "Vells carreres de l'Almudaina," Miquel Ferrá (Mallorcan); "L'Infinit," Rosend Llatas (Catalan); "Sóller," M. Angel Colomar (Castilian) (followed by a brief

description of each of the authors in Castilian, written by Giménez Caballero) (p. 15)

Number 4. February 15, 1927:

1. "Relieves peninsulares. El Humanista de la Vía Layetana (sobre Joan Esterlich)," Editors (pp. 19–20)
2. "Un assaig de revisió: Inteligencia i sentiment," Carles Soldevila (*Catalan*) (p. 21)
3. "El diálogo de las lenguas. Suspicacia poco avanzada," Giménez Caballero (p. 21)
4. "Libros catalanes," Sucre (p. 24)

Number 5. March 1, 1927:

1. "Ciencia i cultura," Joaquim Xirau (*Catalan*) (p. 27)
2. "Joaquim Xirau," drawing by Salvador Dalí (p. 27)
3. "Libros catalanes" (p. 27)
4. "Ateneílo-Hospitalet," Gutiérrez Gili (p. 29)
5. "Les arts i els artistas. Exposición en Galerías Laietanas," Sucre (p. 29)

Number 6. March 15, 1927:

1. "El diálogo de las lenguas," Giménez Caballero (p. 31)
2. "Libros catalanes," Sucre (p. 33)
3. "La Revista," Esclanas (*Catalan*) (p. 33)

Number 7. April 1, 1927:

1. Caricature of the Catalan editor Gili (p. 37)
2. "El diálogo de las lenguas," Giménez Caballero (p. 39)
3. "Les dues muses," Miquel Ferrá (about Joan Alcover) (*Catalan*) (p. 39)
4. "Libros catalanes" (p. 42)

Number 8. April 15, 1927:

1. "El pintor Joan Miró," Sebastià Gasch (*Catalan*) (p. 45)
2. "Literatura catalana: José Plá: *Relacións*, Peer Gynt (Josep Maria Sucre or Juan Alsamora; see Molas, p. 28);
3. "Crónica de Jaume I," Arturo Perucho (p. 45)
4. "El 'Catalan puro.' Carta a Rovira i Virgili," Giménez Caballero (p. 45)

Number 9. May 1, 1927:

1. "Literatura catalana. Un recuerdo a Maragall. El místic del llenguatge," Joan Esterlich; "Pompeyo Fabra," Amado Alonso; "Dos novedades de ruido (*Marcos Villari*, de Barolomé Soler, y *El marido, la mujer y la sombra*, de Mario Verdaguer)," Giménez Caballero (p. 51)

Number 10. May 15, 1927:

1. "Libros catalanes: *Epistolari del segle XV*," Arturo Perucho (p. 57)
2. "Itinerario de revistas: *Revista de Catalonia* y *L'Amic de les Arts*" (p. 58)
3. "Teatro. El teatro de hoy," Jacinto Grau (p. 59)

Number 11. June 1, 1927:

1. "Góngora en Cataluña," Garcés (*Catalan*) (p. 61)
2. "Biblioteca Ibérica. Tomás Garcés: 'La rosa y el laurel'," Melchor Fernández Almagro (photo) (advertisement) (p. 65)
3. "Los raids literarios. Nicolau D'Olwer. El conde de la Mortera en La Habana" (p. 65)

Number 12. June 15, 1927:

1. "La réplica a Darío (1927). Madurez, divino tesoro," Eugenio D'Ors (p. 69)
2. "Una elegía a Joan Alcover," Maristany and Alfons Maseras (p. 71)
3. "Libros catalanes. Ferrán Valls i Ferrán Soldevila: Reseña 'Història de Catalonia,'" Enrique Lafuente (p. 71)

Number 13. July 1, 1927:

1. "Goya desde Barcelona," Sucre (p. 76)
2. "Libros catalanes. L'escultura catalana moderna," Arturo Perucho (p. 77)
3. "S. Sarra Serravinyals," Sucre (p. 77)
4. "Xenius. La nova promoció devant de la companya de descredit orsiá," Sucre (p. 77)
5. "Poemes d'amor y de camí," J. M. Rovira Artigues (p. 77)
6. "Les doctrines politiques en la Catalonia Medieval," F. Valls Taberner (*Catalan*) (p. 77)

Number 14. July 15, 1927:

1. "Memorias literarias. Autobiografía de un seudónimo. Gaziel" (p. 81)
2. "Salvador Dalí," Gasch (p. 85)

Number 15. August 1, 1927:

1. "Gaudi," Josep F. Rafols (*Catalan*) (p. 89)
2. "Música. El Beethovenismo y Cataluña," Subirá (p. 92)
3. "Libros catalanes. J. Navarro Costabella: *Samuel*. Bellafila: *Tres estels i un rosesec*. J. V. Foix: *Gertrudis*," Sucre (p. 92)

Number 16. August 15, 1927:

1. "Conmemoración: La vida y la obra de Salvat Papasseit," Garcés (p. 93)
2. "La llengua catalana," Farran i Mayoral (*Catalan*) (p. 95)
3. "Gabriel Alomar," M. Angel Colomar (p. 95)
4. Poetry from Valencia (*Catalan*) (p. 75)
5. "Francesc Domingo," Gasch (p. 97)

Number 17. September 1, 1927:

1. "Postales Ibéricas. García Lorca se ausenta de Barcelona," Peer Gynt (p. 100)
2. "Un nuevo periódico catalán (*La Nau*)," Anon. (p. 100)

Number 18. September 15, 1927:

1. "Libros catalanes. Sant Vincenç Ferrer (de Almel i Vives)," Anon. (p. 106)
2. "Mapa en Rosa" (Poetry by and about women), "María Tersa Vernet," Sucre (p. 107)
3. "El Teatre Catalá," A. Esclasans (*Catalan*) (p. 109)

Number 19. October 1, 1927:

1. "La Cámara del Libro de Barcelona," Anon. (p. 111)
2. "Libros catalanes: Benjamín Jarnés: *El Conde Güell: Apuntes de recuerdos. El poeta Verdaguer*," "Lluís Capdevila: Angel Samblancat. Lluís Capdevila: *Memoris d'un lit de matrimoni*," Sucre (p. 113)

Number 20. October 15, 1927:

1. "Clásicos catalanes. L'Estética de Maragall," Esterlich (*Catalan*) (p. 119)
2. "La moderna pintura francesa; del cubismo al superrealismo" (Translation from the "Nova Revista" by the author) (p. 121)

Number 21. November 1, 1927:

1. "Poemas en mapa. Cataluña. *Objectes*," Sebastiá Sánchez-Juan (*Catalan*) (p. 125)
2. "Música. La actividad musical catalana (I)," Subirá (p. 127)
3. La librería Catalonia (Barradas drawing) (p. 128)

Number 22. November 15, 1927:

1. "Exposición del libro catalán," Giménez Caballero (p. 129)
2. "Lluís Montanyà. Un 'nou' poeta catala," Sebastiá Sánchez-Juan (with photograph) (*Catalan*) (p. 131)

Number 23. December 1, 1927 (Dedicated to the Exposición del libro catalán):

1. "Saludo a Cataluña," Giménez Caballero (p. 135)
2. "El renacimiento de las letras catalanas y la edición," Anon. (pp. 135–36)
3. Carles Riba, A. Esclasans, Rafael Benet, López-Pico (Reply to survey) (p. 137)
4. "Poetas nuevos de Cataluña": Salvat-Papasseit, "Omega"; Sánchez-Joan, Garcés, Miquel Ferra (All poetry in *Catalan*, except Garcés's poem, which is in Castilian) (p. 139)
5. "Del ritme en la poesía catalana," Esclasans (*Catalan*) (p. 139)

Number 24. December 15, 1927:

1. "Tras la apertura. La exposición del libro catalán," Giménez Caballero (p. 143)
2. "Film-arte, Film-anti-artístico," Dalí (p. 147)

Number 25. January 1, 1928:

1. "La exposición del libro catalán," Giménez Caballero (pp. 151–52)
2. "Perfiles jóvenes. Humberto Pérez de la Ossa," Juan Gutiérrez Gili (p. 154)
3. "Naturaleza y artes," Gasch (p. 155)
4. "La actividad musical catalana," Subirá (p. 155)

Number 26. January 15, 1928:

1. "Castilla a Cataluña. Un raid de LGL," Giménez Caballero (p. 159)
2. "La colección de Ausias March," Almela y Vives (p. 160)
3. "Los catalanes vistos por los demás. Quevedo, J. B. Trend, Laborde, Gracián, Voltaire, Ruben Darío, Unamuno, Baroja," Anon. (p. 161)
4. "Vista de un curioso proceso literario en Barcelona," Anon. (p. 161)
5. "Los carteles de Gecé," Antonio Espina (p. 163)

Number 27. February 1, 1928:

1. "Arte. Madrid: Barcelona. La exposición en Dalmau," Gasch (p. 168)
2. "En torno al libro de Franz Roh. *Panorama de la moderna pintura europea*," Gasch (p. 168)

Number 28. February 15, 1928:

1. "Los carteles de Gecé," Sucre (p. 171)
2. "Superrealismo," Luis Montanyà (p. 175)
3. "Poema (a la Lydia de Cadaqués)," Dalí (p. 175)
4. "Libros catalanes. Joan Arns: *El dolç repós*; Angel Samblancat: *Barro en las alas*," Sucre (p. 175)

Number 29. March 1, 1928:

1. "Marinetti en Barcelona," Anon. (p. 181)
2. "Filmes antiartísticos," Dalí (p. 182)
3. "Etapas: Una : 'Varieté'," Gasch (p. 182)

Number 30. March 15, 1928:

1. "Lorca dibujante," Gasch (p. 186)
2. "La actividad musical catalana (IV)," Subira (p. 186)
3. "El teatro. El Teatre Català," A. Esclassans (*Catalan*) (p. 186)

Number 31. April 1, 1928:

1. "Catolicismo en Cataluña. La Fundación Bíblica Catalana," P. Miquel D'Esplugues (p. 191)
2. "El catolicismo en la música española," Subirá (p. 194)
3. "Un manifiesto—Gasch, Dalí, Montanyà ," Anon. (drawing of the three by Siau) (p. 196)

Number 32. April 15, 1928:

1. "De un orden nuevo," Gasch (p. 200)
2. "Cúpula y Monarquía," D'Ors (p. 201)
3. "Tras nuestro número de catolicismo: Reclamación de D'Ors," Anon. (p. 203)

Number 33. May 1, 1928:

1. "Carteles literarios," Montanyà (p. 211)

Number 34. May 15, 1928:

1. "Un debate: Valery Larbaud y Eugenio d'Ors," Anon. (p. 214)
2. "Bibligrafía artística. Elie Faure: *L'esprit des formes*. Maurice Raynal: *Anthologie de la peinture en France de 1906 à nos jours*," Gasch (p. 216)
3. "Un libro de José Subirá: La música en la casa de Alba," Anon. (p. 216)
4. "Postales ibéricas. Conferencia de Junoy (Ateneo BCN: "Modernitat i Avantguardisme"); *Constel.laciones*, Sebastiá Sánchez Juan," Anon. (p. 218)

Number 36. June 15, 1928:

1. "La actividad musical catalana," Subirá (p. 228)

Number 37. July 1, 1928:

1. "Arte decorativo," Gasch (p. 235)

Number 38. July 15, 1928:

1. "Ramón Gaya," Gasch (p. 240)
2. "Catolicismo y clasicismo," D'Ors (p. 240)

Number 39. August 1, 1928:

1. "Narciso Oller," Sucre (p. 244)
2. "Joan Miró," Gasch (p. 247)

Number 41. September 1, 1928:

1. "Tomás Garcés. Tres poemas," (*Catalan*) (p. 255)
2. "Joan Esterlich. Un griego," Ledesma Ramos (pp. 255–56)

Number 42. September 15, 1928:

1. "El lector obrero en Cataluña," Sucre (p. 262)

Number 43. October 1, 1928:

1. "El acorazado 'Potemkin,'" Jaime Miravitlles (p. 271)
2. "Pintura y cinema," Gasch (p. 272)

Number 44. October 15, 1928:

1. "Cinema y arte nuevo," Gasch (p. 280)
2. "Un escultor: Rebull," Gasch (p. 283)
3. "Realidad y Sobrerrealidad," Dalí (p. 283)

Number 47. December 1, 1928:

1. "Itinerarios jóvenes de España. Gasch, Dalí, Montanyà," Giménez Caballero (p. 303)

Number 48. December 15, 1928:

1. "El arte poético y plástico del pintor Domingo," Gasch (p. 310)

Number 49. January 1, 1929:

1. "Gaceta Catalana" (new section), Directors Tomás Garcés (Barcelona), Juan Chabás (Valencia) (p. 316)
2. "Poemas. José Carner. Invención del beso," Anon. (p. 316)
3. "Belleza y realidad (sobre Dalí)," Gasch (p. 316)
4. "La actividad musical catalana (VI)," Subirá (p. 316)
5. "Arte y artistas," Gasch (p. 319)

Number 50. January 15, 1929:

1. "Gaceta catalana. Tomás Garcés. Pigmalión ochocentista," Editors (p. 324)
2. "¿Qué, he blasfemado quizá," Dalí (p. 324)
3. "Hacia un estado de espíritu peninsular nuevo," José Carbonell (p. 324)
4. "Maragall y Carner," Carles Soldevila (p. 324)

Number 51. February 1, 1929:

1. "Gaceta catalana. Figuras: Alfonso Maseras" (p. 332)
2. "Libros recientes," Garcés (p. 332)
3. "Antología. Josep María López Picó: Al.leluia de la missa de l'Ascensió" (*Catalan*) (poetry) (p. 332)
4. "La actividad musical catalana," Subirá (p. 332)
5. "Obras recientes de Dalí," Gasch (p. 335)
6. "Revistas," Gasch (p. 335)

Number 52. February 15, 1929:

1. "Gaceta catalana. Figuras. Tomás Garcés: *El pintor Vayreda*" (p. 340)
2. "Comentarios. Las exposiciones de Sevilla y Barcelona," Joan Sacs (p. 340)

Number 53. March 1, 1929:

1. "Dos pintores valencianos," Gasch (p. 351)
2. "Libros A. Ozenfant: *L'Art*; Andre Level: *Picasso*," Gasch (p. 351)

Number 54. March 15, 1929:

1. "Con el sol," Dalí (poetry) (p. 353)
2. "Gaceta catalana. Figuras. Carles Riba," Juan Chabás (p. 358)
3. "Antología. Josep María Sagarra. 'Chopa,'" (poetry) (*Catalan*) (p. 358)
4. "Comentarios. El teatro catalán," Anon (p. 358)

Number 55. April 1, 1929:

1. "Picasso y la tradición francesa," Gasch (p. 367)
2. "De un orden nuevo," Gasch (p. 367)

Number 56. April 15, 1929:

1. "Una pluma . . . ," Dalí (poetry) (p. 372)
2. "Narciso: El personaje que encontró a su autor," Montanyà (p. 373)
3. "Bitácora de López-Pico," Chabás (p. 373)

Number 57. May 1, 1929:

1. "Gaceta catalana. Figuras: Josep Pla," Carles Riba (p. 378)
2. "Antología: Salvat-Papasseit" (*Catalan* poem with Castilian translation) (p. 378)
3. "Dos pintores catalanes: Costa y Sandalinas," Gasch (p. 379)

Number 59. June 1, 1929:

1. "Gaceta catalana. Figuras: Millás-Raurell, novelista," Montayá (p. 390)
2. "Antologia. Joaquín Folguera. 'L'orgull,' 'Epigrama de l'abandó,' 'Ambició'" (poetry) (*Catalan*) (p. 390)
3. "Figuras. Joaquín Folguera," Díaz-Plaja (p. 390)

Number 60. June 15, 1929:

1. "Joan Rebull en 'La Galería' de Madrid," Chabás (p. 395)
2. "Juan Pigre," Ribas (p. 395)
3. "Un homenaje íntimo (a Joan Esterlich)," Anon. (p. 395)

Number 61. July 1, 1929:

1. "Fichas: La luna y la nueva poesía," Díaz-Plaja (p. 404)
2. "No veo nada," Dalí (poetry) (p. 404)

Number 63. August 1, 1929:

1. "Una traducción inglesa de la crónica de Desclot," Ferrán Soldevilla (p. 414)
2. "Antología. Jaime Agelet" (poetry) (*Catalan*) (p. 414)
3. "La cuestión de las minorías nacionales," Esterlich (p. 414)

Number 64. August 15, 1929:

1. "La cuestión de las minorías nacionales," Esterlich (p. 418)

Number 65. September 1, 1929:

1. "Paul Morand," Montanyà (p. 424)
2. "Comprensión del Arte Moderno," Gasch (p. 428)

Number 66. September 15, 1929:

1. "Del ambiente intelectual catalán: Problemas del libro y el carácter," Chabás (p. 431)
2. "Antología. Ricardo Permanyer" (poetry) (*Catalan*) (p. 431)
3. "Butlletins del temps," López-Picó (p. 431)

Number 67. October 1, 1929:

1. "La aventura del teatro," Chabás (p. 436)
2. "Antología. A. Esclasans" (p. 436)
3. "Descartes en catalán" (p. 436)
4. "Superrealismo," Gasch (p. 437)

Number 68. October 15, 1929:

1. "Los grandes libros: *Las Dictaduras* de Francisco Cambó," Chabás (p. 442)
2. "Antología: Jaume Agelet y Garriga" (poetry) (*Catalan*) (p. 442)
3. "En la Fiesta del Libro," Carles Soldevila (p. 442)
4. "Aspectos de la Hagiografía," Díaz Plaja (p. 443)

Number 69. November 1, 1929:

1. "Panorama," Gasch (p. 449)
2. "El perro andaluz (declaraciones de Dalí y Buñuel)," Anon. (p. 451)

Number 70. November 15, 1929:

1. "Libros nuevos: *Café, copa i puro*: J. M. Sagarra," Chabás (p. 454)
2. "Antología: J. Millás Raurell: L'Excursió" (poem) (*Catalan*) (p. 454)
3. "Susana en el baño," A. Esclasans (p. 454)

Number 71. December 1, 1929:

1. "Salón de Otoño en París," D'Ors (p. 459)
2. "La inaugural de las galerías Dalmau," Gasch (p. 461)

Number 72. December 15, 1929:

1. "El juego lúgubre y el doble juego (sobre Dalí)," D'Ors (p. 467)
2. "Teatro leído," Díaz Plaja (p. 468)

APPENDIX I

~

Periodicals Consulted

A partial list of the periodicals consulted for the completion of this book, listed in chronological order and indicating the name of the magazine (without subtitles), the city or cities in which it was headquartered, date of foundation, and end date when available.

1. *Garba* (Barcelona, 1905–6)
2. *Renacimiento* (Madrid, 1907)
3. *Futurisme* (Barcelona, 1907)
4. *Prometeo* (Madrid, 1908–12)
5. *Futurisme* (Tarrasa, 1908)
6. *Los Contemporáneos* (Madrid, 1909)
7. *España Futura* (Madrid, 1909–10)
8. *Futurisme* (Vilafranca del Penedés, 1910)
9. *El Peregrino* (Madrid, 1912)
10. *El Arte Español* (Madrid, 1912–23, 1925, [1927], 1928–31)
11. *Correo de las letras & de las artes* (Barcelona, 1912)
12. *La Esfera* (Madrid, 1914–31)
13. *Revista Nova* (Barcelona, 1914–16)
14. *España* (Madrid, 1915–24)
15. *Los Quijotes* (Madrid, 1915–18)
16. *Vell i Nou* (Barcelona, 1915–21)
17. *Iberia* (Barcelona, 1915–19)
18. *La Revista* (Barcelona, 1915–36)

19. *Filosofía y Letras* (Madrid, 1915–36?)
20. *Cervantes* (Madrid, 1916–20)
21. *Troços* (Barcelona, 1916)
22. *391* (Barcelona/New York/Zurich/Paris, 1917–24)
23. *La Revista Quincenal* (Barcelona, 1917–19)
24. *La Nau* (Barcelona, 1917)
25. *Hermes* (Bilbao, 1917–22)
26. *Un Enemic del Poble* (Barcelona, 1917–19)
27. *La Columna de Foc* (Reus, 1918–20)
28. *Trossos* (Barcelona, 1918)
29. *El Camí* (Barcelona, 1918)
30. *D'ací, d'allà* (Barcelona, 1918–36)
31. *Arc-Voltaic* (Barcelona, 1918)
32. *L'Instant* (Paris/Barcelona, 1918–19)
33. *Grecia* (Sevilla/Madrid, 1918–20)
34. *Cosmópolis* (Madrid, 1919–22)
35. *Studium* (Figueres, 1919)
36. *Perseo* (Madrid, 1919)
37. *Terramar* (Sitges, 1919–20)
38. *Alfar* (A Coruña, 1920–54)
39. *Perfiles* (Madrid, 1920)
40. *Gran guiñol* (Sevilla, 1920)
41. *La Pluma* (Madrid, 1920–24)
42. *Reflector* (Madrid, 1920)
43. *Centauro* (Huelva, 1920)
44. *Monitor* (Sitges, 1921–23)
45. *Ultra* (Madrid, 1921–22)
46. *Proa* (Barcelona, 1921)
47. *Creación/Création* (Madrid/Paris, 1921–24)
48. *La Mainada* (Barcelona, 1921–23)
49. *Índice* (Madrid, 1921–22)
50. *Tableros* (1921–23)
51. *Prisma* (Barcelona/Paris, 1922)
52. *Horizonte* (Sevilla, 1922–23)
53. *Paraules* (Barcelona, 1922–23)
54. *Ambos* (Madrid, 1923)
55. *Parábola* (Burgos, 1923–28)
56. *Revista de Occidente* (Madrid, 1923–36)
57. *Vértices* (Madrid, 1923)
58. *Gaseta de les Arts* (Barcelona, 1924–30)

59. *Ronsel* (Lugo, 1924)
60. *Revista de Catalunya* (Barcelona, 1924–31)
61. *Tobogán* (Madrid, 1924)
62. *La Mà Trencada* (Barcelona, 1924–25)
63. *Plural* (Madrid, 1925)
64. *Revista de Poesia* (Barcelona, 1925–27)
65. *Amauta* (Lima, 1926–32)
66. *Residencia* (Madrid, 1926–34)
67. *Ciutat* (Manresa, 1926–28)
68. *L'Amic de les Arts* (Sitges/Barcelona, 1926–29)
69. *Mediodía* (Sevilla, 1926–29, 1933, 1939)
70. *Favorables París Poema* (Paris, 1926)
71. *Sagitario* (Mexico, 1926–27)
72. *Litoral* (Málaga, 1926–29)
73. *Carmen* (Gijón, 1927–28)
74. *Post-guerra* (Madrid, 1927–28)
75. *La Gaceta Literaria* (Madrid, 1927–32)
76. *La Nova Revista* (Barcelona, 1927–29)
77. *Verso y Prosa* (Murcia, 1927–28)
78. *La Rosa de los Vientos* (Santa Cruz de Tenerife, 1927–28)
79. *Papel de Aleluyas*, (Huelva-Sevilla, 1927–28)
80. *Arts i Bells Oficis* (Barcelona, 1927–30)
81. *Gallo* (Granada, 1928)
82. *Circunvalación* (Mexico, 1928)
83. *Les Arts Catalanes* (Barcelona, 1928–)
84. *Almanaque de las artes y las letras para 1928* (Madrid, 1928)
85. *Meridiano* (Huelva, 1929–30)
86. *Nueva Revista* (Madrid, 1929–30)
87. *Mirador* (Barcelona, 1929–37)
88. *Hèlix* (Barcelona, 1929–30)
89. *Atlántico* (Madrid, 1929–30)
90. *Fulls grocs* (Barcelona, 1929)
91. *Anti* (Caldas de Montbui, 1931)
92. *AC* (Barcelona/Madrid/San Sebastian, 1931–37)
93. *Art: Revista Internacional de les Arts* (Lleida, 1933–34)
94. *Quaderns de Poesia* (Barcelona, 1935–36)

~

Bibliography

Primary Documents

391. Francis Picabia, ed. Barcelona/New York/Zurich/Paris, 1917–24. http://sdrc.lib. uiowa.edu/dada/391/index.htm (accessed February 13, 2011).

ABC, "Clausura de la exposición de Artistas Catalanes," February 2, 1926.

Abril, Manuel. "Un artista precoz." *Blanco y Negro*, January 17, 1926.

———. "Sociedad de Artistas Ibéricos." *El Heraldo de Madrid*, June 16, 1925.

AC. Documentos de actividad contemporánea, nos. 1–25. Barcelona/Madrid/San Sebastian, 1931–37. Barcelona: Gili, 1975.

Albert, Salvador. "Cataluña, el estatuto de autonomía." *España* 370 (4–5), May 19, 1923.

Alcantara, Francisco. "En el salón de artistas ibéricos. Los escultores." *El Sol*, June 24, 1925.

———. "Exposición de los artistas Ibéricos. II." *El Sol*, June 1, 1925.

———. "La primera Exposición de la Sociedad de Artistas Ibéricos. I." *El Sol*, May 29, 1925.

———. "Obras de la Exposición de Artistas Ibéricos. IV." *El Sol*, June 12, 1925.

Alfar. Revista de Casa América-Galicia, nos. 21–62. La Coruña, September 1922– Montevideo, February 1929. La Coruña: Nos, 1983.

Alomar, Gabriel. "Las dos capitales." *España Futura* 5 (May 15–31, 1909): 259.

———. "El Futurisme." In *Assaig*, edited by Jaume Brossa and Gabriel Alomar, 72. Barcelona: Edicions 62, 1985.

———. *El futurisme i altres assaigs*. Barcelona: Edicions 62, 1970.

———. "Futurismo." *Prometeo*, September 1907.

———. "Futurismo." *Prometeo*, November 1907.

———. "Futurismo." *Renacimiento* 2 (September 1907): 257–276.

———. "Futurismo." *Renacimiento*, 2 (November 1907), 575–597.

———. "Spotula: El Futurisme a Paris." *El Poble Català*, March 9, 1909.

———. "En el umbral de España Futura." *España Futura* 2 (April 1–15, 1909): 65–68.

Amauta. Revista mensual de doctrina, literatura, arte, polémica. Lima, Peru 1926–32.

Arca. Arxiu de revistes catalanes antigues. http://www.bnc.cat/digital/arca/index. html (accessed February 13, 2011).

Arc-Voltaic. http://www.cervantesvirtual.com/obra-visor/arc-voltaic--0/html/ (accessed February 13, 2011).

Art. Revista Internacional de les Arts, nos. 1–10. Lleida, 1933–1934. Barcelona: Letradura, 1977.

Atlántico. Revista mensual de la vida hispanoamericana, nos. 1–18. Madrid, June 5, 1929–March 16, 1933.

Bargas, Corpus. *La exposición de los residentes españoles en París.* March 20–25, 1929. Catalogue. Madrid: Residencia de Estudiantes, 1929.

Barradas, Rafael. *Atocha.* Madrid: Museo Nacional Centro de Arte Reina Sofía, 1919.

Benet, Rafael. "La vida artistica." *La Ciutat*, March 2, 1926.

———. "Salvador Dalí." *La Veu de Catalunya*, November 27, 1925.

Breton, André. "Surrealist Manifesto." http://wikilivres.info/wiki/Surrealist _Manifesto.

Cambó, Francesc. *Per la concòrdancia.* Madrid: Alianza, 1986.

Cervantes. Revista Hispanoamericana, nos. 1–53. Madrid, August 1916–March 1920.

Ciutat. Ideari d'art i cultura, nos. 1–30. Manresa, February 1926–28.

Columna de Foc. Fulla de subversió espiritual, nos. 1–10. Reus, 1918–20.

Correo de las letras y de las artes, nos. 1–3. Barcelona, November 1912–January 1913.

Dalí, Salvador. "Temes artístics. El decàleg de Salvador Dalí. Resposta a unes al·lusions." *La Nau*, June 28, 1928.

———. *Figure at Window.* 1925.

———. *Seated Girl from the Back (Portrait of the Artist's Sister).* 1925.

———. *Sleepwalking Dreams.* 1922.

———. *Venus and Sailor. Homage to Joan Salvat-Papasseit.* 1925.

Díaz-Plaja, Fernando. *La preguerra española en sus documentos (1923–1936).* Barcelona: Ediciones G.P., 1969.

Doménech, Rafael. "Exposiciones de arte." *ABC*, January 28, 1926.

Domingo, Marcelino. "¿Qué es España y qué es Cataluña?" *España* 74 (June 22, 1916), 23.

D'Ors, Eugeni. "La exposición de Artistas Ibéricos." *ABC*, June 3, 1925.

———. "La hazaña de Salvador Dalí." *El Día Gráfico*, Barcelona, December 19, 1924.

El Amic de les Arts, nos. 1–31. Sitges, April 1926–March 1929. Sabadell (Barcelona): Ausa D. L., 1990.

El Día Gráfico, "En la vide en la corte…," February 21, 1926.

El Sol, "Corpus Barga y la nueva pintura," March 22, 1929.

———, "Guía del lector," March 21, 1929.

———, "La clausura de una Exposición. Discurso de D. José Ortega y Gasset," February 2, 1926.

———, "Manuel Abril en la exposición del Botánico," March 26, 1929.

Encina, Juan. "La nueva generación artística." *La Voz*, January 26, 1923.

Enemic del Poble, Una fulla de subversió espiritual, nos. 1–18. Barcelona, March 1917–May 1919. Barcelona: Leteradura, 1976. http://www.cervantesvirtual.com/obra-visor/un-enemic-del-poble-fulla-de-subversio-espiritual--11/html/ (accessed February 13, 2011).

España. Semanario de la vida nacional, nos. 1–415. Madrid, January 1915–March 1924. Vaduz, Liechtenstein: Topos Verlag, 1982. http://hemerotecadigital.bne.es/cgi-bin/Pandora.exe?fn=select;collection=cabeceras_internet;query=id:0000000766;x slt=header-details;lang=; (accessed February 24, 2011).

España Futura. Revista quincenal: ciencia, industria, economía, agricultura, comercio, artes, literatura, política, nos. 1–19. Madrid, March 1909–February1910.

Esterlich, Joan. *Catalonia endins.* Barcelona: Catalònia, 1930.

Exposición del Libro Catalán. Madrid (5–21 Diciembre 1927). Algunas notas sobre el libro en catalán 1900–1927. Barcelona: López Llausás, 1927.

Francés, José. "Arte joven." *Heraldo de Madrid*, January 22, 1926.

Frollo, Claudio. *España Futura.* 1 (March 15–31, 1909): 60–62.

Futurisme, Revista Catalana, nos. 1–3. Barcelona, June 1907–July 1907.

Gallo, Revista de Granada, nos. 1–2. Granada, February 1928–April 1928. Barcelona: Leteradura, 1977.

Garcès, Tomás. *La rosa y el laurel.* Prologue by Melchor Fernández Almagro. Madrid: Biblioteca Iberia, 1927.

García Maroto, Gabriel. *El año artístico.* Madrid: José Fernández Arias, 1913.

———. "Carta a Juan de la Encina." *La Voz*, February 24, 1923.

———. "Exposiciones artísticas. 'Heraldo de Madrid.' Crítica de pintor." *Heraldo de Madrid*, January 20, 1926.

———. Illustration. "La Gaceta Literaria." *La Gaceta Literaria*, January 1, 1927.

———. *La nueva España 1930. Resumen de la vida artística española desde el año 1927 hasta hoy.* Prologue by José Luís Morales y Marin. Madrid: Tecnos, 1988.

———. "Un mecenas catalán." *La Voz*, February 1, 1923.

Gasch, Sebastià. "Arte. Madrid : Barcelona. La Exposición en Dalmau." *La Gaceta Literaria* February 1, 1927, 168.

———. *Federico García Lorca. Cartas a sus amigos. Sebastián Gasch, Guillermo de Torre, Ana María Dalí, Angel Ferrant y Juan Guerrero.* Barcelona: Cobalto, 1950.

———. "Atlántico," in Ernesto Giménez Caballero, *Cataluña ante España,* 107. Madrid: La Gaceta Literaria, 1930.

———. "Un manifest i un full groc." *Serra d'Or* 107 (August 1968): 27–30.

Gaseta de les Arts, Publicació quinzenal de Informació Artística. Barcelona, March 1924–January 1930.

Giménez Caballero, Ernesto. *Amor a Cataluña.* Madrid: Ruta, 1942.

———. "L'aventura en la concòrdia." *Revista de Catalunya* 13.67 (1931): 233–40.

———. *Carteles*. Madrid: Espasa Calpe, 1927.

———. *Casticismo, nacionalismo y vanguardia [Antología, 1927–1935]*. Edited by José-Carlos Mainer. Madrid: Fundación Santander Central Hispano, 2005.

———. *Cataluña ante España*. Madrid: La Gaceta Literaria, 1930.

———. "El diálogo de las lenguas." *La Gaceta Literaria*, February 15, 1927.

———. "El diálogo de las lenguas." *La Gaceta Literaria*, March 15, 1927.

———. "El diálogo de las lenguas." *La Gaceta Literaria*, April 1, 1927.

———. *Ernesto Giménez Caballero entre la vanguardia y el fascismo*. Edited by Enrique Selva. Valencia: Pre-Textos, 2000.

———. *Ernesto Giménez Caballero: Prosista del 27 (antología)*. Edited by Enrique Selva Roca de Togores. Barcelona: Anthropos, 1988.

———. *Genio de España: exaltaciones a una resurrección nacional y del mundo*. Barcelona: Planeta, 1983.

———. "La República española como asunto catalán." *La Gaceta Literaria*, October 1, 1931.

———. *Lengua y literatura de España*. 9 vols. Madrid: Ernesto Giménez Caballero, c. 1940–1946.

———. Letter to Sánchez Cuesta. November 2, 1927. Madrid: Residencia de Estudiantes, 1927.

———. "Literatura española, 1918–1930," in *The European Caravan. An Anthology of the New Spirit in European Literature Part I: France, Spain, England and Ireland*. Putnam, Samuel, Maida Castelhun Darnton, George Reavey, J. Bronowski, eds. New York: Brewer, Warren & Putnam, 1931: 301–308.

———. *Los toros, las castañuelas y la virgen*. Madrid: Caro Raggio, 1927.

———. *Notas marruecas de un soldado*. Barcelona: Planeta, 1983.

———. "Por la pluridad a la unidad." *La Gaceta Literaria*, January 15, 1927.

———. "Qué es el superrealismo?" *La Gaceta Literaria*, May 1, 1997.

———. "Salutación." *La Gaceta Literaria*, January 1, 1927.

———. "Teorema de la nueva literatura española." *La Gaceta Literaria*, April 15, 1928.

———. *Trabalenguas sobre España. Itinerarios de Touring-Car. Guía de Touring-Club. Baedeker espiritual de España*. Madrid: Giménez, 1931.

———. *Universo de la literatura española contemporánea*. Illustration. *La Gaceta Literaria* 14 (July 1927), 4.

———. *Visitas literarias de España (1925–1928)*. Edited by Nigel Dennis. Valencia: Pre-textos, 1975.

Gómez de la Serna, Ramón. "Nuevos caprichos." *Un enemic del Poble* 12 (Feb. 1918): 2.

———. "Nuevos caprichos." *Un enemic del Poble* 13 (March 1918): 1.

———. "Fundación y manifesto del Futurismo." *Prometeo* 6 (1909).

———. "Proclama futurista a los espanoles." *Prometeo* 20 (1910).

Grecia. Revista de literatura, nos. 1–50. Seville, October 12, 1918–Madrid, November 1, 1920. Malaga: Centro Cultural de la Generación del 27, 1998.

Gris, Juan. *Espanyol*. Illustration. Madrid: *Exposición de Españoles Residentes en París*. 1929.

Guinart, Roque. "Una cena casi platónica." *El Sol*, June 6, 1925.

Hèlix, nos. 1–10. Vilafranca del Penedès, February 1929–1930. Barcelona: Leteradura, 1977.

Heraldo de Madrid, "Exposiciones artísticas. El arte catalán moderno," January 16, 1926.

———, "Exposiciones artísticas. Los grandes acontecimientos en la exposición de arte catalán," January 16, 1926.

———, "Iniciativas de 'Heraldo de Madrid'. Exposición de arte catalán moderno. Éxito franco y verdadero expectación," January 18, 1926.

Hermes, Revista del País Vasco, nos. 1–85. Bilbao, January 1917–1922. Bilbao: Idat Ekintza, 1988.

Iberia, nos. 1–187. Barcelona, April 10, 1915–1919. http://www.bnc.cat/digital/arca/titols/iberia.html.

Índice, Revista mensual, nos. 1–4. Madrid, July 1921–April 1922. Madrid: El Museo Universal, 1987.

Iribarne, Francisco. "Consideracions sobre el futurisme." *Revista Nova*, November 5, 1914.

Jarnés, Benjamín, "El libro catalán," in Ernesto Giménez Caballero, *Cataluña ante España*, 90. Madrid: La Gaceta Literaria, 1930.

La Gaceta Literaria. Ibérica Americana Internacional: letras, arte, ciencia, nos. 1–123. Madrid, January 1927–May 1932. Prologue by Ernesto Giménez Caballero. Vaduz, Liechtenstein: Topos Verlag, 1980.

———, "Dietari Epiritual." 33, February 1917, 91.

———, "Dietari Epiritual." 47, February 1917, 332.

La Mainada. Barcelona, June 10, 1921–1923.

La Nova Revista, Publicació Mensual de Literatura i d'Art, nos. 1–30. Barcelona, January 1927–June 1929.

La Revista. "Dietari Epiritual." 33 (February 1917), 91.

———. "Dietari Epiritual." 47 (September 1917), 332.

La Rosa de los vientos, nos. 1–5. Tenerife, April 1927–January 1928. Las Palmas de Gran Canarias: Mancomunidad de Cabildos, 1977.

La Vanguardia, "Clausura de la Exposición de Arte Catalán," February 2, 1926.

———, "Conferencia," January 29, 1926.

———, "El arte catalán en Madrid," January 16, 1926.

———, "Exposición de arte catalán," January 16, 1926.

Les Arts Catalanes, nos. 1–8. Barcelona, October 1928–May 1929.

L'Instant, Revue franco-catalane d'art et littérature. Paris/Barcelona, July 1918–January/February 1919. Barcelona: Leteradura, 1977.

Litoral, Poesía, música y dibujos, nos. 1–12. Málaga November 1926–June 1929. Madrid: Turner, 1975.

L.P.B. "Exposiciones artísticas" de 'Heraldo de Madrid.' El arte catalán moderno." *Heraldo de Madrid*, January 26, 1926.

"Los antigermanófilos. Manifesto." *El Liberal*, January 7, 1917.

Los Residentes Españoles en París. March 20–25, 1929. Catalogue. Madrid: Residencia de Estudiantes, Sociedad de Cursos y Conferencias, 1929.

Lucientes, Francisco. "¡Hurra a la vanguardia! El ruidoso, 'jazz artístico' del Botánico." *Heraldo de Madrid*, March 22, 1929.

Marquina, Rafael. "Arte catalán moderno. Sugestiones y comentarios." *Heraldo de Madrid*, January 27, 1926.

———. "L'art nou al Botànic." *Mirador*, April 4, 1929.

———. *Heraldo de Madrid*, January 22, 1926.

———. "Exposició d'Art Català," *La Veu de Catalonia*, January 26, 1926.

———. "De Madrid estant. Una exposició interessant." *La Veu de Catalonia*, June 10, 1925.

Martínez Sierra, Gregorio. "Introducción." *Renacimiento*, March 1907.

Mà Trencada, Revista quinzenal de totes les arts, nos. 1–6. Barcelona, November 6, 1924–January 31, 1925. Barcelona: Leteradura, 1977.

Mediodía, Revista de Sevilla, nos. 1–16. Sevilla May/June 1926–February, 1929. Sevilla: Renacimiento, 1999.

Méndez Casal, Antonio. "En el Círculo de Bellas Artes. Cataluña y su arte contemporáneo." *Blanco y Negro*, February 7, 1926.

Meridiano, Revista de orientación estética. Huelva, November 1929–1930.

Mirador, Setmanari de Literatura, Art i Política, nos. 1–380. Barcelona, January 31, 1929–July 16, 1936.

Monitor, Gaseta nacional de política, art i literatura, nos. 1–8. Sitges, 1921–23.

Montaner, Joaquín. "Azorín." *Correo de las letras y las artes*, December 1912.

Montanyà, Lluís. "Gertrudis." *Mediodía* 11 (n.d.): 15–16.

———. "Carteles." *La Gaceta Literaria*. May 1, 1928.

Moreno Villa, J. "Nuevos artistas. Primera Exposición de la Sociedad de Artistas Ibéricos." *Revista de Occidente*, July 25, 1925.

Mori, A. "Artistas Ibéricos." *El Proceso*, June 5, 1925.

Ortega y Gasset, José. "Clausura de la exposición de Arte Catalán Moderno." *El Heraldo de Madrid*, February 1, 1926.

———. *La deshumanización del arte y otros ensayos de estética*. Prologue by Valeriano Bozal. Madrid: Austral, 1987.

———. "Sobre un periódico de las letras." *La Gaceta Literaria*, January 1, 1927.

Papel de Aleluyas, Hojillas del calendario de la nueva estética, nos. 1–7. Huelva, July 1927–Sevilla, July 1928. Huelva: Instituto de Estudios Onubenses "Padre Marchena," 1980.

Parábola, Cuadernos mensuales de valoración castellana, nos. 1–8. Burgos, June 1923–1928.

Paraules, Fulls mensual d'arts i literatura, nos. 1–5. Barcelona, December 1922–April/May 1923.

Paszkiewicz, Marjan. "La construcción sólo puede ser elemento pictórico como engarce del color y la línea." *Heraldo de Madrid*, January 27, 1926.

"Patria." In *Pombo: La sagrada cripta*, edited by Ramón Gómez de la Serna. Madrid: G. Hernández y Galo Sáez, 1918.

Pla, Josep. "La Publicitat," in Ernesto Giménez Caballero, *Cataluña ante España*. Madrid: La Gaceta Literaria, 1930, 48.

Plandiura, Luis. "Hay que crear el Salón de Independientes." *La Voz*, July 3, 1923.

Plural, Revista mensual de literatura, nos. 1–2. Madrid, January 1925–February 1925.

Prisma, Revista internacional de poesía, nos. 1–8. Barcelona, January 1922–Paris, August 1922.

Proa, Fulls de poesia i guerra, nos. 1–2. Barcelona, January 1921. Barcelona: Parsifal, 1994.

Prometeo, Revista mensual social y literaria, nos. 1–38. Madrid, November 1908–1912.

Pujols, Francesc. "Cubisme i Futurisme." *Revista Nova*, June 6, 1914.

Reflector, Revista internacional de arte, literatura y crítica, no. 1. Madrid, December 1920. Madrid: Visor, 1993.

Renacimiento, nos. 1–10. Madrid, March 1907–December 1907.

Revista, La, Quaderns de publicació quinzenal. Barcelona, May 15, 1915–1936.

Revista de Catalunya. Barcelona, July 1, 1924–1934.

Revista Nova, nos. 1–46. Barcelona, April 11, 1914–January 1917.

Revista de Poesia, nos. 1–11. Barcelona, January 1925–March 1927. Barcelona: Leteradura, 1978.

Rivas Cherif, Cipriano. "Divagaciones de un aprendiz de cicerone. Palabras y colores para ojos que entienden y oídos que ven." *Heraldo de Madrid*, January 28, 1926.

———. "Divagaciones de un aprendiz de cicerone. Venus y un marinero." *Heraldo de Madrid*, January 21, 926.

———. "El caso de Dalí." *España*, n.d.

Ronsel, Revista de arte, nos. 1–6. Lugo, May 1924–October/November 1924. Barcelona: Sotelo Branco, 1982.

Sagitario, Revista del siglo XX, nos. 1–14. Mexico, July 15, 1926–May 31, 1927.

Sala, Rafael. "Els futuristes i el futurisme." *Themis*, March 20, 1916.

Sánchez-Juan, Sebastià. "Barradas, geni idealista." *La Nova Revista*, 9 (1929), 411–12.

———. "Lluís Montanyà. Un nou poeta català." *La Gaceta Literaria*, November 15, 1927.

Sucre, Josep Maria de. "L'angelic laic Rafael Barradas." *La Nova Revista* 5 (1928): 337–39.

———. "Les arts i els artistes. Exposición en Galerías Laietanes." *La Gaceta Literaria*, March 1, 1927.

———. "El lector obrero en Cataluña." *La Gaceta Literaria*. September 15, 1928.

———. "Madrid." *Un enemic del Poble*, May 1919.

———. *Memorias*. Edited by Francesc Miralles. Barcelona: Barna, 1963.

————. "Rafael Barradas." *La Nova Revista*. 1 (January 1927): 179–80.

Tableros, Revista internacional de arte, literatura y crítica, nos. 1–4. Madrid, November 15, 1921–February 28, 1922.

Tobogán, Revista de afirmación literaria, nos. 1–3? Madrid, August, 1924–?.

Torre, Guillermo de. *Literaturas europeas de vanguardia*. Madrid: Rafael Caro R. Fagio, 1925.

Torres-García, Joaquín. "El futurisme." *Vell i nou*, February 1916.

————. "Devem caminar . . ." *Un Enemic del Poble*, 7 (1917), 2.

————. *Un Enemic del Poble*. November 1917.

Troços, nos. 1–4. Barcelona, 1916–April 1918. Barcelona: Leteradura, 1977.

Ultra, Poesía–Crítica–Arte, nos. 1–24. Madrid, January 27, 1921–February 1922. Madrid: Visor, 1993.

Unamuno, Miguel de. "Salutación." *Iberia*, April 1, 1915, 3.

Vell i nou, Revista Quinzenal d'Art. Barcelona, April 1915–March 1921.

Verso y Prosa, Boletín de la joven literatura, nos. 1–12. Murcia, January 1927–October 1928. Murcia: Galeria Chys, 1976.

Vértices, Revista literaria, nos. 1–3. Madrid, October 15, 1923–December 1, 1923.

Secondary Documents

AC. Las vanguardias en Cataluña 1906–1939. July 16–September 30, 1992. La Pedrera, Barcelona.

Ades, Dawn, Ana Beristain, and Fèlix Fanés, ed. *Dalí joven. 1918–1930*. Vizcaya: Banco Bilbao, 1994.

Aisa, Ferran. *Salvador Dalí y Federico García Lorca: la persistencia de la memoria*. Barcelona: Viena Ediciones, Gerneralitat de Catalunya, Department de Cultura, 2004.

Aisa i Pàmpols, Manel. "Josep Maria de Sucre." http://manelaisa.com/34-agrupacion-pro-cultura-faros/articulo-15-josep-maria-sucre/ (accessed in January 2012).

Anderson, Andrew A. *Ernesto Giménez Caballero: The Vanguard Years (1921–1931)*. Newark: Juan de la Cuesta, 2011.

————. "Federico García Lorca y Sebastià Gasch: Escenas de una amistad epistolar." *Boletín de la Fundacion Federico García Lorca* 23 (1998): 83–105.

————. "Futurism and Spanish Literature in the Context of the Historical Avant-Garde." In *International Futurism in Arts and Literature*, edited by Günter Berghaus, 144–181. Berlin: Sonderdruck, 2000.

————. "Ramón Gómez de la Serna y F. T. Marinetti: sus contactos epistolares y la génesis de una proclama." *Boletín Ramón* 7 (2003): 34–41.

————. "Sebastià Gasch y Federico García Lorca: Influencias reciprocas y la construcción de una estética vanguardista. In *Federico García Lorca i Catalunya*, edited by Antonio Monegal and José María Micó, 93–108. Barcelona: Universitat Pompeu Fabra, 2000.

Arenas, Carme, and Glòria Bordons. *Avantguardes i literatura a Europa i a Catalunya*. Barcelona: Universitat Oberta de Cataluna, 2000.

Ascunce, Aránzazu. "Building Bridges: Joan Salvat-Papasseit's Contribution to the Poetic Avant-Garde Movement in Madrid." *Catalan Review: International Journal of Catalan Culture* 17.2 (2003): 9–33.

Badaracco, Joseph L. *The Knowledge Link. How Firms Compete Through Strategic Alliances.* Boston: Harvard Business School Press, 1991.

Balcells, Albert. *Catalan Nationalism: Past and Present.* New York: St. Martin's Press and Macmillan, 1996.

Balfour, Sebastián. *The End of the Spanish Empire 1898–1923.* Oxford: Clarendon Press, 1997.

Barcelona and Modernity: Gaudí to Dalí. March 7–June 3, 2007. The Cleveland Museum of Art, the Metropolitan Museum of Art, New York, and Museu Nacional d'Art de Catalunya, Barcelona.

Barradas/Torres-García. Madrid: Galería Guillermo de Osma, 1992.

Bassolas, Carmen. *La ideología de los escritores: literatura y política en La Gaceta Literaria (1927–1932).* Barcelona: Fontamara, 1975.

Bohn, Willard. *Modern Visual Poetry.* Newark: University of Delaware Press, 2001.

Bonet, Juan Manuel. "Barradas y el Ultraísmo." In *Barradas/Torres-García.* Madrid: Galería Guillermo de Osma, 1992.

———. *Diccionario de las vanguardias en España 1907–1936.* Madrid: Alianza, 1999.

———. "Ramón Gómez de la Serna: intento de cronología." In *Los ismos de Ramón Gómez de la Serna y un apéndice circense.* Museo Nacional Centro de Arte Reina Sofia. Madrid, June 5–August 25, 2002. Madrid: Sociedad Estatal para la Acción Cultural Exterior, 2002.

Borès, Francisco. *El ultraísmo y el ambiente literario madrileño.* Madrid: Residencia de Estudiantes, 1999.

Borràs, Maria Lluïsa, Arnau Puig, and Pilar Garcia-Sedas. *Josep Maria de Sucre i l'art de la primera postguerra.* October 15–November 30, 2003. Barcelona. Barcelona: Generalitat de Catalunya, Departament de Cultura, 2003.

Brass, D. J. "A Social Network Perspective on Human Resource Management." In *Research in Personnel and Human Resource Management,* edited by K. M. Rowland and G. R. Ferris, 39–79. Greenwich, CT: JAI Press, 1995.

Brenan, Gerald. *The Spanish Labyrinth: The Social and Political Background of the Spanish Civil War.* Cambridge: Cambridge University Press, 2000.

Brihuega, Jaime. *Arte y política en España, 1898–1939.* Seville: Instituto Andaluz del Patrimonio Histórico, Junta de Andalucía, Conserjería de Cultura, 2002.

———. "La ESAI y el arte español en la bisagra de 1925." In *La Sociedad de Artistas Ibéricos y el arte español de 1925.* Madrid: Museo Nacional Centro de Arte Reina Sofía, 1995.

———. *Las vanguardias artísticas en España: 1909–1936.* Madrid: Istmo, 1981.

———. *Manifiestos, proclamas, panfletos y textos doctrinales: Las vanguardias artísticas en España, 1910–1930.* Madrid: Istmo, 1981.

Buckley, Ramón, and John Crispin, eds. *Los vanguardistas espanoles (1925–1935).* Madrid: Alianza, 1973.

Cano, José L. "Un epistolario: Unamuno y Maragall." *Insula: Revista de Letras y Ciencias Humanas* 27 (1972): 8–9.

Cano Ballesta, Juan. *Literatura y tecnología. Las letras españolas ante la revolución industrial, 1900–1933*. Madrid: Editorial Origenes, 1981.

Carr, Raymond. *Modern Spain 1875–1980*. Oxford: Oxford University Press, 1980.

Casanova, Julián. "Terror and Violence: The Dark Face of Spanish Anarchism." *International Labor and Working-Class History* 67 (2005): 79–99.

Cassasas Ymbert, Jordi, ed. *La dictadura de Primo de Rivera (1923–1930)*. Barcelona: Anthropos, 1983.

Casassas, Jordi, Agusti Colomines, Eduardo González Calleja, and Francesc Santolaria. *Els fets del Cut-Cut!, cent anys després*. Barcelona: Centre d'Història Contemporània de Catalunya, 2006.

Corredor-Matheos, José. *Antología esencial de la poesía catalana contemporánea*. Madrid: Espasa Calpe, 2001.

———. "Garcia Lorca y las vanguardias catalanas." In *Federico Garcia Lorca i Catalunya*, edited by Antonio Monegal et al., 111–16. Barcelona: Universitat Pomeu Fabra, 2000.

Dada. Zurich, Berlin, Cologne, Hanover, New York, Paris. February 19–May 14, 2006. The National Gallery of Art, Washington, D.C.; the Centre Pompidou, Paris; and the Museum of Modern Art, New York.

Dalí, Salvador. *Oui. The Paranoid-Critical Revolution. Writings 1927–1933*. Edited by Robert Descharnes. Translated by Yvonne Shafir. Boston: Exact Change, 1998.

———. *Dalí joven*. 1918–1930. October 18, 1994–January 16, 1995. Madrid: Museo Nacional Centro de Arte Reina Sofía.

Davidson, Robert. "Observing the City, Mediating the Mountain: *Mirador* and the 1929 International Exposition of Barcelona." In *Visualizing Spanish Modernity*, edited by Susan Larson and Eva Woods, 228–44. Oxford: Berg, 2005.

Dennis, Nigel. "De la palabra a la imagen: La crítica literaria de Ernesto Giménez Caballero, cartelista." In *El universo creador del 27. Literatura, pintura, música, cine*, edited by Cristóbal Cuevas García and Enrique Baena, 363–77. Málaga: Publicaciones de Literatura Española Contemporánea, 1997.

Díaz-Plaja, Fernando. *L'avantguardisme a Catalunya i alters notes de crítica*. Barcelona: Publicacions La Revista, 1932.

———. *La preguerra española en sus documentos (1923–1936)*. Barcelona: G.P., 1969.

Domínguez Álvarez, Alexia. *La Setmana Tràgica de Barcelona, 1909*. Valls, Tarragona: Cossetània, 2009.

El Heraldo de Madrid, "Se ha inaugurado la Exposición de arte catalán moderno," January 16, 1926.

Epps, Brad, and Luis Fernandez Cifuentes. *Spain beyond Spain: Modernity, Literary History and National Identity*. Lewisburg, PA: Bucknell University Press, 2005.

Evans, Steve. "The Little Magazine A Hundred Years On: A Reader's Report." *The Modern Review* 2.2 (2006). http://www.thirdfactory.net/archive_little_magazine .html (accessed in January 2012).

Fanés, Fèlix. *Salvador Dalí. The Construction of the Image 1925–1930*. New Haven and London: Yale University Press, 2007.

———. "The First Image–Dalí and His Critics: 1919–1929." In *Salvador Dalí: The Early Years*, 90–96. Michael Raeburn, ed. London: Thames Hudson, 1994.

Foard, Douglas. *The Revolt of the Aesthetes: Ernesto Giménez Caballero and the Origins of Spanish Fascism*. New York: P. Lang, 1989.

Foix, J. V. *Catalans de 1918*. Barcelona: Edicions 62, 1981.

Fuster, Joan. *Contra el Noucentisme*. Barcelona: Crítica, 1977.

Galinsoga, L. de. "La revolucionaria Sociedad de Artistas Ibéricos." *Las Provincias*, Valencia, June 3, 1925.

García Gallego, Jesús. *La recepción del surrealismo en España, 1924–1931. La crítica de las revistas literarias en castellano y catalán*. Granada: A. Ubago, 1984.

García García, Isabel, and Javier Pérez Segura. *Arte y política, 1898–1939*. Sevilla: Instituto Andaluz del Patrimonio Histórico: Junta de Andalucía, Consejería de Cultura, 2002.

García Lorca, Federico. *Cartas a sus amigos Sebastián Gasch, Guillermo de Torre, Anna María Dalí, Angel Ferrant y Juan Guerrero*. Barcelona: Cobalto, 1950.

———. *Epistolario a Federico García Lorca desde Cataluna, la Comunidad Valenciana y Mallorca*. Edited by Roger D. Tinnell. Granada: Fundación Federico García Lorca: Caja de Granada; Albolote, Granada: Editorial Comares, 2001.

García-Sedas, Pilar. *Joaquim Torres-García i Rafael Barradas. Un diàleg escrit: 1918–1928*. Barcelona: Publicacions de l'Abadia de Montserrat, 1994.

Gibson, Ian. *Lorca–Dalí: el amor que no pudo ser*. Barcelona: DeBols!llo, 2004.

———. *The Shameful Life of Salvador Dalí*. New York London: W. W. Norton and Company, 1998.

Giest, Anthony L., and José B. Monleón, eds. *Modernism and its Margins: Reinscribing Cultural Modernity from Spain and Latin America*. New York: Garland, 1999.

Giménez Caballero, Ernesto. *Memorias de un dictador*. Barcelona: Planeta, 1979.

Gómez de la Serna, Ramón. "Nuevos caprichos." *Un enemic del Poble* 12 (Feb. 1918): 2.

———. "Nuevos caprichos." *Un enemic del Poble* 13 (May 1918): 1.

———. *Pombo*. Madrid: Trieste, 1986.

———. *La sagrada cripta de Pombo*. Vol. 2. Madrid: Trieste, 1986.

González Garcia, Ángel, Francisco Calvo Seraller, and Simón Marchán Fiz. *Escritos de arte de vanguardia (1900–1945)*. Madrid: Istmo, 2003.

Graham, Helen, and Jo Labanyi, eds. *Spanish Cultural Studies: An Introduction: The Struggle for Modernity*. Oxford: Oxford University Press, 1995.

Guxà, Pere. "Tras los pasos de la Setmana Tràgica." *365 Culturas. La Vanguardia*. June 17, 2009.

Harris, Derek. *The Spanish Avant-Garde*. Manchester: Manchester University Press, 1995.

Hearn, Jonathan. *Rethinking Nationalism*. New York: Palgrave, 2006.

Hernández, Mario. *Line of Light and Shadow. The Drawings of Federico García Lorca*. Translated by Christopher Maurer. Durham: Duke University Press, 1991.

Hernando, Miguel Ángel. "*La Gaceta Literaria*" *(1927–1932). Biografía y valoración.* Valladolid: Universidad de Valladolid, 1974.

Holguín, Sandie. *Creating Spaniards. Culture and Identity in Republican Spain.* Madison: University of Wisconsin Press, 2002.

Ilie, Paul. *Documents of the Spanish Vanguard.* Chapel Hill: University of North Carolina Press, 1969.

The International Dada Archive. http://sdrc.lib.uiowa.edu/dada/collection.html (accessed February 13, 2011).

Jiménez-Blanco Carrillo de Albornoz, María Dolores. *Arte y estado en la España del siglo XX.* Prologue by Francisco Clavo Serraller. Madrid: Alianza, 1989.

Labanyi, Jo, ed. *Constructing Identity in Contemporary Spain. Theoretical Debates and Cultural Practice.* Oxford: Oxford University Press, 2002.

Larson, Susan, and Eva Woods, eds. *Visualizing Spanish Modernity.* Oxford: Berg, 2005.

Lentzen, Manfred. "Marinetti y el futurismo en España." In *Actas del IX Congreso de la Asociación Internacional de Hispanistas,* 700–749. Frankfurt: Vervuert, 1989.

Little Magazine Collection. University of Wisconsin Memorial Library. Humanities and Social Sciences. Introduction. http://memorial.library.wisc.edu/collections/littlemags.html (accessed February 13, 2011).

Litvak, Lily. "Alomar and Marinetti: Catalan and Italian Futurism." *Revue des Langues Vivantes* 38 (1972): 585–603.

Llera Esteban, Luis de. *La modernización cultural de España 1898–1975.* Madrid: Actas Editorial, 2000.

López Guerra, Luis. "National and Regional Pluralism in Contemporary Spain." In *Iberian Identities: Essays on the Nature of Identity in Spain and Portugal,* edited by Richard Herr and John Herman Polt, 19–27. Berkeley: Institute of International Studies, University of California, Berkeley, 1989.

Luskey, Matthew. "The Little Magazine 'Others' and the Renovation of Modern American Poetry (review)." *Modernism/Modernity* 15, no. 4 (2008): 822–24.

Madrigal Pascual, Arturo Ángel. *Arte y compromiso. España 1917–1936.* Madrid: Fundación Anselmo Lorenzo, 2002.

Mainer, José-Carlos. *La edad de plata (1902–1931). Ensayo de interpretación de un proceso cultural.* Barcelona: Libros de la Frontera, 1975.

Marinetti, Filippo Tommaso. "Proclama futurista a los españoles." In *Documents of the Spanish Vanguard,* edited by Paul Ilie, 73. Chapel Hill: University of North Carolina Press, 1969.

Mas, Ricard. *Dossier Marinetti.* Barcelona: Universitat de Barcelona, 1994.

Maurer, Christopher. *Sebastian's Arrows: Letters and Mementos of Salvador Dalí and Federico García Lorca.* Chicago: Swan Isle Press, 2004.

Menocal, Rosa María. "Beginnings." In *The Cambridge History of Spanish Literature,* edited by David Gies, 58–74. Cambridge: Cambridge University Press, 2004.

Minguet, Joan M. Batllori. *El manifest Groc: Dalí, Gasch, Montanyà i l'antiart.* Barcelona: Galàxia Gutenberg, 2004.

———. *El manifiesto amarillo: Dalí, Gasch, Montanyà y el antiarte.* Translated by Joan Riambau. Barcelona: Galaxia Gutenberg, Círculo de Lectores, 2004.

Molas, Joaquim. "Las vanguardias literarias: imitación y originalidad," in *Las vanguardias en Cataluña 1906–1939: Protagonistas, tendencias, acontecimientos.* Barcelona: Olimpíada Cultural, 1992.

———. *Las vanguardias literarias en Cataluña: imitación y originalidad.* Lleida: Milenio, 2010.

———. *La literatura catalana d'avantguarda (1916–1938). Selecció, edició i estudi.* Barcelona: Bosch, 1983.

Monge, Peter R., and Nochir S. Contractor. "Network Concepts, Measures, and Multitheoretical Multilevel Analytical Framework." Chap. 2 in *Theories of Communication Networks.* Oxford: Oxford University Press, 2003.

Mur, Pilar. "El papel del arte vasco." *La Sociedad de Artistas Ibéricos y el arte español de 1925.* Madrid: Ambit, 1995, 67–75.

Murgades, Josep. "Eugeni d'Ors, Xènius." http://lletra.uoc.edu/ca/autor/eugeni-dors (accessed February 3, 2011).

Olmedo, Soria A. *Vanguardismo y crítica literaria en España.* Madrid: Istmo, 1988.

Ortega y Gasset, José. *Genio de España exaltaciones a una resurrección nacional y del mundo.* Barcelona: Planeta, 1983.

———. "Sobre un periódico de las letras," *La Gaceta Literaria,* January 1, 1927, 1.

Osma de, Guillermo, Juan Manuel Bonet and Robert S. Lubar. *Barradas/Torres-García.* November–December 1991. Madrid: Galería Guillermo de Osma, 1991.

Osuna, Rafael. *Revistas de la vanguardia española.* Sevilla: Renacimiento, 2005.

Paniagua, Domingo. *Revistas culturales contemporáneas.* Madrid: Ediciones Punta Europa, 1964.

Payne, Stanley G. *Fascism in Spain 1923–1977.* Madison: University of Wisconsin Press, 1999.

———. *The History of Spain and Portugal.* Vol. 2. http://libro.uca.edu/payne2/index. htm (accessed February 3, 2011).

Peran, Martí, ed. *Madrid–Barcelona.* "Carteles literarios" de Gecé. Madrid / Barcelona: Museo Nacional Centro de Arte Reina Sofia / Universitat de Barcelona–Balmes 21, 1994.

Pérez-Segura, Javier. "Anatomía de un re-encuentro: el 'Arte Catalán Moderno' en Madrid." *La Sociedad de Artistas Ibéricos y el arte español de 1925.* Madrid: Ambit, 1995, 77–84.

———. *Arte moderno, vanguardia y estado. La Sociedad de Artístas Ibéricos y la República (1931–1936).* Madrid: Consejo Superior de Investigaciones Científicas, 2002.

Perloff, Marjorie. *The Futurist Moment: Avant-Garde, Avant-Guerre and the Language of Rupture.* Chicago: Chicago University Press, 1986.

Plataforma. *Diccionario de la Falange.* 2003. http://www.plataforma2003.org/diccionario-falange/ (accessed May 2007).

Poggioli, Renato. *The Theory of the Avant-Garde.* Cambridge, MA: Belknap Press of Harvard University Press, 1968.

Pound, Ezra. "Small Magazines." *The English Journal* 19 (1930): 9.

Raeburn, Michael, ed. *Salvador Dalí: The Early Years*. London: Thames and Hudson, 1994.

Resina, Joan Ramon, ed. *El aeroplano y la estrella: El movimiento de vanguardia en los Países Catalanes (1904–1936)*. Amsterdam: Rodopi, 1997.

———. "The Catalan Avant-Garde." In *The Cambridge History of Spanish Literature*, edited by Davis Gies, 545–52. Cambridge: Cambridge University Press, 2004.

———. "The Last Look from the Border." In *Visualizing Spanish Modernity*, edited by Susan Larson and Eva Woods, 329–39. Oxford: Berg, 2005.

Rial, James H. *Revolution from Above. The Primo de Rivera Dictatorship in Spain 1923–1930*. Fairfax, VA: George Mason University Press, 1986.

Rodrigo, Antonina. *García Lorca, el amigo de Cataluña*. 1st ed. Barcelona: Edhasa, 1984.

———. *García Lorca en el país de Dalí*. Barcelona: Editorial Base, 2004.

———. *Lorca, Dalí: una amistad traicionada*. 1st ed. Barcelona: Planeta, 1981.

———. *Margarita Xirgu*. Madrid: Aguilar, 1988.

Rojo Martín, María del Rosario. *Evolución del movimiento vanguardista. Estudio basado en La Gaceta Literaria (1927–1932)*. Madrid: Fundación Juan March, 1980.

Salvat, Ricard. "Margarida Xirgu, su trabajo en Barcelona y Madrid." In *Dos escenarios: intercambio teatral entre España y Argentina*, edited by Osvaldo Pellettieri, 117–31. Buenos Aires, Argentina: Galerna, 2006.

Sánchez Vidal, Agustín. *Buñuel, Lorca, Dalí: el enigma sin fin*. Barcelona: Planeta, 2004.

Sánchez Vigil, Juan Miguel. "Ortega y Gasset. Director editorial de CALPE." *Revista de Estudios Orteguianos* 10–11 (2005): 177–96.

Sansone, Giuseppe E. "Gabriel Alomar e il Futurismo italiano." In *Les avantguardes literàries a Catalunya: Bibliografia i antologia crítica*, edited by Joaquim Molas et al., 119–38. Madrid: Iberoamericana, 2005.

Santos Torroella, Rafael. *Dalí residente*. Madrid: Publicaciones de la Residencia de Estudiantes, 1992.

———. *Dalí. Epoca de Madrid*. Madrid: Residencia de Estudiantes, 1994.

———. "The Madrid Years," in *Salvador Dalí: The Early Years*, M. Raeburn, ed. London: Thames Hudson, 1994, 81–89.

———. *"Los putrefactos" de Dalí y Lorca. Historia y antología de un libro que no pudo ser*. Madrid: Residencia de Estudiantes, 1995.

———. "Salvador Dalí en la primera exposición de la Sociedad de Artistas Ibéricos." In *La Sociedad de Artistas Ibéricos yel arte español de 1925*. Museo Nacional Centro de Arte Reina Sofia. Madrid: Ambit, 1996.

"Segadors, Els." Museu d'Història de Catalunya. http://www.en.mhcat.net/the_mhc_offers/permanent_exhibition/on_the_edge_of_the_empire/the_reapers_war (accessed July 10, 2011).

Selva Roca de Togores, Enrique, ed. *Ernesto Giménez Caballero entre la vanguardia y el fascismo*. Valencia: Pre-Textos, 2000.

———, ed. *Ernesto Giménez Caballero: Prosista del 27 (antología)*. Barcelona: Anthropos, 1988.

———. "Giménez Caballero en los orígenes ideológicos del fascismo español." *Estudis d'Història Contemporània del País Valencià. El franquisme* 9 (1990): 183–213.

Sferraza, María. *Ernesto Giménez Caballero en la literatura española de la Dictadura y de la República*. Venezzia: Instituto Universitario Ca'Foscari, 1963–64.

Soberanas i Lleó, Amadeu J. *Epistolari de Joan Salvat-Papasseit*. Barcelona: Edicions 62, 1984.

La Sociedad de Artistas Ibéricos y el arte español de 1925. Museo Nacional Centro de Arte Reina Sofia. Madrid: Ambit, 1996. Catalog.

La Sociedad de Artistas Ibéricos y el arte español de 1925. Museo Nacional Centro de Arte Reina Sofia. Madrid. October 17–January 22, 1996. Pamphlet.

Solé i Sabater, Josep Maria. *Salvador Dalí i Federico García Lorca: la persistència de la memòria*. Barcelona: Viena Ediciones: Generalitat de Catalunya, Departament de Cultura, 2004.

Soler Serrano, Joaquin. *Ernesto Gimenez Caballero*. Madrid: Ediciones Trasbals Multimedia, 2000.

Tandy, Lucy, and María Sferrazza. *Ernesto Giménez Caballero y "La Gaceta Literaria" o la Generación del 27*. Madrid: Turner, 1977.

Torres-García, Joaquín. *Historia de mi vida*. Barcelona: Paidós, 1990.

———. *Universalismo constructivo*. Madrid: Alianza, 1984.

Ucelay-Da Cal, Enric. *El imperialismo catalán. Prat de la Riba, Cambó, D'Ors y la conquista moral de España*. Barcelona: Edhasa, 2003.

Universitat Oberta de Catalunya. *Lletra. L'Espai Virtual de Literatura Catalana*. 2007. http://www.uoc.edu/lletra/

Valcárcel, Eva. *La vanguardia en las revistas literarias*. La Coruña: Universidad de Coruña, 2000.

Vallcorba Plana, Jaume. *Noucentisme, mediterraneisme i classicisme: apunts per a la història d'una estètica*. Barcelona: Quaderns Crema, 1994.

Valle-Inclán, Joaquín del. "Introduction" in *Luces de bohemia: esperpento*. Madrid: Espasa Calpe, 2006.

Ventalló, Joaquim. *Los intelectuales castellanos y Cataluña. Tres fechas históricas: 1924, 1927 y 1930*. Barcelona: Galba, 1976.

Verdú, Daniel. "Una obra de Lorca y Barradas." *El País digital*. http://www.elpais.com.uy/Suple/DS/08/03/30/sds_337982.asp (accessed January 2012).

Vidal, Mercè. 1912. *L'Exposició d'Art Cubista de les Galeries Dalmau*. Barcelona: Universitat de Barcelona, 1996.

Vidal i Oliveras, Jaume. *Josep Dalmau. L'aventura per l'art modern*. Manresa: Fundació Caixa de Manresa, 1993.

Videla, Gloria. *El ultraísmo. Estudios sobre movimientos poéticos de vanguardia en España*. 2nd ed. Madrid: Gredos, 1971.

Villalón, Emilio Marcos. *Luis Bagaría entre el arte y la política*. Madrid: Biblioteca Nueva, 2004.

Vilanova Ribas, Mercedes, and Xavier Moreno Juliá. *Atlas de la evolución del analfabetismo en España de 1887 a 1981*. Madrid: Centro de Publicaciones del Ministro de Educación y Ciencia, 1992.

Visa, Miquel. "Dalí–Lorca. Evolucion identificativa de una amistad." In *Intermedialidad e hispanística*, edited by Angelica Rieger, 103–16. Frankfurt: Sonderdruck, 2004.

Wellman, Barry. "Structural Analysis: From Method and Metaphor to Theory and Substance." In *Social Structures: A Network Approach*, edited by S. D. Berkowitz and Barry Wellman, 19–61. Cambridge: Cambridge University Press, 1998.

Ybarra, Lucia. *La Sociedad de Artistas Ibéricos y el arte español de 1925*. Madrid: Museo Nacional Centro de Arte Reina Sofía, 1995.

Index

~

About the Author

Aránzazu Ascunce Arenas earned her B.A. in English and Spanish literatures at Duke University and her Ph.D. in Spanish literature at the University of Virginia. She received a Fulbright grant to research this volume. She is assistant professor at the University of Hawaii in Honolulu where she has received commendations for her teaching of Spanish language, literature, and culture. She has studied at the University of Girona and the University of Salamanca, and she has taught at the University of Seville and the University of Valencia. Her experience working in cultural programming, film, theater, public relations, television, and the press have been especially formative in her development as an artist, scholar, and educator.

CPSIA information can be obtained at www.ICGtesting.com
Printed in the USA
BVOW020712050312

284352BV00002B/2/P